Law, Visual Culture, and the Show Trial

Addressing the relationship between law and the visual, this book examines the importance of photography in Central, East, and Southeast European show trials.

The dispensation of justice during communist rule in Albania, East Germany, and Poland was reliant on legal propaganda, making the visual a fundamental part of the legitimacy of the law. Analysing photographs of trials, this book examines how this message was conveyed to audiences watching and participating in the spectacle of show trials. The book traces how this use of the visual was exported from the Soviet Union and imposed upon its satellite states in the immediate aftermath of the Second World War. It shows how the legal actors and political authorities embraced new photographic technologies to advance their legal propaganda and legal photography. Drawing on contemporary theoretical work in the area, the book then challenges straightforward accounts of the relationship between law and the visual, critically engaging entrenched legal historical narratives, in relation to three different protagonists, to offer the possibility of reclaiming and rewriting past accounts. As its analysis demonstrates, the power of images can also be subversive; and, as such, the cases it addresses contribute to the discourse on visual epistemology and open onto contemporary questions about law and its inherent performativity.

This original and insightful engagement with the relationship between law and the visual will appeal to legal and cultural theorists, as well as those with more specific interests in Stalinism, and in Central, East, and Southeast European history.

Agata Fijalkowski is Reader in Law at Leeds Beckett University, UK.

Discourses of Law

for information about the series and details of previous and forthcoming titles, see https://www.routledge.com/Discourses-of-Law/book-series/SE1036

The publisher gratefully acknowledges the support of the Jacob Burns Institute for Advanced Legal Studies of the Benjamin N. Cardozo School of Law to the series *Discourses of Law*.

A GlassHouse Book

Law, Visual Culture, and the Show Trial

Agata Fijalkowski

Routledge
Taylor & Francis Group
a GlassHouse book

First published 2024
by Routledge
4 Park Square, Milton Park, Abingdon, Oxon OX14 4RN

and by Routledge
605 Third Avenue, New York, NY 10158

a GlassHouse book

Routledge is an imprint of the Taylor & Francis Group, an informa business

British Library Cataloguing-in-Publication Data
A catalogue record for this book is available from the British Library

Library of Congress Cataloging-in-Publication Data
A catalog record has been requested for this book

ISBN: 978-0-367-42960-7 (hbk)
ISBN: 978-1-032-52253-1 (pbk)
ISBN: 978-1-003-40577-1 (ebk)

DOI: 10.4324/9781003405771

Typeset in Bembo
by Taylor & Francis Books

For Marjorie,
Who said, 'Yes, do it!'

Contents

Figures

Acknowledgements

There are many people I wish to thank for making this project possible.

The idea for this project started with the image of Musine Kokalari, my hero. Linda Kokalari was extremely generous with time and information about her great-aunt's remarkable life story. Rozeta Kokalari, Musine Kokalari's first cousin once removed, provided a fabulous family tree. My research trips to Albania were full of adventure. I had two outstanding research assistants, Florian Agalli and Davjola Ndoja. I could not have navigated the national archives nor the interviews without their assistance. Their enthusiasm and support for my work made the research even more rewarding. The archivists at the Albanian Telegraphic Agency and at the Central State Archive, both in Tirana, were incredibly patient and went out of their way to help: a special thanks goes to Sokol Çunga at the Central State Archive. I also am grateful to the UK-based Anglo-American Association and to the former Albanian Ambassador to the UK, H.E. Mal Berisha, who heard early versions of my work on Musine Kokalari. A big thank you to Dr Elidor Mëhilli at Hunter College, City University of New York, for invaluable comments and critical insights on the chapter on Albania, and to Teuta Skenderi.. The country is truly under my skin, not least because of the help of you all: *faleminderit*!

In Germany, I am indebted to Dr Andrea Feth, Hilde Benjamin's biographer. Dr Feth is a remarkable person and lawyer. Our interviews in Berlin were a highlight and always took place at wonderful cafés where discussions centred on the temporal and professional contexts in which Hilde Benjamin worked. Dr Feth took time to read drafts of my chapter on East Germany and Hilde Benjamin closely. Special thanks go to Marcus Behaimi at the German Federal Archives Berlin, who drew my attention to the Frieda Lehmann case. I am grateful to Lennart Schuett at the Stasi Records Archive for careful guidance and advice when looking at the materials, and for introducing me to the building's paternoster. *Danke schön* to you all!

In Poland, I was very lucky to have Krzysztof Poznański as my excellent research assistant, who stepped in immediately and accessed materials at the Institute of National Remembrance in Warsaw in between periods of lockdown because of COVID-19. I also thank the staff at the Institute of National Remembrance in Warsaw; Bożena Rudzińska explained the procedures and assisted me in finding and holding the documents for me. And, finally, I am grateful to Dr Piotr Łubiński for his ongoing support. *Dziękuję Wam bardzo!*

Back in the UK support came from funding from Lancaster University Faculty of Arts and Sciences and Lancaster Law School and made trips to all the countries comprising my case studies possible. My former Law School colleague and dear friend, Dr Bela Chatterjee, offered unwavering encouragement; Bela is second to none. I am grateful to Prof. Adam Geary, from Birkbeck's School of Law, for advice, and his overall generosity when talking to me about Lyotard and my book's main arguments.

In 2017 I had a Neil MacCormick Fellowship at Edinburgh Law School, where I started to advance my ideas for this project. I was part of a vibrant community and I met several amazing people. I could not have asked for a better mentor than Dr Andy Aydīn-Aitchison. I have fond memories of discussing law and aesthetics, and all things Polish, with Prof. Zenon Bańkowski, over endless coffees at Machina. Many of their insights appear in the book.

In Chicago, my former teacher and mentor at the University of Illinois at Chicago and now dear friend, Prof. Matthew Lippman, is a constant source of support; I am always grateful for his wise words of advice.

At GlassHouse Books, from the start Prof. Peter Goodrich and Colin Perrin helped to put the reviewers' comments into action. Peter was especially helpful in helping me think about photographs as a sensory experience and pointed me to some fun reading. Thank you to Naomi Round Cahalin for guiding me through the publication process.

I am very lucky to have had special research assistance from my family. Friends and colleagues know my love for our 'menagerie'. Ushba, our long-haired German Shepherd dog was a companion for most of the writing. She was a joy and losing her during lockdown was heartbreaking. But Sputnik, another German Shepherd dog appeared on the scene, as did Max the Belgian Malinois puppy. Both were surprises and both provide the sort of boost and unconditional love that one needs when one is writing, doubting what is on the paper, and hitting writers' block. Together they, along with our three cats, Sugar the Maine Coon, Majik the Siberian forest cat, and Modi the Norwegian forest cat, have been unswerving in their interest by forcing me to get up, get some fresh air, and making the writing fun, in between stroking their fur and just enjoying their company. There are the animals but there also is my amazing husband Mark, and if not for him, this project would not have been realised. He has been an ongoing source of support and a good reviewer of different sections of my book.

I am writing this at the Institute for Research in the Humanities at the University of Wisconsin-Madison, where I am an Honorary IRF Fellow. The 2022 Fellowship, and financial support from Leeds Law School, has brought me to the finish line. The IRH colleagues and community are amazing in terms of resources, support, and camaraderie. During my stay, I had such a rewarding experience presenting vignettes from my book to colleagues at The Center for

Russia, East Europe, and Central Asia (CREECA). And I can think of no better place to complete this project that I have loved researching and writing over the years.

Some images, like those of my protagonists, linger in my mind from the moment that I came across them.

Excerpts of my article 'Musine Kokalari and the Power of Images: Law, Aesthetics and Memory Regimes in the Albanian Experience', (2015) 28(3) *International Semiotics of Law* 577–602, namely pages 588–589 and 591–592, have been reprinted with permission.

Excerpts of my article co-authored with Sigrun Valderhaug, 'Legal Decisions, Affective Justice, and "Moving On"?' (2017) 7(2) *Oñati Socio-Legal Series* 337–364, namely pages 346–348 and 349–350, have been reprinted with acknowledgement and permission.

A huge thank you to Lorraine Slipper for checking the book in manuscript. All mistakes are my own.

Madison, WI, USA
November 2022

Introduction

The uniqueness of *Law, Visual Culture, and the Show Trial* lies in its unravelling of the cultural, historical, and political implications of visualising law. It is the first full-blown exploration of law and visual culture situated squarely in the context of Central, Eastern, and Southeast European show trials, as broadly understood.[1] Emphasis on the case studies of Albania, East Germany, and Poland contributes to the discourses about law and the dispensation of justice in a specific time in the legal history of communism, involving the notions of effective and affective justice. This study hopes to cement the relationship between law and visual culture, making it a viable dimension in the field, and to contribute to its recognition more widely as an integral legal discourse.

A show trial, broadly speaking, is a trial that is held in public with the underlying purpose not of achieving justice but of influencing public opinion. The show trial continues to capture the imagination, because the subject matter is exciting, intriguing, and contains an element of the unknown. A question mark hangs over the individuals who participate in show trials – an untold story. As an academic research topic it is revisited by writers, many of whom provide much-needed and engaging analyses from various disciplinary lenses across the social sciences and the humanities.[2] These different perspectives have contributed to ongoing, dynamic discussions about exposing conventional constructs of law, justice, and violence, and the meaning attached to the dispensation of justice and the judge as an individual.[3] The discussion shows how

1 I define 'Central and Eastern Europe' as including Poland and East Germany – the former was a 'People's Democracy' and the latter an independent communist state – although I understand the rejection of the term by scholars. I find Melissa Feinberg's approach to these questions illuminating: see Melissa Feinberg, *Curtain of Lies: The Battle over Truth in Stalinist Eastern Europe* (Oxford University Press 2017), xii. For the purposes of this book, I follow Feinberg: the phrase is used to refer to a geographical space. In the same way, I define Southeast Europe as including Albania. Beyond this reference I discuss the three case studies separately but will refer to works that consider the region more widely.

2 Feinberg, *Curtain of Lies.*

3 Leslie J. Moran, *Law, Visual Culture and Judges* (Routledge 2021), addressing visual depictions of judges in various formats within the common law context. For

DOI: 10.4324/9781003405771-1

the visual depictions of show trials, such as the photograph, add to their affective power and influence. Photographs delimit what is knowable, what is true, what can be seen.[4] They possess a transformative authority; in relation to law, photographs point to the affectivity of the law, because of the image and law's performativity. In other words, performativity is an attribute of the law. For the purposes of this book, the show trial is understood as a kangaroo court, sham trial, or judicial murder. It is the maladministration of justice. It can be argued that all trials are show trials, and while this is a question that is not directly tackled in this book's discussion, it is a theme that is relevant and resonates. Current developments, namely the Russian invasion of Ukraine, and Russian efforts to set up show trials of Ukrainian prisoners of war, have revived discussions about the show trial.[5]

My starting point is a collection of photographs that I have gathered from Albanian, German, and Polish archives. Most of the photographs, taken in the years between 1944 and 1963, are of trials, and all are related to the dispensing of justice. This era is noted for its application of political justice, as well as a presentation of legitimacy of law in action, which was an integral feature of communist rule. This aspect of communist rule involved a variety of political and judicial officials working behind the scenes, some of whom understood the power of a performance. The photographs were taken in order to accelerate the performance's reach and provide a visual account of court proceedings for the public eye, especially of the key participants – the defendant, the judge or judiciary, the prosecutor. It was an effective way to demonstrate that the law was for the people and that the aims of justice – punishing the enemies of the state – were achieved. As well as focusing on the principal participants in the trial, at other times the symbols of justice are the main features in the image, as well as the venue itself, both of which can also be seen as key participants. The dissemination of images involved individuals who worked behind the scenes. Several photographs also include the photographer. These images show the law and legal participants at work and collaborating to stage the enactment of the law – activities that include the image makers as an active part of the process of creating a visual account of how the law was applied.

The relationship between law and visual culture is one that goes back to ancient times.[6] The discourses to emerge from this relationship focus on the

contemporary examples, see the reality television competition to find the next drag superstar, *RuPaul's Drag Race*, in which RuPaul is the host, mentor, and head judge.

4 Kathryn A. Heard, 'Unframing the Death Penalty', in Austin Sarat and Jurgen Martschukat (eds), *Is the Death Penalty Dying? European and American Perspectives* (Cambridge University Press 2011) 126–149, 130.

5 'Russia's Mariupol Show Trials', Editorial Board, *Wall Street Journal*, 30 August 2022.

6 Addressed in Austin Sarat, Lawrence Douglas, and Martha Merrill Umphrey (eds), *Law and Performance* (University of Massachusetts Press 2018).

nature of the image and our ability to understand what we are seeing: whether through a literacy skill or an emotional response. The way that the public display of images relating to law has been controlled by authorities is in itself a legal historical record of the perceived threat that some images posed.[7] While this relationship might be strong, it does not result in the viewer acquiring an understanding about the meaning of what they are seeing. Although scholars lack the training to read images, because they were trained in reading text, Peter Burke reminds us that images are read and are treated as documents.[8] The images could have been intended to communicate a message of their own, but writers frequently do not acknowledge this, or try to identify different meanings. The image maker will have different purposes – the image maker's gaze is rarely objective and innocent. For Burke, these questions do not have to be too problematic if we, as researchers, acknowledge the challenges[9] and recognise that 'what we see never resides in what we say'.[10] The visual is then the nonverbal.

Visual efficacy is the ability to effectively view visual information. It entails taking in and processing that information. Writing about the history of art, Georges Didi-Huberman argues that as long as it remains 'subject to the tyranny of the visible', the history of art will fail to understand the visual efficacy of images.[11] A key theme in Didi-Huberman's work asks: What do pictures want? Didi-Huberman's position engages with the relationship with thought and with seeing or looking when contemplating the possibility of discourse on images.

Other writers have also asked this question. For example, in *Camera Lucida*[12] Roland Barthes discusses whether images produce a system of signs or a cluster of symbols. The reading of images becomes a question of semiotics because of the way language is conveyed – through speaking or writing. If the meaning is contained in an image, then it becomes an exploration of how meaning is retrieved through seeing or looking at it. Barthes's notions of *studium* and *punctum* relate to photographic meaning. The *studium* is connected with the historical, social, or cultural meaning deriving from the image. Its reading follows semiotic analysis. The *punctum* produces a meaning that does not follow a

7 Considered in Costas Douzinas and Lynda Nead (eds), *Law and the Image: The Authority of Art and the Aesthetics of Law* (University of Chicago Press 1999).

8 Peter Burke, *Eyewitnessing: The Uses of Images as Historical Evidence* (Reaktion Books 2001) 13.

9 Burke, *Eyewitnessing*, 19.

10 Burke, *Eyewitnessing*, 34. For others, witnessing is connected to human dignity and sees ethical and political considerations trump aesthetics. See Carolyn J. Dean, 'Atrocity Photographs, Dignity, and Human Vulnerability' (2015) 6(2) *Humanity: An International Journal of Human Rights, Humanitarianism, and Development* 239–264.

11 Georges Didi-Huberman, *Confronting Images: Questioning the Ends of a Certain History of Art* (tr. John Goodman, Pennsylvania State University Press 2005) 52.

12 Roland Barthes, *Camera Lucida: Reflections on Photography* (tr. Richard E. Howard, Vintage 2000).

system because it is connected with the specific viewer's response to the image but is also meant to be disconnected from the image maker. The notion is a commentary about time, in relation to life and death. Barthes's notion of the *punctum*, despite criticisms, is a compelling starting point for the consideration of the affective nature of images and visual epistemology, although it is hard for Barthes to defend it as it does present the viewer with a vivifying experience.

Sontag discusses the meaning of photography in her consideration of its lingering effect.[13] Likewise, Feyertag points out that images catalyse a reflective process that never quite disappears.[14] And importantly, as Mondzian reminds us, what is visible cannot be understood as apparent, because invisibility is just as important.[15] Returning to Didi-Huberman, Ferrari notes:

> [Didi-Huberman] regards the acts of seeing not as the act of a machine perceiving the real as composed of tautological evidence. The act of making visible is not the act of giving visible evidence to a pair of eyes that unilaterally seize the 'visual gist' to unilaterally satisfy themselves with it.[16]

Didi-Huberman turns to Walter Benjamin's notion of the 'aura' when writing about visibility and virtuality; Benjamin's writing about childhood perceptions of colours was an important theme in his own reflections on images.[17] The common theme binding these writers – the meaning of the image – as an issue becomes critical for visual epistemology where

> [i]n our contemporary world, images have become widely used as a means of communication. This makes it urgent to understand the process of reading and interpreting images and effects of this paradoxical experience; particularly when it comes to challenging artistic images. The relationship with artistic images makes possible to experience active and passive reception of colours, thus awakening our faculty of imagination.[18]

13 Susan Sontag, *On Photography* (Penguin Books 1979) 19–20.

14 Karoline Feyertag, 'The Art of Vision and the Ethics of the Gaze: On the Debate on Georges Didi-Huberman's Book *Images In Spite of All*', transversal texts (April 2008). https://transversal.at/transversal/0408/feyertag/en#_ftn17 (accessed 21 July 2022).

15 Marie-Jose Mondzian, 'What is an Image?' https://www.psupress.org/books/titles/978-0-271-05064-5.html (accessed 21 July 2022), as quoted in Sonia Campaner Miguel Ferrari, 'Images beyond Representation: Evidence and Depth of Meaning', in Asun López-Varela Azcárate (ed.), *Mind and Matter* (Interchopen 2021), note 2 https://www.intechopen.com/chapters/79021 (accessed 21 July 2022).

16 Ferrari, 'Images beyond Representation', note 2.

17 Didi-Huberman, *Confronting Images*, 191.

18 Ferrari, 'Images beyond Representation'.

Different schools of thought posit questions pertaining to visual thinking and non-visual thinking. The question of whether visual thinking has any epistemic value is one raised regarding mathematics.[19] In this field, both are used together to consider concepts, for example. As noted by Harald Klinke, 'It might be said that ideas can be both abstract and visual, and that they can be communicated accordingly in words or images'.[20]

In law, the study of the image as a source of knowledge is growing in significance, but more can be done to reinforce the relationship between law and visual culture within the wider discourse about visual epistemology. In other words, the difference between knowing and looking will be addressed within the framework of visual epistemology, at least to acknowledge that the detail is understood through a layered interpretive lens; as Didi-Hubermann puts it, 'Nothing is harder to analyse than a phenomenon that can be known in two different orders of magnitude'.[21] For Didi-Hubermann, the part consumes the whole;[22] the exchange is between the discourse and the image. Both Didi-Huberman and Lyotard valorise the eye and the visual over the written text, amplifying the sensual and affect – in other words, the sensory form. Recognising the sensory form of an image of the enactment of law informs our knowledge about these specific accounts. Given the nature and purpose of the show trial, which embraces the performativity of the law, this monograph reasserts the value of visual epistemology within law and in legal historical discourses.

In his 1971 work *Discourse, Figure*, Lyotard considers the way in which that discourse – or the written text central to studies in semiotics and structuralism – and the figural – or the visual – are differentiated. His work is a critique of the dominance of the written text in structuralism and of the position that the intellectual has over the sensual. Instead, the eye and the ways it sees figures challenge the ascription to a single meaning.[23] While Lyotard is central to these exchanges, this monograph will engage with different approaches adopted in the way we understand images. It does, however, return to the contention that the visual possesses a rhythm that points to an order to the emotional sense of the written text. Because I focus on the narratives emerging from the legal life accounts of the depicted individuals, the sentient dimension of what we are seeing strikes me as unavoidable. It is intrinsically tied to the performativity of the law, making its enactment an important way to reach the viewer. This

19 'The Epistemology of Visual Thinking in Mathematics', *Stanford Encyclopedia of Philosophy* (19 February 2020), https://plato.stanford.edu/entries/epistemology-visual-thinking/ (accessed 20 June 2022).

20 Harald Klinke, 'Introduction: The Image and the Mind', in Harald Klinke (ed.), *Art Theory as Visual Epistemology* (Cambridge Scholars Publishing 2014) 1–10, 3.

21 Didi-Hubermann, *Confronting Images*, 232.

22 Didi-Hubermann, *Confronting Images*, 268.

23 See 'Jean François Lyotard', *Stanford Encyclopedia of Philosophy* (21 September 2018) https://plato.stanford.edu/entries/lyotard/#LimiRepr (accessed 20 June 2022).

reach includes wider society, key in the eyes of authorities who embraced the performative value of the performance, including the photograph of a trial.

The dynamic depiction of 'justice being done', as in the collection of photos presented in this monograph, is only part of the story. After all, '[s]how trials are not judicial procedures but media events'.[24] Turning the trial into a media event does not necessarily mean that the proceedings thereby become those of a kangaroo court, but rather this imbues the trial with legitimacy and purpose.[25] The rhetoric that accompanied the trials depicted in this collection of photographs and that is found in the trial transcripts is evidence that the quest for 'truth and just punishment' are not the ultimate goal.[26] The visual record of this collection goes beyond any immediate ideological message. It is an ongoing process and taps into different skill sets related to visual literacy. For example, visual literacy is at the heart of Les Moran's work, which is aimed at raising awareness of pictures of judges.[27] To do so, the management of the pictures, namely their reproduction and dissemination, is key, as visual depictions of judges makes them seem more accessible. This does not come without its challenges. The audience's ability to 'see' and 'read' judges and understand the subject matter cannot be assumed.[28]

Viewing the images takes us on a journey that is led by those working in the background. But there is more than one journey. The other path might be personal. In both cases the performativity of the law, and its enactment, results in some sort of engagement with the manner in which the law is enacted. In other words, we are implicated in the dispensation of justice and the fate of the key participants in the trial. The performativity of images and the way that photographs assume an active role in the viewer's understanding of the subject matter have been subjected to much scholarly scrutiny. An understanding of conceptual and material components is crucial, and the situating of this study of visualising law in visual discourse also solidifies the relationship between visual and legal discourses; they are interrelated.

The study of law and visual culture has developed over the years. This rich area comprises studies in history, as well as contemporary studies in communication theory, and propaganda and mass media more generally. There are works on specific high-profile trials,[29] and in addition to the writing on visual

24 Karl Schlögel, *Moscow, 1937* (Polity 2012) 69.
25 Julie A. Cassiday, *The Enemy on Trial: Early Soviet Courts on Stage and Screen* (Northern Illinois University Press 2000).
26 Schlögel, *Moscow, 1937*, 69.
27 Moran, *Law, Visual Culture and Judges.*
28 Burke, *Eyewitnessing.*
29 Such as the 1893 Lizzie Borden trial (Cara Roberston, *The Trial of Lizzie Borden* , Simon and Schuster 2019), the 1924 Leopold and Loeb trial (Nina Barrett, *The Leopold and Loeb Files: An Intimate Look at One of America's Most Infamous Crimes*, Agate Publishing 2018), the 1950 Julius and Ethel Rozenberg trial (Anne Sebba, *Ethel Rozenberg: An American Tragedy*, St Martin's Publishing Group 2021), the 1960 Adolf Eichmann trial (Hannah Arendt, *Eichmann in Jerusalem: A Report on the*

as sensory noted above, there is much in the field of visual semiotics. A few that will inform the book's approach are worthy of note here, as they raise questions of power and address both the aesthetics underpinning the operationalisation of the visualisation of justice and the reach of affective justice, and why it is vital to informing our understanding of the law.

One position maintains that photographs are taken, brokered, and published with a specific interpretation or meaning in mind. Zeynep Devrim Gürsel argues that seeing through another's eyes is a myth, and that it is really a question of cultural construction. She aptly refers to this as 'powerful fantasy' and bases her claim on anthropological studies concerning the role of storytelling in societies. The point is that it is a fallacy to believe that we can understand the local from the local's point of view – the constructed understanding of the constructed local's constructed point of view. In this convincing account fictions are layered to obscure hierarchy and power relations. To read these images is also to be aware of the decisions that underpin the processes of brokering, as well as the complicated layers of attitudes and behaviours. And in fact there are many participants in a legal propaganda machine. The meaning of these images is entangled in their reproduction and transformation.[30] It is futile to assume that we can look over the shoulder of the image maker, because she is part of the power relations of the image brokers, who converge and diverge on their respective interpretations of justice, as portrayed in the images. Gürsel's research reinforces the point of power relations. John Tagg also provides an important account of knowledge production in the 19th century arising from record-keeping in disciplinary institutions.[31]

Scholars have noted how aesthetic formulations may serve to create law's 'foundational fantasy'.[32] Both law and art contribute to various forms of representation that relay the truth, and can do so in legal or in aesthetic terms.[33] Affective representations both arouse emotion and actualise 'that

Banality of Evil, Penguin 1963), 1969–1970 Chicago Seven trial (Mark L. Levine, George C. McNamee, and Daniel L. Greenberg, eds, *The Trial of the Chicago 7*, Simon and Schuster 2020), the 1992 Rodney King trial (Charles Goodwin and Marjorie Harness Goodwin, 'Contested Vision: the Discursive Constitution of Rodney King', (1997) in B.L. Gunnarsson, Per Linell, and Bengt Nordberg, eds, *The Construction of Professional Discourse*, Routledge 2014 292–316), or the 1995 O. J. Simpson trial (William J. Bowen, James J. Duane, and Benson P. Fraser, 'Media Coverage and Public Opinion of the OJ Simpson Trial: Implications for the Criminal Justice System' (1997) 2(2) *Communication Law and Policy* 261–287).

30 Zeynep Devrim Gürsel, *Image Brokers: Visualising World News in the Age of Digital Circulation* (University of California Press 2016) 10.

31 John Tagg, *The Burden of Representation: Essays on Photographies and Histories* (Macmillan 1988).

32 Julia J. A. Shaw, *Law and the Passions: Why Emotions Matter for Justice* (GlassHouse Books 2019) 28–51.

33 Shaw, *Law and the Passions*, 50. Agata Fijalkowski and Sigrun Valderhaug, 'Legal Decisions, Affective Justice, and "Moving On"?' (2017) 7(2) *Oñati Socio-Legal Series* 337–364.

which can otherwise only be accessed abstractly'.[34] Aesthetic confrontations with justice and injustice guide societal development through narratives that speak to the individual person as well as to the wider community.[35] Upon closer inspection, we discover that the law is immersed in performance.[36] The performance is not only counsel's speech, but also what is immersed in the lawyer's surroundings. Meaning is afforded to those narratives that purport to tell the truth in the legal context, while collectively the same stories represent a lived narrative that can also instruct and assist people in their engagement with the world.[37]

To further emphasise law's performativity, law and visual culture have looked at architecture and the narratives contained in brick, stone, and emblems.[38] The performativity of space is addressed in research dedicated to the court as a space, an aspect as integral to trial proceedings as the stage is to a theatre performance.[39]

As noted above, the photograph collection studied here contains images of the dispensation of justice, the courtroom venue (whatever space was adopted for this purpose, always chosen with great care), and the faces of those involved in the trial. Often the venues was the cinema, a space that

> constitutes a world of its own – a world that exists under artificial lights and that comes alive solely to nourish the daydreams of moviegoing crowds. The doors of the projection hall are hung with velvet curtains. The graceful curve of its huge balcony and the rich

34 Shaw, *Law and the Passions*, 50. Fijalkowski and Valderhaug, 'Legal Decisions, Affective Justice, and "Moving On"?'.
35 Shaw, *Law and the Passions*, 50. Sarat, Douglas, and Umphrey *Law and Performance*.
36 Sarat, Douglas, and Umphrey, *Law and Performance*.
37 Shaw, *Law and the Passions*, 50.
38 Fijalkowski and Valderhaug, 'Legal Decisions, Affective Justice, and "Moving On"?'. See also Judith Resnik and David E. Curtis, *Representing Justice: Invention, Controversy, and Rights in City-States and Democratic Courtrooms* (Yale University Press 2011).
39 Carol Rosenberg, 'Inside America's War Court: Clothing and Culture at Guantánamo Bay', *The New York Times*, 28 December 2019. Within the court's physical space, justice is dispensed, staged, and performed. There are a variety of elements, beginning with the decor, the furniture, the seating arrangements, the line of vision, the clothes worn, and various other aspects that may have an impact on the event. More recently scholars have been looking at the interplay between art and international justice. This approach views the nature of law as formulaic and working towards creating a normative framework that either resolves a particular conflict or details guidelines of general applicability. Art does not concern itself with outcomes to the same degree. The process of international justice is defined as a ritual, and specific details pertaining to the judicial process play a role as they contribute to thoughtful reflection. Marina Aksenova, 'Symposium on Art, Aesthetics, and International Justice' (2020) 114 *AJIL Unbound* 103–107.

> fixtures make the spectators feel that they are entering a – modern – baroque palace.[40]

The venue offered a new aspect to daily reality and 'while the moviegoers' imaginations may roam far from the quotidian, their bodies remain enveloped in a sphere that fills the gap between the quotidian and film plots'.[41]

In addition to the narratives contained in bricks and mortar, the visual representation of the face has its location in the relevant literature. Research in law and visual culture has examined portraits of judges; these depictions contain the same visual codes and hierarchies of law, as do painted portraits.[42] In other words, because of the overrepresentation of men in law, a discourse that centres on masculinity and masculine attributes marginalises women, and the male role in legal developments, past and present, emerges as dominant. Writers instruct us that the silence in terms of the representation of women and LGBTQ+ in visual depictions of judges does not mean that their presence cannot be read into these accounts.[43] Portraits may offer traces of individual legal life stories, which can be put to use in legal life writing.[44] In my collection, most of the photographs are of the faces of defendants and of judicial officials. While they are not portraits, the main point for many researchers of portraiture is that a photo records that someone was in front of a camera when the photo was taken – what Barthes refers to as 'presence'.[45] Whether an image can tell us anything about how people actually looked is less easy to determine. A person will look different depending on how a photo has been made, taking into account conventions of genre and aesthetics, so that a professional portrait will differ from a police mug shot, for instance. Taking a photograph of someone can be both political and visual, presenting us with the 'complexity of entangled relations' between various participants and their particular interests and agendas.[46] Moran, in his study of pictures of judges, links this agenda to the

40 Hans Ulrich Gumbrecht, *In 1926: Living at the edge of Time* (Harvard University Press 1997)141. See also Kirsty Duncanson and Emma Henderson (eds), *Courthouse Architecture, Design and Social Justice* (Routledge 2021).

41 Gumbrecht, *In 1926*, 142.

42 Nikki Godden-Rasul, 'Portraits of Women of the Law: Re-envisioning Gender, law and the Professions in Law Schools' (2019) 39(3) *Legal Studies* 415–431, 429. Les Moran, Gary Watt, Linda Mulcahy, and David Isaac, 'Four Reflections on "The Art of Justice: the Judge's Perspective"' [book review] (2013) 7(1) *Law and Humanities* (2013) 113–128.

43 Moran, *Law, Visual Culture and Judges*, 42.

44 Linda Mulcahy and David Sugarman, *Legal Life-Writing: Marginalised Subjects and Sources* (Wiley-Blackwell 2015).

45 Barthes, *Camera Lucida*, 87.

46 Ariella Azoulay, 'The Lethal Art of Portraiture' (2015) 8(2) *Photography and Culture* 213–226, 214. See also Hannah Parker, 'Face to Face Encounters: Letter Writers and Portrait Photographers in the Russian State Archive', *History* (3 November 2021) https://historyjournal.org.uk/2021/11/03/face-to-face-encounter

white male domination of the profession[47] that promotes values emanating from whiteness and masculinity. At the same time he offers a way to read pictures and develop our visual literacy, but this requires participation in reading the picture to avoid becoming trapped in its narrative.[48]

The performativity and affectivity of the image is tied to the biography of the photograph, located within the photograph's narrative, including its roots in art, performance, and theatre, serving as it does to disseminate messages about law and justice. The law has the capacity to capture the relevant social and political contexts of the period. An image also captures the social context that ordered the lives lived at that juncture. A photograph becomes a live, tangible biography, a material source from the time period of events in that specific country. Manipulation of biography is connected to the mutability of the law, and the fine lines between hero and villain are on display, at different moments, similar to an Italo Calvino story.[49] By and large, such definitions depend on the social, cultural, and political contexts. Photographs, like those in this collection, are simply the most remarkable instance of stories and storytelling, of Stalinist justice, conveyed through non-verbal communication.[50] The photograph certainly merits a place in research pertaining to the visual enactments of the performativity of the law. Trial proceedings retain their intrinsic performativity, rendering the image rich in narratives.

This study's focus is on a specific period; and on this point it is vital to note that it is not the aim of this book to set out a definitive history of Stalinism, or the communist histories of my case studies, or show trials in general, all of which have been done elsewhere.[51] Rather, this work is concerned with situating law and visual culture within the context of the show trial in order to show how an analysis of the performativity of the law can introduce new questions about some of the key individuals involved, as well as about the nature of law and the meaning of achieving justice at the time the photos were

s-letter-writers-and-portrait-photographs-in-the-russian-state-archive/ (accessed 16 November 2021).

47 Moran, *Law, Visual Culture and Judges*, 42.

48 Cited in Azoulay, 'The Lethal Art of Portraiture', 214.

49 Agata Fijalkowski, 'Musine Kokalari and the Power of Images: Law, Aesthetics and Memory Regimes in the Albanian Experience' (2015) 28(3) *International Journal for the Semiotics of Law* 577–602. Italo Calvino, *The Castle of Crossed Destinies* (tr. William Weaver, Vintage 1998).

50 Thank you to Prof. Neil Walker for making this point: Neil MacCormick Fellow seminar, University of Edinburgh (June 2017).

51 See Feinberg, *Curtain of Lies*. For communist histories, see Robert Conquest, *Harvest of Sorrow: Soviet Collectivisation and Terror-Famine* (Oxford University Press 1986) and Robert Service, *Comrades: Communism: A World History* (Harvard University Press 2008). For Soviet show trials, see Viola Lynee, *Stalinist Perpetrators in Trial: Scenes from the Great Terror in the Soviet Ukraine* (Oxford University Press, 2018) and Donald Rayfield, *Stalin and His Hangmen: The Tyrant and Those Who Killed for Him* (Random House 2004). By no means is this list complete.

taken. The work argues for the deployment of art in our legal research. Moreover, the law cannot maintain a discourse that is separate from the circumstances of everyday life. It is imprinted with the past, and its implementation will, in certain circumstances, invoke certain ghosts, i.e. memories.[52] My focus on a collection of photographs warrants consideration for three reasons.

First of all, these images are the ideal starting point for appreciating how a slight shift in our engagement with an image, as an element of visual discourse, has the potential to unlock important narratives about justice. As noted above, the narratives can be released through an ordered rhythm of emotional sense that derives from these images. This dimension will be discussed in relation to three unconventional figures. My protagonists lived in Stalinist Albania, East Germany, and Poland, but in spite of this tried to rise above the dangerous political climate, where no one was immune from being targeted. And they managed to succeed in this endeavour.[53]

Their narratives, like their image, are not fixed per se, and the discourses in question cut across several different temporalities. Because they possess an order to their emotional sense, this movement is critical to our appreciation of visual epistemology. I am interested in our continued fascination with show trials from this period, and how they interact with the present, as a means to complete legal historical accounts. These components continue to be brokered, reproduced, and disseminated. This ability to cross temporalities is the subject of the 'aura' in Walter Benjamin's discussion of mechanical reproduction, or Didi-Huberman's on virtuality.[54] Although writing about fascism, Benjamin's work is also relevant to the context of Soviet justice and the way in which time advances our understanding of key legal discourses at the point where the image irrupts. This point will be picked up in the case studies. Through what I argue is the process of visualising law and justice, we, as viewers, can experience the law as a 'live' event. This occurs at the moment we perceive and identify the law and relive the moment depicted in the visual account. It is the injustice captured by the photographer that is lived through in experience or feeling in our imagination or memory. In art, there is a notion of a 'presentiment of fate' that is located at the heart of the longevity of art. In other words, at each moment of reproduction the image must experience its fate and its story must be retold.[55]

52 For some writers a legal ruling has as much to do with feelings as with intellectual understanding: Shaw, *Law and the Passions*, 13.

53 Karl Schlögel recognises the significance of the individual's pre-history to key historical developments. Schlögel, *Moscow, 1937*, 8.

54 Walter Benjamin, 'The Work of Art in the Age of Mechanical Reproduction', in Walter Benjamin (ed.), *Illuminations* (tr. Harry Zohn, Fontana 1973) 219–253. Didi-Huberman, *Confronting Images*, 191.

55 Lindsay Smith, 'The Wont of Photography, or the Pleasure of Mimesis', in Luisa Calè and Patrizia Bello (eds), *Illustrations, Optics and Objects in Nineteenth-Century Literary and Visual Cultures* (Palgrave 2010) 65–86.

Benjamin's idea of history is an approach that sits comfortably with legal photography. Images are stamped in a mechanical way, which makes them speak out. The viewer is not a passive participant in this process; the viewer retrieves the suppressed message. The retrieval occurs following a summons to respond to the knock of the image and redeeming the image's message. The liberation is temporal, so that the future is what leaves behind traces that will do the redeeming, whereas the redemption is found in the past. In this way, Benjamin undermines the sequences of past, present, and future. The actual present time coexists alongside virtual time. The former is closed and concrete and the latter fluid and open. Both have a role to play at the moment that the individual loses control of the situation and experiences the blind spot of illumination. The camera also undermines the viewer's sovereignty:

> It reproduces the images beating traces of what the photographer intends to capture in the frame, but also what has escaped the photographer's view and succeeded in penetrating the surface of the image. The photograph is not the record of the moment at which the human eye was present. Only by making the visible speak out, which is always performed after the fact, can the photographer or the addressee of the photograph recognise what appears in the image.[56]

A new concept of history was created by acknowledging the psychoanalytic and cultural-technological model of photography. In this approach, history is not yet completed. There continue to be gaps in our knowledge about the period in question. To address these slippages, art can be used as a bridge between the viewer and what is depicted in the image, or between law and society, when the law has run out of space to address the maladministration of justice. The viewer uses art to make the subject legal and part of a folk tale of justice, which makes it understood and connects with members of society.[57]

Second, communist rule in Europe, as well as the dispensation of justice under it, continues to be discussed and dissected through a 21st-century perspective. An account of legal photography and legal photojournalism has the potential to unlock hitherto unknown elements within visual legal and written records. As Peter Goodrich observes, 'the visual rendering – the *veritas falsa* – of law's social presence can be tracked to sources of various jurisliterary forms'. We will see how embracing the various portals noted above inform and change

56 Ariella Azoulay, 'The Darkroom of History' (2005) 10(3) *Angelaki: Journal of the Theoretical Humanities* 57–77, 67.

57 Robert Cover, 'The Folktales of Justice: Tales of Jurisdiction' (1984–1985) 14 *Capital University Law Review* 179–203 https://openyls.law.yale.edu/bitstream/handle/20.500.13051/2048/The_Folktales_of_Justice.pdf?sequence=2&isAllowed=y (accessed 22 December 2021). See also Martha Minow, Michael Ryan, and Austin Sarat (eds), *Narrative, Violence and the Law: the Essays of Robert Cover* (University of Michigan Press 1995).

our understandings of juridical practice. Law is not a singular discipline, but a mix of 'practices and inventions the drivers and instigations of decisions and the scope and inclusiveness of *nomos* at any given time'.[58]

While remnants of communist rule can be found in the present day, our perspective is laden with knowledge that can prejudice our reading of an image. The photograph, however, has the power to override this, to liberate, if we allow it to. This shift in our viewing can lead us to appreciate efforts to achieve justice and extend the reach of the law in seemingly unbelievable contexts; it also allows for an engagement with law's failure. According to Benjamin, 'history isn't only a science that makes definitive statements but also a form of remembering that can change the definitive statements of the past'.[59] Thinking about the past in this way introduces an active materiality that emerges from the intersection of experiences and imaginings of the past.[60] The photograph releases a paradox when it brings a bit of the past to the viewer's attention. This split-second temporal flash can have long-lasting significance.

In contrast to Barthes, writing about 'presence',[61] Benjamin makes the past active in the present. This has wide implications for the law and our understanding of justice during the period of Stalinism.[62] At the time of writing, this point has particular relevance as the Russians prepare show trials along the lines of the Moscow Trials discussed in Chapter 2[63] following the Russian invasion of Ukraine in February 2022. Russian officials have indicated that the Mariupol Tribunal, created to hear trials of Ukrainian prisoners of war, will be modelled on the Soviet war crimes trials of the early 1940s. Officials point to the 'international precedent' that was set in laying a foundation for Nuremberg.

Finally, I turn to the law and how law acts. I explain this through its performativity and how it is enacted in the image. I contend that the key element of political justice, namely 'speaking legally', is an important lens through which to view the photographs. It operates in partnership not only with an understanding of the key brokers of these images, but also with the concept of the here-now and then-there. Using Otto Kirchheimer's formulation of 'speaking legally', we can develop this concept in such a way that it allows the

58 Peter Goodrich, 'Vision and Decision', (2021) 40(1) *Rhetorik* 47–64, 51.

59 Cited in Azoulay, 'The Darkroom of History', 63.

60 Elizabeth Edwards, 'Photography and the Material Performance of the Past' (2009) 48 *History and Theory* 130–150.

61 Barthes, *Camera Lucida*, 87.

62 More recently the work of Ariella Azoulay, *Potential History: Unlearning Imperialism* (Verso 2019), 162–169, provides further impetus for the turn to the visual on the part of law. '[It is l]inear temporality – concretised by the historical timeline – that makes the past into the sealed province of the archive. With the assistance of documents people are made captives of the past': interview with Ariella Azoulay.

63 Francine Hirsch, 'Russia is counting on the media to spread propaganda about show trials', *The Washington Post*, 23 June 2022, https://www.washingtonpost.com/outlook/2022/06/23/russia-is-counting-media-spread-propaganda-about-show-trials/ (accessed 20 July 2022).

viewer to manoeuvre between Stalinist justice and the subject matter of the photograph and its temporality so as to unlock excluded and suppressed narratives.[64] It is not this book's intention to critique Kirchheimer's work on political justice, but to utilise this novel feature to help ground the visual investigation of the law in the disciplinary category of law.[65] This is accompanied by an understanding of visual epistemology that can assist in the study of legal photography and photojournalism of the trial more broadly. Ultimately, this book contends that we need art, such as photography, to bring the subject matter closer. Law inevitably creates a distance between viewers or spectators and the subject matter, including within the context of the show trial. Art is needed in order to begin to understand what the law has totalised or accumulated as evidence. Totalisation leaves the evidence outside the reach of scrutiny; art introduces an affective point of view.[66]

My study will reinforce the importance of interdisciplinarity,[67] an approach that

> does not always require us to fully grasp the new discipline. It is enough to offer inspiration or a tool that helps us better understand the facts to which we want to apply the law. When seen from this perspective, the interdisciplinary approach resembles what courts regularly do when they invite experts to assess a situation. Thus, in practice and in research, law needs extra-legal knowledge.[68]

64 Otto Kirchheimer, *Political Justice* (Princeton University Press 1961) 419.

65 In addition to cadre of socio-legal scholars working on situating visual law in law, I draw inspiration from Robert Darnton's *The Great Cat Massacre* (Penguin 1984). Darrnton applies anthropology to cultural history to produce an engaging work about the French history of mentalities. I am grateful to Dr Andy Aydīn-Aitchison for drawing my attention to this fabulous book.

66 Shoshana Felman, 'Theaters of Justice: Arendt in Jerusalem, the Eichmann Trial, and the Redefinition of Legal Meaning in the Wake of the Holocaust' (2000) 1(2) *Theoretical Inquiries in Law* 466–507, 467.

67 Linda Mulcahy, 'Eyes of the Law: A Visual Turn in Socio-Legal Studies?' (2017) 44(S1) *Journal of Law and Society* S111–S128.

68 Caroline Omari Lichuma, 'Thinking Outside the (Methodological) Box: Teaching New Dogs Old Tricks' (11 December 2020), BAR Socio-Lab Blog, https://barblog.hypotheses.org/3485 (accessed 22 July 2022), emphasis in original. See also Felman, 'Theatres of Justice', 3: 'We needed limits to be able both to close the case and to enclose it in the past. Law distances the Holocaust. Art brings it closer. We needed art – the language of infinity – to mourn the losses and to face up to what in traumatic memory is not closed and cannot be closed. Historically, we needed law to totalize the evidence, to totalize the Holocaust, and, through totalization, to start to apprehend its contours and its magnitude. Historically, we needed art to start to apprehend and to retrieve what the totalization left out. Between too much proximity and too much distance, the Holocaust becomes today accessible, I will propose, precisely in this space of slippage between law and art. But it is also in this space of slippage that its full grasp continues to elude us'.

In short, law does not work in a vacuum. It is in tune with its surroundings and engages in a dynamic process of imprinting, transforming, and mutating. Not only is law capable of being a focal point, it can also leave tiny clues at the fringe of a discussion. It is hidden. Law can take many forms, both physical and non-physical, and its materiality can be felt and seen through various formats. Importantly, law is affective. Its affectivity is a key consideration in this work, which explores the power of the photograph, which in turn allows us to engage with the law through the photograph. Law cannot be separated from visual culture; this is shown in the number of writings on this subject over the years.

This introduction has pointed to several dominant positions that diverge with respect to the meaning of the image, whether it is attached to its system of signs or to its sentient character, or dependent on the viewer's way of seeing and looking. Didi-Huberman's question 'What does the image want?' is an important point to take forward in the case studies.

The chapters in this book cover a wide range of concerns and issues of biography and history that do not only reflect, but also rethink and rework the photograph. It does so by looking at the context of the time in which the image was taken and discusses its relevance to the dispensation of justice at that time, and what has endured by way of the image in terms of the law, justice, and individuals caught in that moment.[69] In other words, the discussion reaches out to extra-legal sources – a process familiar to lawyers and legal scholars alike. It is the most effective means to engage with legal problems, which again acknowledges that law does not work in a vacuum. Reaching out to art is intentional for it 'inscribes what we do not yet know of our lived historical relation to the events of our times'.[70]

Conceptualising the Photograph

I have identified performativity as the key connection between the law and the visual. I contend that in order to think about visualising law, we need to shift the way in which we engage with the image. Drawing on key writings about narrative, I argue that the image should be read against the grain to allow it to speak legally and disclose other histories.

As my collection of photographs comes from different national archives – the Albanian Telegraphic Agency (ATSH) and the Albanian Central State Archives (CSA); the Federal German Archives and Stasi Records Archive (BArch); and the Polish National Institute of Remembrance (IPN) – there are notable selections and absences in these archives, and any neutrality assumed by the

69 Felman refers to contextualisation and textualisation. Shoshana Felman and Dori Laub, *Testimony: Crises of Witnessing in Literature, Psychoanalysis, and History* (Routledge 1992), xv.

70 Felman and Laub, *Testimony*, xx.

archive is an illusion, confirming Allan Sekula's assertion that archives are not neutral depositories.[71] All three archives preserve certain historical discourses that are also reworked and obscured. While this is not central to my research questions, it is central to the ethos of the project, which has self-reflection at its core. It is important to be aware of the micro-intentions in the practices at archives concerning the organisation of respective holdings. As Steve Edwards points out, 'Photographs might be truthful ... but the descriptions of pictures are not at all reliable'.[72]

Many photographs were produced in the past, but few remain in circulation decades after they were taken, and researchers are often interested in how and why particular images are reused. To explore the historical trajectory of a single photograph requires attending to captions, and to the changing placement and context of an image (newspaper, art gallery, etc.). Furthermore, what is visible shifts due to cropping and alteration. Reflecting on why a photo was made in a particular way and tracing its trajectory raises questions about whether researchers can use photographs to learn about a photographer's attitudes and conscious or unconscious viewpoint. Discovering a photographer's intentions is not straightforward, but the contexts in which the photographer's work is encountered can provide vital clues. I will reflect on specific related points when I turn to individual collections, most evident in the Albanian case study.

I address key themes relating to the way in which the image irrupts in the three case studies. Photographs are meant to generate questions about the events, people, and things that are photographed and how they connect to a wider world.[73] As Susan Sontag states, 'It was not a question of knowledge ... but of alertness, a fastidious transcription of what *could* be thought about something, once it swam into the stream of attention'.[74]

Chapter 1: Stalinist Justice in Central and Eastern Europe

This chapter addresses law and the dispensation of justice within the broader context of Stalinist justice in Central and Eastern Europe. The discussion introduces key criminal legal provisions and characteristics of Stalinist rule by looking at the writings of Andrei Vyshinsky and Leon Petrażycki, before

71 Allan Sekula, 'Reading an Archive: Photography between Labour and Capital', in P. Holland, J. Spence, and S. Watney (eds), *Photography/Politics: Two* (Comedia Publishing 1986) 153–159. And by the same author, 'The Body and the Archive', in R. Bolton (ed.), *The Contest of Meaning: Critical Histories of Photography* (MIT Press 1996) 343–388.

72 Steve Edwards, *Photography: A Very Short Introduction* (Oxford University Press 2006) 68.

73 Howard Becker, 'Do Photographs Tell the Truth?', in T. Cook and C. Reichardt (eds), *Qualitative and Quantitative Methods in Evaluation Research* (Sage 1979) 99–117.

74 Susan Sontag, 'Remembering Barthes', *New York Review of Books*, 15 May 1980, https://www.nybooks.com/articles/1980/05/15/remembering-barthes/ (accessed 22 July 2022), emphasis in original.

addressing the example of the 1949 Rajk trial. These key themes will be part of the backdrop to the discussion about the way in which the image irrupts in the three case studies.

Chapter 1 also provides a brief account of Stalin's life story and the evolution of Stalinist justice. It sets up the context concerning developments in Soviet legal photography and photojournalism that served to bring images of show trials to the public, all based on the performativity of the law and tradition of performing agitation trials, which will be looked at in Chapter 2. It also considers that at the heart of the appeal of the trial was the confession and the *samokritika*.

Chapter 2: Law, Visual Culture, and the Show Trial in Soviet Times

This chapter discusses visual law in Soviet Russia, namely the advancement of legal propaganda from staged trials to photography. It engages with Elizabeth Wood's work on agitation trials, which identifies the significance of ritual and enactment of moral codes in a public venue.[75] With technology, Lenin saw its potential in presenting the political message and legal propaganda in a proactive and direct fashion. This visual legal model was brought to and imposed on the communist satellite states through a rigorous campaign of legal propaganda that had performance at its centre. It was dependent on Soviet photographers and photojournalists, who played a critical role in relaying messages about the law that were both educational and punitive, especially of the class enemy. Each state applied the model in different ways, as will be shown in the three case studies of Albania, East Germany, and Poland. Its success rested with the people involved and the appreciation of performance, including the performance of the law. With photography, the reach of the power of the image could be amplified through the dissemination of shots from the proceedings.

Chapter 3: Law, Visual Culture, and the Show Trial in Albania

This chapter discusses visual law in Albania. Albania is one of the most important examples of a European dictatorship. The consideration of the wider context that includes the Soviet setting in the Albanian context will rely on Elidor Mëhilli's research.[76] Albanian communism was highly centralised and communists dominated all aspects of everyday life. From 1945 to 1951 the Enver Hoxha regime consolidated its power over the country, and six critical trials were held during this period. Albanian photography has an important

75 Elizabeth Wood, *Performing Justice: Agitation Trials in Early Soviet Russia* (Cornell University Press 2005).

76 Elidor Mëhilli, *From Stalin to Mao: Albania and the Socialist World* (Cornell University Press 2017).

history and played a significant role at this time. This part of the discussion will engage with Gilles de Rapper's work.[77] Key studios were established in the country by photographers who had trained in Istanbul and Paris. Those who trained at these studios – and survived the Second World War – would later work at the state-run Telegraphic Agency, where they could hone their skills. They photographed the trials, and their images were published in the principal broadsheets of the day. The images are deeply captivating, a quality attributable in part to the photographers' experience and training. The photographs taken at the six main trials did much to ensure that speaking legally also meant acting legally: in other words, stifling and eliminating any independent thought. The images are also powerful because of the courtroom setting – capacious theatre venues that provided space for a large audience. In scrutinising the Albanian case study we need to bear in mind the importance of private photography for family biographies. Finally, the images are compelling because of the subject matter itself. The combination of the material and visual culture, and the narratives contained within some of the images, disclose the law's *punctum*. Research and archival materials show the driving force underpinning the law's sentient presence in specific images in the Albanian case study and point to the image maker.

Chapter 4: Law, Visual Culture, and the Show Trial in East Germany

Otto Kirchheimer notes that the policy of the East German administration served a dual purpose: speedy integration with other communist-directed states and furthering social change, paving the way for eventual absorption into the Eastern bloc.[78] Law in East Germany had its foundations in the Soviet experience. This came in the form of Evgeny Pashukanis (representing legal nihilism) and Andrei Vyshinsky (representing the value of formal law).[79] A new High

77 Gilles de Rapper, 'Photography and Remembrance. Questioning the Visual Legacy of Communist Albania', in Jonila Godole and Idrit Idrizi (eds), *Between Apathy and Nostalgia: Private and Public Recollections of Communism in Contemporary Albania* (IDMC 2019) 103–119, 103. See also Gilles de Rapper and Anouk Durand, 'Family Photographs in Socialist Albania: State Photography and the Private Sphere', in Eckehard Pistrick, Nicola Scaldaferri, and Gretel Schwörer (eds), *Audiovisual Media and Identity Issues in Southeastern Europe* (Cambridge Scholars Publishing 2011) 210–229; Gilles de Rapper, 'Photographs and *Régime d'historicité*: Past, Present, and Future in Two Photographic Albums on Communist Albania', in Nataša Gregorič and Smoki Musaraj (eds), *Remitting, Restoring and Building Contemporary Albania* (Palgrave 2021) 51–73.

78 Otto Kirchheimer, 'The Administration of Justice and the Concept of Legality in East Germany' (1958–1959) 68 *Yale Law Journal* 705–749, 705, fn. 1. He refers to Harold Berman, 'Soviet Law Reform: Dateline Moscow 1957' (1957) 66(8) *Yale Law Journal* 1191–1215, 1212.

79 Peter C. Caldwell, *Dictatorship, State Planning, and Social Theory in the German Democratic Republic* (Cambridge University Press 2003) 57.

Court (*Obersten Gericht*) and the Office of the Attorney General were created in 1949, when the state was permitted to take its final shape. These two bodies became the central focus for directing legal developments.

This chapter examines the vital role that legal photography and legal photojournalism played in the administration of law. Visual accounts included in the main broadsheet newspapers further demonstrate the particular approach to the administration of justice in East Germany. This unique characteristic manifested itself in the way that the legal system wholly embraced Vyshinsky's notion of educating to throttle and throttling to educate. In some ways the application of Vyshinsky's theories exceeded the Soviet prosecutor's wildest dreams.[80] This accelerated version of Vyshinsky's programme was facilitated by judge Hilde Benjamin.[81] Benjamin is chiefly known for her unwavering commitment to communism, and during the 1950s as High Court judge she delivered judgments in cases concerning capital crimes that earned her the nickname 'Bloody Hilde' or 'The Red Guillotine'. Benjamin presided over all of the decisions in political cases. State-employed photographers photographed the trials, and the images were published in the main broadsheets of the day. As in the Albanian case study, the images are captivating and the viewer is drawn to a certain aesthetic in the photograph. They are also powerful because of the courtroom setting – large theatre venues, as in the Albanian case. Finally, they are compelling because of the subject matter. The driving force underpinning the law's *punctum* in the East German case study points to the performance of education and throttling during the trial proceedings, so effectively captured in the images, which possess an emotive power.

Chapter 5: Law, Visual Culture, and the Show Trial in Poland

Polish judicial officials always nursed an underlying mistrust of the Soviet authorities. Poland historically had anti-Russian sentiments and the Second World War offered the Poles, even if members of the Polish Communist Party, no reason to change their minds. For future Polish leaders of the Communist Party it was not possible to attain Soviet objectives (in terms of imposing the Soviet model across all walks of life) without bearing in mind Polish realities, namely the resentment of Polish civil society towards the Soviets. For the Soviets this raised suspicion, and during 1933 to 1938 all the leaders of the Polish party, intellectuals and prominent functionaries, were murdered.[82] These themes are present in the images depicted in this chapter.

80 Hilde Benjamin and Ernst Melsheimer, 'Zehn Jahre demokratischer Justiz in Deutschland' (1955) 9 *Neue Justiz* 259–266.

81 Hilde Benjamin, 'Feierliches Gedenken von Andrej Januarjewitsch Wyshinski' (1954) 8 *Neue Justiz* 678.

82 Timothy Snyder, *Bloodlands: Europe between Hitler and Stalin* (Bodley Head 2010) 95–98.

The pro-communist Committee for National Liberation (*Polski Komitet Wyzwolenia Narodowego*, PKWN) issued the relevant decrees that played a key role in prosecuting Poles who were charged with treason. The visual records focused on the main judicial figures within a legal framework that was in a state of flux. This chapter discusses a specific war crimes trial, that of Albert Forster, held before the Polish Supreme National Tribunal (*Najwyższy Trybunał Narodowy*) and one of the prosecutors, Mieczysław Siewierski. As Gerry Simpson argues, all trials are show trials.[83] But in this case the prosecutor became the defendant overnight, by violating the same law as the German war criminal. The images largely concern the judicial gatherings, symbols, and specific shots of defendants.

The Polish visual record played a different role for the Polish state, where the legal discourses concerned the attempt to create the new judicial official, who was, above all, politically reliable. This yielded different results. The driving force underpinning the law's *punctum* in the Polish case study points to this specific subject matter found within these photographs, many of which have never been seen in a wider, English-speaking context.

Conclusion

This chapter draws on common themes and diverging narratives in the Albanian, East German, and Polish case studies, and show how images cut across temporalities and have the ability to challenge seemingly entrenched legal narratives. We are thus concerned here with three narratives that are at odds and diverge but come together at law's *punctum*: Albania and its image makers; East Germany and its redefinition of Vyshinsky's school of education and throttling; and Poland and its visual account of judges and those suspected of political crimes. The selected images point to the law's *punctum* and a consideration of the 'presence' of the dispensation of justice. The material quality enables the image to travel across temporalities and to become part of new historical legal discourses as society is challenged by new representations of law and justice. The power of the materiality of the image transforms it into an actant to mobilise and affect the viewing audiences.

This visual law project employs cross-disciplinary and interdisciplinary frameworks that test the boundaries of law and transcend them. The visual account testifies to the fact that the law does not exist in isolation. Because it does not, it is vital to identify what is law within the parameters of the individual's life. Does this knowledge have an emotional response? How is it ordered in one's mind? There is an aspect of the 'album' about this collection, for there are connections between the case studies, much as there are in a family album, where people, events, and settings are connected. The image also captures the

83 Gerry Simpson, *Law, War and Crime: War Crimes Trials and the Reinvention of International Law* (Polity Press 2007).

social context that ordered everyday life at that time. The photograph becomes a tangible biography, a material source for the time period of events in the specific country. Photographs are the most effective non-verbal communication art form to retell the story of the show trials without ignoring the sensory component that is entangled in the image's narrative.

Chapter 1

Stalinist Justice in Central and Eastern Europe

This chapter sets the backdrop to the nature of Stalinist justice in the three case studies, which will provide further context to the key themes emerging from the image and the way that it irrupts. Justice, and the enemy, were defined in the Stalinist period, and the way that these ideas became tangible in a trial were dependent on a variety of factors, namely the photograph's ability to 'speak legally' in visual depictions of the dispensing of justice and the visual literacy of the average citizen. It is important not to ignore the sentient dimension of these depictions, felt by past and present viewers. This chapter considers the main parameters of Stalinist justice. It is not intended to provide a comprehensive analysis, which has been done elsewhere, but to show that general points can be made about the law during this time, as a means to illustrate the discourses about law under communism, the effect and affect of show trials, justice and legitimacy, and photography and evidence.[1] The legal photography and legal photojournalism in the case studies are linked to key developments in the Soviet Union, as Chapters 1 and 2 will demonstrate.

Otto Kirchheimer's central idea lives on in discussions about the legacy of the Stalinist period, in terms of 'speaking legally'. According to Kirchheimer, political justice operates in a system that adheres to a special kind of communication. Above all, however, political justice relies on procedure, understood as an integral part of the administration of justice. The first examples of Kirchheimer's reminded readers of the fact that it is not an innovation to discredit or to destroy a political opponent by accusing them of having committed a common crime. The role of the trial is twofold: as a weapon of attack but also as a defence of the existing regime. To be accepted as legitimate in the public eye, a certain degree of reasonableness in the exercise of state power must be demonstrated. The show trial should have the appearance of authenticity. The specific task of legitimising cases of state power that are directed at an alleged opponent falls to the courts; the judge is the legitimiser of the exercise of governmental power. At the same time, the judiciary enters into a

1 Melissa Feinberg, *Curtain of Lies: The Battle over Truth in Stalinist Eastern Europe* (Oxford University Press 2017).

DOI: 10.4324/9781003405771-2

role that is as formidable as it is fragile. The notion of speaking legally is 'a veritable key to the clarification of the problematic role of the judiciary in the political fabric'.[2] Yet '[w]hy do governments resort to courts at all? Why do they run the risk of being rebuffed by the courts and the danger of the political trial being used by the accused and his group as a public forum of the potentially highest efficiency?'[3] The right balance between judicial independence and judicial obedience must be found: 'Courts cannot serve as legitimisers of governmental power unless they can follow their own judgment independent of the views of the government'.[4] Soviet justice involves a dichotomy between the notion of legality and that of force, or between the political and non-political, and also between the way in which the relation between legality and the party is operationalised. In this grey area, a dictatorship is capable of creating a legal order that operates with considerable stability and independence in matters considered non-political.[5]

The Reinvention of Stalin and the Creation of Stalinist Justice

It is not possible to consider the performativity of Stalinist justice without a brief consideration of Joseph Stalin, who himself was reinvented with the help of visual culture. The main commentators of show trials refer to Stalin as a central driver in the show trials. There are many excellent biographies written about Stalin.[6] The purpose of this section is to identify some key facts.

Stalin was born in 1878 in Gori, Georgia, and studied at an Orthodox seminary in Georgia. For some scholars, this formed an important part of his attitude towards the visual.[7] Although he rejected Orthodox teaching and any form of religion in favour of atheism, Stalin appealed to the religious nature of the Russian (and other Soviet) people and supported the construction of an image of himself resembling an Orthodox saint. He did this by having images of himself displayed in many public places, often as statues. A false account of his childhood was created to make him appear as a Christlike figure, born to lead his people. In the arts, operas and films were made to show him in a

2 Otto Kirchheimer, *Political Justice* (Princeton University Press 1961) 419.
3 Kirchheimer, *Political Justice*, 199.
4 Kirchheimer, *Political Justice*, 200.
5 Otto Kirchheimer, 'The Administration of Justice and the Concept of Legality in East Germany' (1958–1959) 68 *The Yale Law Journal* 705–749.
6 See Stephen Kotkin, *Stalin: Waiting for Hitler, 1929–1941* (Penguin 2018); Simon Sebag Montefiore, *Stalin: The Court of the Red Tsar* (Weidenfeld & Nicolson 2003); Phillip Boobbyer, *The Stalin Era* (Routledge 2000); Robert Conquest, *Stalin: Breaker of Nations* (Harmondsworth 1998). See also Orlando Figes, *The Whisperers: Private Life in Stalinist Russia* (Picador 2007) and Sheila Fitzpatrick, *Everyday Stalinism: Ordinary Life in Extraordinary Times: Soviet Russia in the 1930s* (Oxford University Press 2000).
7 George H. Hodos, *Show Trials: Stalinist Purges in Eastern Europe, 1948–1954* (Praeger 1987) 1–2.

heroic light, for example in Soviet director Sergei Eisenstein's *Ivan the Terrible*.[8] Significantly, Stalin's name was kept constantly before the Soviet people. As one writer remarked, '[y]ou only have to listen to the radio programme about our achievements, and every fifth or tenth word will be the name of Comrade Stalin'.[9] Stalin had thus controlled and became part of master historical, political, cultural, and legal narratives. People across all sectors of society played an important role in maintaining these discourses. With practically no dissent and his image constantly before the Soviet people, Stalin was able to impose his will with some skill and efficiency.

Stalinist justice would rework the purpose of the trial to suit Marxism–Leninism–Stalinism[10] and the performative element of Stalinist justice successfully personalised the abstract political enemy by placing her in the dock in flesh and blood and, with the aid of the law, transforming abstract political-ideological differences into easily intelligible common crimes. Once Lenin had died and Stalin assumed leadership in 1928, legal reform was expected to conform to the principles of Marxism–Leninism–Stalinism. Up until that point, legal drafters introduced innovations to Soviet criminal law based on current thinking about criminal behaviour related to the Italian positivist school of Enrico Ferri.[11] Crime was redefined as social danger; the act against the interests of the working class was a social danger if it was a commission or omission. The concept of guilt was debated by the key thinkers of the period, and at one point Pashukanis and his school drafted a legal system that would conform to ideological objectives of a law withering away.[12]

Stalinism, for its part, refers to the actual style of government and it needed and relied on the law and a legal system. Stalin's closest associate played a key role in the show trials of the 1930s. In relation to the judiciary, Andrei Vyshinsky wrote that the proletarian dictatorship is assisted by the courts in ensuring compliance with the state's orders, in particular during the transitional period 'to crush exploiters'.[13] The Unified State Political Administration (*Obyedinyonnoye gosudarstvennoye politicheskoye* upravleniye, OGPU, the new name that Stalin had given to the state security police, previously known as Vecheka/Cheka) was also an expression of the proletarian dictatorship that was given the task of '*crush[ing] the resistance* of class enemies of the toilers'.[14] The intensification of the class struggle did not recognise the 'withering away of the

8 Hodos, *Show Trials*, 1–2. See also Sergei Loznitsa's *The Trial* (2018).
9 Hodos, *Show Trials*, 1–2.
10 Hodos, *Show Trials*, 1–2.
11 Soviet jurists denied that they were greatly influenced by Ferri. See Harold J. Berman, 'Principles of Soviet Criminal Law' (1947) 56 (5) *The Yale Law Journal* 803–836, fn. 9.
12 Berman, 'Principles of Soviet Criminal Law', 803, fn. 4.
13 Andrei Vyshinsky (ed.), *The Law of the Soviet State* (tr. Hugh W. Babb, Macmillan 1948) 50.
14 Vyshinsky, *The Law of the Soviet State*, 154, emphasis in original.

law'. One of Vyshinsky's main contributions to criminal legal writing was his emphasis on the confession, the 'queen of the truth'. The significance of the confession was identified by Stalin, as has been noted,[15] linking the dictator's writings with his upbringing and education at the seminary. The show trial was a dynamic event that engaged the wider audience in the process of defining the enemy. This process, which drew on legal innovations and certain social and cultural contexts, developed the notion of 'enemy' at the domestic level and had a role to play internationally as well. Stalin controlled every detail of the policy of the moment; he himself underpinned the political culture that would shape the definition of a perpetrator[16] to be carried into the dominant legal discourse, nationally and internationally.

As to the latter, the main Nuremberg trial following the Second World War was a political and a legal event on an unprecedented scale, but also a remarkable media undertaking: it was broadcast and recorded. Moreover, photographs, films, and audio recordings were used as evidentiary material during the proceedings. Stalin had already made use of such a show trial of German war criminals in Kharkov (now Kharkiv, Ukraine) in December 1943. It is therefore not surprising that in 1945 Stalin sought to establish the International Military Tribunal, and to organise another round of show trials of German leaders.[17]

The Importance of the Confession

One of the drivers of the discourse was the confession. Stephanie K. Decker, in her study of this period, finds that the prevalent agreement among authorities was that confessions were a necessary form of additional social control, as they framed conflicts rooted in societal contradictions as deviant behaviour.[18] Decker argues that by using valuable criminological frameworks of degradation ceremonies and spectacle, public confessions intended to reframe larger contradictions within the social order as acts of deviance are unlikely to be

15 Mark D. Steinberg, *Proletarian Imagination: Self, Modernity, and the Sacred in Russia, 1910–1925* (Cornell University Press 2002). See also Lynne Viola, 'The Question of the Perpetrator in Soviet History' (2013) 72(1) *Slavic Review* 1-23, https://www.jstor.org/stable/10.5612/slavicreview.72.1.0001 (accessed 8 September 2021), on the discourse concerning the perpetrator, where the distinction between the perpetrator and victim is not clear-cut; Golfo Alexopoulos, 'Stalin and the Politics of Kinship: Practices on Collective Punishment, 1920s–1940s' (2008) 50(1) *Comparative Studies in Societies and History* 91–117.

16 Viola, 'The Question of the Perpetrator in Soviet History'.

17 Valentyna Polunina, 'Soviet War Crimes Policy in the Far East: The Bacteriological Warfare Trial at Khabarovsk, 1949', in Morten Bergsmo, Wui Ling Cheah, and Ping Yi (eds), *Historical Origins of International Criminal Law: Volume 2* (Torkel Opsahl Academic EPublisher 2014) 539–562.

18 Stephanie K. Decker, 'The Role of Public Confessions in Show Trials: An Analysis of the Moscow Show Trials' (2019) 32(4) *Journal of Historical Sociology* 459–477.

successful for long periods of time, as the deep-rooted contradictions within the social order will exist after the trials have come to their conclusion. The spectacle of the dramatised trial would come to represent the 'inverted image of society',[19] whereby authentic social life is replaced with its representation. Gradually the audience comes to identify with the trial performances that increasingly superseded real activities and perceptions of law and justice. The confession becomes an important component of the enactment of the law.

Assisted by the aesthetic of the trial,[20] photographs of defendants making their confession served as evidence of the spectacle's authenticity. They also played a role in the transformation of the spectacle into the real. Decker concurs that a well-selected venue makes for an especially advantageous setting. Courts represent truth and neutrality; thus any narratives that emerge contain grains of legitimacy.[21] This legitimacy coexists with the educational role of the law. The final component requires effective management of the audience through selection of what is to be reported and published for wider dissemination.[22] This involved the brokers, who were negotiating and arranging the identity of the 'enemy', who sealed her fate by way of the confession. The response of the audiences and the circulation of information attests to the power of images and how we interpret what we see. The confession is the connection to the criminal legal process. These final two components in Decker's analysis conform to the criteria of 'speaking legally', but also rely on subject matter that captures the audience's attention, and the correct technology to disseminate the images of the spectacle and performance. Finally, political developments underpin the success of the show trial through its popularity: authorities understood the value of law and drama and, importantly, how to write and perform the story that is rooted in a confession that was a very real part of the case against the defendant and her ultimate sanction, often death or a prolonged period of imprisonment.

The Construction and Deconstruction of the Definition of the Enemy

The confession or admission of guilt is located within the wider context of a new criminal legal framework, which saw the introduction of new terminology and approaches to social danger, guilt, and punishment. This section will briefly discuss key terms and context.

19 Guy Debord, *The Society of the Spectacle* (tr. Donald Nicholson-Smith, Black and Red 1970). Debord's work develops Marx's concept of fetishism of commodities found in *The German Ideology*, published in 1867.

20 Julie A. Cassiday, *The Enemy on Trial: Early Soviet Courts on Stage and Screen* (Northern Illinois University Press 2000) 5–6.

21 Decker, 'The Role of Public Confessions in Show Trials'.

22 Decker, 'The Role of Public Confessions in Show Trials', 462.

Inspired by new terminology, the drafters filled the criminal code with provisions that were framed in it. At the same time, the use of indefinite terms and clauses covering a wide range of crimes left room for loose interpretation and arbitrariness. The claim that Soviet law was entering a new path in the treatment of crime and punishment was advanced but not entirely supported. While the People's Commissar for Justice, Nikolai Krylenko, advocated the elimination of personal guilt as a basis of punishment, he also supported the idea of social danger.[23] In essence, a social danger may be presented in the act of a person who is not capable of controlling herself; or a responsible person may commit an act through the force of circumstances; likewise, a person may be dangerous although there is no evidence of her participation in a given crime.[24] If the measure is protective, it should be applied against any dangerous person.

The idea of social danger itself came to be reflected in the concept of aggravating circumstances. For example, section 47 (as amended in 1927 and again in 1930) of the Soviet Criminal Code saw aggravating circumstances also occurring if there was a possibility that the interests of the state or the workers could have been endangered by the crime, even though the crime was not specifically directed against the interests of the state or the workers. Not surprisingly, the concept of social danger as a substitute for guilt was used by the Soviet state security police. These powers were first used in 1934 in a series of legal provisions. Section 1(3) of the Statute on Political Crimes of 8 June 1934 introduced guilt by association, for example, and was later incorporated into section 58(1)(c) of the Criminal Code.[25] Section 58 entered Soviet public discourses quickly and was greatly feared; it continues to lurk in the shadow across the images discussed in this book.

These legal amendments would also lead to the creation of various counter-revolutionary crimes. This development was justified on the grounds of necessity, namely taking energetic steps to suppress class enemies, according to Stalinist theory. In other words, responsibility extended to all and was represented as a collective responsibility. Individual counter-revolutionary crimes were defined in broad terms and, in addition to definitions of particular crimes given in 14 sections, there was a 'species' definition of counter-revolutionary crime:

> Section 58(1). Any act intended to overthrow, to undermine, or to weaken the power of workers' and peasants' soviets, and of the workers' and peasants' governments of the USSR, the constituent and autonomous republics elected by the soviets in accordance with the constitutions of the

23 Berman, 'Principles of Soviet Criminal Law', 810–811, also fn. 16. But see George V. Starosolsky, 'Basic Principles of Soviet Criminal Law' (1950) 28(4) *North Carolina Law Review* 359–374, 365.

24 Berman, 'Principles of Soviet Criminal Law', 811–813.

25 Berman, 'Principles of Soviet Criminal Law', 825–826 and Robert W. Thurston, 'The Soviet Family during the Great Terror' (1991) 43(3) *Soviet Studies* 553–574, 556.

> USSR and the constituent republics, or to undermine or weaken the external safety of the USSR or the basic economic, political and national conquests of the proletarian revolution shall be considered counter-revolutionary.

For example, in the statute from 5 November 1934 a person need not be found guilty to be subject to penalties.[26] Under the law in section 16, if a socially dangerous act was not directly specified by the Code, the basis and limits of punishment for it would be determined by applying the sections of the Code which specified crimes of the kind closely resembling the act.[27] Guilt by association was key: wide-reaching and carried out in the context of the class struggle. The Soviet science of criminal law openly declared that the interpretation of criminal laws were essentially a political interpretation. This meant that the only correct and truly scholarly interpretation of criminal law was one that protected working-class interests. The smallest departure from this principle might show sympathy with the position of bourgeois objectivity, which in turn would result in the heaviest violation of socialist legality.

Leon Petrażycki

Vyshinsky had a disdain for the intuitive sense of justice that underpinned workers' ideas. The intuitive law doctrine that would later accommodate Marxist thought created a new order by institutionalising a centralised hierarchy of command that was equated with the legal order. Templates in textbooks set out different frames of legality related to different social structures. On the other hand, scholars such as the Polish legal philosopher Leon Petrażycki tried to look at the role of law as an instrument of power.[28] Petrażycki's writings offer an important counterpoint to Vyshinsky's works. His view provides an important way through which to consider developments in Soviet justice and serve as a counterpoint to Vyshinsky's approach.

Petrażycki's rejection of a narrow legal positivism was formed by Polish history.[29] He did not equate law with the external coercion exercised by the state.

26 Starosolsky, 'Basic Principles of Soviet Criminal Law', 360. For a personal account, see Evgenia Ginsburg, *Journey into the Whirlwind* (Harcourt Brace 1975).

27 Starosolsky, 'Basic Principles of Soviet Criminal Law', 369.

28 See Leon Petrażycki, 'O dopełniających prądach kulturalnych i prawach rozwoju handlu' [On Complementary Cultural Trends and Laws of Commercial Development] (Nakładem Towarzystwa im. Leona Petrażyckiego 1936). See also 'Prawo a Sad' [Law and Court] (Nakładem Towarzystwa im. Leona Petrażyckiego 1936).

29 Russia was having the same legal debates as Continental Europe. B. Chicherin, representing the legal idealism school, included in his main works *A History of Political Theories* (5 vols, Macmillan Company 1877–1902) and Vladimir Soloviev, *The Crisis of Western Philosophy: Against the Positivists* (1874, reprinted by SteinerBooks 1996). P. I. Novgorodsteff supported the revival of natural law; his main works include *The Historical School in Jurisprudence* (1896) and *Kant and Hegel* (1901)

He argued that only a man suffering from a total inability to have legal experiences, or the experience of having a legal right or a legal obligation, could assume that law was simply a set of commands. Instead he looks at the individual experiencing the legal phenomena.[30] Law was not a system of abstract norms but a part of social reality which had to be studied causally. For Petrażycki, the ethical function of law was paramount. The goal was to make purposeful, conscious law.[31]

Petrażycki was best known for his emphasis on 'intuitive law', and he frequently identified the superiority of intuitive law over statutory law. He presented relevant examples in contemporary Russian history.[32] In Petrażycki's view, legal expertise was institutionally underdeveloped in Russia. He pointed to the excessive growth of the institutions and the arbitrary and detailed explanations of existing laws that was dangerous because the authority of law was not justified. He observed that the objective meaning of a statute law was always less important than the opinions of influential people. Russian statutes had too many references to subjective factors, such as 'good will' or 'conscience', which judges were supposed to consider when adjudicating.

(both available at https://etherwave.wordpress.com/2012/08/19/paul-vinogradoff-historical-jurisprudence-and-the-critique-of-sociology/, accessed 15 August 2022). As for the legal positivism school, the writings of N. Korkunoff – *Lectures on the General Theory of Law* (tr. W.S. Hastings, Macmillan Company 1888) and *Russian Constitutional Law* (St Petersburg 1893–1901) – influenced both Russian jurists and Petrażycki. See W.E. Butler, 'Towards an Introduction to Russian Legal Theory', in W.E. Butler (ed.), *Russian Legal Theory* (Dartmouth 1996) xxxv–xxxvii.

30 William R. Jentes, 'Petrazycki: Law and Morality' (1955) 54 *Michigan Law Review* 160–163, 161.

31 Petrażycki was drawn to psychology when creating this new legal policy. During his law studies, Petrażycki was in Berlin to participate in a seminar run by the expert in Roman Law at that time, Heinrich Dernburg. Petrażycki published *Fruchtverteilung beim Wechsel des Nutzungsberichtigten* (Berlin 1892) and *Die Lehre vom Einkommen* (2 vols, 1893–1895) https://archive.org/details/dielehrevomeink00petrgoog/page/n15/mode/2up (accessed 27 September 2022). The appendix to the second volume contained the source of his original ideas. It was published in Russia, entitled *Introduction to Legal Policy*. See discussion in Agata Fijalkowski, *From Old Times to New Europe: The Polish Struggle for Democracy and Constitutionalism* (Ashgate 2010) 45–50.

32 Petrażycki returned to Russia to defend his doctoral thesis. He was appointed to the Encyclopaedia of Law at the University of St Petersburg. Petrażycki's influence grew with the creation of the first Russian newspaper, *Pravo*, dedicated to the struggle for legal culture in the tsarist empire. The editors were members from minority groups (Jewish and Polish) who were most affected by the lack of civil liberties in the Russian empire. Petrażycki was tried for illegal propaganda and sentenced to a brief term in prison. For further details about the Kadet Party, see Judith Zimmerman, 'The Kadets and the Duma 1905–1907', in Charles E. Timberlake (ed.), *Essays in Russian Liberalism* (Columbia University of Missouri Press 1972) 119–138 and William Rosenberg, 'Kadets and the Politic of Ambivalence', in Charles E. Timberlake (ed.), *Essays in Russian Liberalism* (Columbia University of Missouri Press 1972) 139–163.

Petrażycki claimed that law was to be found in inner experience and knowledge which could be achieved by means of introspection. Law, according to him, was a psychic phenomenon, a part of our spirit. He saw it as an inner voice which tells us what our duties are in relation to others and, more importantly, what our rights are, and what we can legitimately demand from others. The only way to study law, then, was to analyse our inner experiences. Petrażycki felt, however, that states of mind did not suggest the existence of a state or any other form of social organisation issuing commands and backing them by force. His work informs our understanding of the Russian agitation trials and what was at the heart of the dramatised trial: the critique of the official (tsarist) law and morality.

Petrażycki's work would be developed further by Marxists, but cut short by the Stalinist purges[33] and Vyshinsky's change of direction. Vyshinsky's notion of socialist legality started with the premise that '[w]hat *was* good, no longer *is* good'. A new term of reference was needed, so proletarian dictatorship replaced the rule of law.[34] His observations continue to be relevant with respect to the success of photography in the Soviet Union, and the manner in which it was embraced by the early Soviet photographers, who could now capture purposeful, conscious law in action.

Stalinist Justice in Action

Even when the political climate changed, the tension about what constituted the core of Soviet justice remained. For Vyshinsky, proletarian dictatorship referred to a specific mode of legality and power not limited by any laws. This did not mean anarchy or chaos, but rigid order and unconfined power. It was a new type of democracy – proletarian democracy. For this to be operationalised, the state could not refrain from violence, state force, and stifling of political opposition. It could not refrain from throttling exploiters. The process of throttling would be brought about by the masses themselves, by virtue of their education. In one phase, one therefore educates the masses for throttling, while at another one throttles in order to educate. This was enthusiastically applied to old Russian capitalists, tsarist officials, thousands of Polish officers, and more than 20 million ordinary Soviet citizens who were

33 After the Russian Revolution, there was an attempt to incorporate Petrażycki's theories to explain Marxist ideology. M. Reisner, the Vice-Commissar of Justice, tried to convince his superiors that the legislation of the tsarist regime could be incorporated alongside that of the provisional government since a replacement already existed in the form of intuitive law of the working class. See Timasheff, 'Introduction', xxxvii–xxxviii. Petrażycki's thinking continues to resonate. See Edoardo Fittipaldi and A. Javier Treviño (eds), *Leon Petrażycki: Law, Emotions, Society* (Routledge 2023).

34 Jacek Kurczewski, *The Resurrection of Rights in Poland* (Clarendon 1993) 43, emphasis in original.

shot or starved.[35] Significantly, under Stalinism, administrative orders were based on law and were fully legal, so extending the scope of throttling and education. It rewrote power relations between the state and the people. Image makers were part of the power relations because their role was to disseminate the official message about the dispensation of justice, no matter that it contained two seemingly contradictory elements of throttling and education. But what if we disassociate ourselves from this specific narrative of the image and try and read another potential history? As Todorov instructs, the unanimity of the narrative between good and evil is anything but neatly divided.[36]

For some, trials incited the masses against the evil embodied by the defendants and showed them the risks they would run in supporting any potential opposition. Stalinist justice included not only public show trials before handpicked audiences and broadcasts on the radio, but also secret trials, news of which was disseminated by 'clever whispering campaigns among party members. In their secrecy and with the silent disappearance of the accused, these were no less effective as instruments of terror than were the public trials'.[37] As reported by one American journalist:

> there was no room for mercy in that surcharged courtroom; it was crowded out by the unseen audience of uncounted thousands of tortured and massacred Ukrainian men, women, and children whose blood the defendants and others like them had shed. The sentence of hanging was read by the chief judge around midnight in the final blaze of krieg projectors.[38]

The visual account added a sense of glamour to the trial proceedings. 'Speaking legally' fully embraced the notion of performance and drama, because this was entangled with the presentation of legitimacy. The new ideological framework provided for this at the moment that law became a political weapon and a powerful performative tool. As Marxism–Leninism–Stalinism theory advanced, the connection between education and throttling could be utilised in the courtroom drama, and a visual account could further support the interrelationship between the two. Accounts of the 1937 show trials in Moscow described the reactions of people who knew that everything had already been decided and that their actual appearance in court would not change anything. Everything unfolded in an authoritative manner; it was all formal and even accommodating – everything had been rehearsed and prepared in advance.[39]

35 Kurczewski, *The Resurrection of Rights in Poland*, 44–45.
36 Tzevtan Todorov, *Hope and Memory: Lessons from the Twentieth Century* (tr. David Bellos, Atlantic 2004) and by the same author, *A French Tragedy: Scenes of Civil War* (tr. Mary Byrd Kelly, Dartmouth College Press 1996).
37 Hodos, *Show Trials*, xii–xiii.
38 Edmund Stevens, *Russia Is No Riddle* (Greenberg 1945) 115.
39 Karl Schlögel, *Moscow, 1937* (Polity 2012) 129.

'As a rule, efforts to understand the Moscow show trials are directed at what took place, or is said to have taken place, 'behind the scenes'.[40]

The fine line between hero and villain was continuously redrawn, affecting as it did the legal and political discourses of the day. What society saw was a repeat loop of performances about the meaning of law and justice, depicting and representing a societal value. The visual lens of justice changed the way that innocence and guilt were viewed and defined. Yet, despite Vyshinsky's attempts to eliminate intuitive law, the effect was precisely the opposite. These visual accounts had an impact on the official public and unofficial private faces pertaining to justice. The depiction of hero and villain embodied in the defendant are found in these visual accounts. These boundaries would radically redefine personal, legal, political, historical, and social discourses, a process that continues to the present day.

At the end of the Second World War, Stalinist justice took on a wider, international role. It introduced the 'growing intensity of class struggle' into the phase of transition from capitalism to socialism. Vigilance became a paramount concern. The theory implied that the enemy, beaten and cornered, finds covert, desperate, devious methods to conspire against the people's democracies and to sabotage the construction of socialism. The party itself was no exception:

> Imperialist agents disguised as communists would try to subvert from within the newly won empire. Soon the most dangerous enemy became the one who held a party card and occupied an important post in the hierarchy. Tito's revolt served as proof to Stalin and it led directly to show trials.[41]

The negotiation and organisation of the enemy would permeate all levels of personal and professional lives and go beyond what was expected in internal state affairs. It was successful owing to vigilance, which became an integral part of the courtroom proceedings. Images of Stalin adorned the courtroom walls and represented the watchful eye on one and all, serving to maintain their vigilance. As will be discussed in the case studies, space that takes on the legal role contains within its walls historical narratives about the performativity of the enactment of the law. This vigilance reverberated back to the viewer, creating a fluid channel of control and education. Such attentiveness was shaped by political developments of the time. Yugoslavian leader Marshal Tito's break with Stalin and his brand of communism provided the Soviet leader with concrete reasons to intensify and multiply purges within the inner and outer communist circles,[42] with the Cominform being the most effective way to

40 Schlögel, *Moscow, 1937*, 69.

41 Hodos, *Show Trials*, 2.

42 Three elements encouraged the need for show trials in the Soviet satellite countries: the Cold War, Stalin's increasing paranoia and the Soviet-Yugoslav split. Hodos, *Show Trials*.

reach the communists of the peoples' democracies.[43] This provided a basis for continued vigilance. Many scholars speculate that by this time Stalin's personal paranoia was increasing.[44] The Cominform provided the centralised control system that Moscow needed to keep the governments of the Eastern bloc in check.

The Rajk Trial

The Rajk trial in Hungary was the first 'pure' post-Second World War show trial in Eastern Europe that marked the start of purges of political party members. László Rajk was an important communist official in Hungary: he was Minister of the Interior and Minister of Foreign Affairs from 1948 to 1949. Rajk was part of the sweep that was catalysed by the Stalinist justice machinery in response to Tito's break from the Soviet Union. Rajk was accused of being a 'Titoist spy'.

Rajk's trial took place from 16 to 24 September 1949 and served as a model for all the satellite countries, in many of which show trials were being prepared. When referring to Stalinist justice in the communist states, it is not possible to ignore the effect that this trial had on the dispensation of justice in the region. The trial arguably demonstrates the quest of lawyers engaged in pedagogic pursuits. What was at stake was an issue rather than an answer to the questions that the judge had posed. This succeeded in confirming a specific historical narrative. In this constellation the truth has no place, unless it is an illusory truth.[45] The photographic record would differ from the trial record. The latter is unreliable, while the former, even if presented, is legitimate even if it is performed. It is the image that contains both truth and misinformation, bringing these versions of the past to the present to experience them time and time again.

As will be the case in the examples discussed in this monograph, accompanying the international press were representatives of the security services of Poland, Czechoslovakia, and East Germany, who came to Budapest to study the organisation and procedure of the Rajk trial. It was at this trial that the legend of Noel Field was first created. The Field association would connect the show trials held in the newly set-up communist states. According to this record, Field was the master spy from the US who, during the Second World War,

43 The Cominform, or the Information Bureau of the Communist Parties, was created in September 1947. It consisted of nine countries: the Soviet Union, Poland, Czechoslovakia, Hungary, Romania, Bulgaria, Yugoslavia, France, and Italy. Its headquarters were in Belgrade, and a newspaper issued fortnightly in numerous languages was disseminated. With the Soviet–Yugoslav rupture, the headquarters were moved to Bucharest.

44 Hodos, *Show Trials*, 4.

45 Gerry Simpson, 'History of Histories', in Kevin Jon Heller and Gerry Simpson (eds), *The Hidden Histories of War Crimes Trials* (Oxford University Press 2013) 1–9.

recruited communists in exile for the US espionage network and who ended up serving as liaison between the imperialists and Tito in order to undermine the East European communist parties. The account of Noel Field resulted in the death and imprisonment of hundreds of communists in Albania, Hungary, Bulgaria, Romania, Poland, Czechoslovakia, and East Germany. As noted by Hodos, '[t]he story of Noel Haviland Field is part of the most exciting, darkest, and hopeless periods of world history'.[46] Field was the connection between the communists who were later exposed as 'traitors'.[47]

The indictment in the Rajk trial, signed by the president and chairman of the state public prosecutor's office, was in fact drawn up by the leader of the Hungarian Central Committee, edited by the Soviet security police, and approved by both Lavrentiy Beria (chief of the state security police) and Stalin. The Hungarian Minister of Justice provided names of politically reliable defence attorneys; their texts were likewise dictated by the 'legal experts'. The selection of politically reliable judges and judicial officials was vital. The venue was also of critical importance, since it had to possess a semblance of transparency and at the same time act as a grand stage.

Before the trial, every defendant received a typewritten copy of their confession, the questions to be posed by the president of the people's court, and the answers to those questions, each to be learned by heart. Soviet stage managers oversaw repeated rehearsals. Prosecutors and judges also rehearsed. Witnesses were screened and instructed as to what they should say, having been forced to sign false statements. The statements were subsequently examined by Russian and Hungarian legal officials, who pieced together the show trial, and ensured that the 'confessions' fitted into the scheme.[48]

Prior to the start of the trial, the state prosecutor called in the chairman and handed in the script of the trial, including the defendants' questions and answers. Strict instructions were given not to deviate from the text. Were a defendant in fact to deviate from the approved script, the chairman was told to adjourn the proceedings for the day. No witnesses for the defence were present, only for the prosecution. Witnesses were not treated any better by virtue of their having provided falsified testimony – after the trial, they were usually sentenced in secret trials to longer sentences on trumped-up charges. The interrogations were 'achieved with rubber truncheons, rifle butts, electric shocks, sleeplessness, hunger, and cold – a mixture of the most advanced and barbaric methods of physical and psychological tortures'.[49] The legal experts

46 Further details are beyond the scope of this study. See the personal accounts of Noel's brother Hermann Field, *Trapped in the Cold War: The Ordeal of An American Family* (Stanford University Press 2002) and Erica Glaser Wallach, *Light at Midnight* (Doubleday 1967).

47 Hodos, *Show Trials*, 35.

48 Fijalkowski, *From Old Times to New Europe*, 81–82.

49 Hodos, *Show Trials*, 46.

could boast that the techniques of the show trials of the 1930s were perfected in the Rajk trial.

But the Rajk trial was subjected to some criticism. Internal reports submitted by representatives from the Comintern offer a glimpse into the role of law and the legal system. Some spectators admitted to a degree of disappointment.

> In my opinion, I do not think that the prosecutor … Gyula Alapi demonstrated to the court in the summations that this was a group of paid agents … The president of the court … Janko Peter, was weak before the court when the defendant Rakosi showed up.[50]

The same observer was also not impressed by the line of questioning, which he thought could have been more centred on the Yugoslav betrayal.[51]

The show trial was a tool especially designed to control and purge: controlling political opponents and purging the Communist Party ranks of any dissident and opposition elements.[52] At the same time the show trial demonstrated to society the ever-present, almost omnipotent, role of the Party. The press presented the show trials as a victory over counter-revolutionaries. Some writers comment many people continued to believe that the Party knew best.[53] Quite a few individuals still had faith in the Communist Party. Even in the face of arrest and mistreatment people were convinced that the mistake would ultimately be rectified.[54] Personal accounts show that confidence that Stalin knew what was best prevailed: belief in the Party was paramount, even in the face of death. Their dreadful plight, and the torture to which they had been

50 'Dve Zapiski Referenta tov. Zawolshkova svezu s poezdkoj v g. Budapesht' [Two Summaries from the Report of Zawolszki in Relation to the Process in Budapest], 29 September 1949, p. 206, fond 575, opis 1, delo 95, RTsKhIDNI, Moscow, Russia. Discussed in Fijalkowski, *From Old Times to New Europe*, 81–82.

51 On revealing the evil of the opposition's actions, see Feinberg, *Curtain of Lies*, 2.

52 See Zuzana Justman's *A Trial in Prague* (2001).

53 Certainly public opinion was behind the courts in the political trials of the 1930s. One of the trials resulted in the deaths of prominent technical specialists, who were accused of wrecking, subversion, and espionage, with links to the president of France. Raymond Poincaré issued a special declaration, refuting the charges, which was subsequently published in *Pravda* and entered in the court record. Poincaré pleaded: 'If by chance there are still judges in Moscow, they would do well to unmask the accusers and the accused, who are acting against their own interests in this strange affair and are participating in the dissemination of falsehood.' Most people believed that the declaration was part of a plot.

54 See Ginsburg, *Journey into the Whirlwind*. Hodos writes: 'Even I, the true believer, had some difficulty understanding and explaining the excommunication of Marshal Tito … But I knew that the party was always correct. Stalin knew what he is doing and why he is doing it [*sic*] … In May, the *Neue Zürcher Zeitung* began to serialize [Arthur Koestler's] Darkness at Noon … I did not believe one word of the novel, considered it a dirty slander, and soon stopped reading the installments'. Hodos, *Show Trials,* 42.

subjected, often led defendants to 'recognise' their guilt, and the righteousness of the Party. What mattered was a proactive engagement with *samokritika*,[55] about which Eric Ambler's *Judgment on Deltchev* is instructive.[56] Julie Cassiday identifies *samokritika* as an important part of the melodrama in which the defendant has a religious conversion.[57]

Concluding Remarks

This chapter looked briefly at Stalin's personal background and its relevance to the construction of Stalinist justice with the assistance of Soviet lawyers like Andrei Vyshinsky. The main features of Stalinist justice come in the form of the absolute control over the political context, the confession, the internal and external enemy, the sense of justice, and the blueprint of a trial. The images in this book contain all of these features, leading to their value as evidence of dispensing justice, but also an awareness that these features carry an affective response that more often than not leaves the viewer feeling slightly uncomfortable.

This chapter looked at the main parameters of Stalinist justice. It referred to examples of the changing nature of the criminal legal framework, specifically the introduction of new terms associated with social danger, guilt, and punishment. These terms emanate from the legal photography and legal photojournalism of the period. At the centre of these themes is Stalin and how his position with respect to the law was translated in specific statutes. Tensions in and contradictions between the terminologies and state goals were explored through a look at the positions of Vyshinsky and Leon Petrażycki (rationale of the criminal law), before contemplating law's Janus face. Procedural standards are present, but they are reinterpreted to suit political goals, as seen in the example of the Rajk trial. Legal thinkers of the time were compared to show how the performativity of the law was practically present in the tension within actions – good if fulfilling the socialist political project or dangerous if undermining it, even in thought. This point is the basis for the successful staging of the law in theatre and on screen that results in an emotional entanglement on the part of the viewer. Chapter 2 will engage these themes when considering visual culture and the visualisation of law, broadly understood, in Soviet Russia.

55 Peter Steiner, 'Justice in Prague, Political and Poetic: Some Reflections on the Slansky Trial (with Constant Reference to Franz Kafka and Milan Kundera)' (2000) 21(4) *Poetics Today* 653–679.

56 Eric Ambler, *Judgment on Deltchev* (Thriller Book Club 1952).

57 Cassiday, *The Enemy on Trial*, 5–6. See also the films of Hungarian film maker Márta Mészáros, *Diary for My Children* (1984), *Diary for My Lovers* (1987), and *Diary for My Mother and Father* (1990).

Chapter 2

Law, Visual Culture, and the Show Trial in Soviet Times

This chapter explores how images can be regarded as a powerful tool both of propaganda and of political justice in the Soviet context. Before the camera became the preferred medium to visually record social and political change, political justice was performed on stage. Visualising law is understood here to include the agitation trials under the rule of Lenin (1917–1924) and of Stalin (1924–1953), and also the role of photography in Soviet Russia. The discussion will focus on two key features: the basis of the Soviet experience of visualising law and of Stalinist justice. First, it will consider the examples of visualising law upon which the Soviet model was founded. This model was subsequently 'exported' to other countries and applied in the three case studies under review here. These examples of visualising law provided wider society with important visual accounts that worked in conjunction with written accounts and public discourses about criminal trials. There would seem to be a strong case for a legal discipline capable of exploring all visual legal communication practices. Second, the chapter will consider the notions of Stalinist justice within this context. Otto Kirchheimer's classic notion of political justice[1] will be addressed first. Kirchheimer and notions of Stalinist justice will form the backdrop to this present inquiry.

Political Justice

The art of political justice will rely on a legitimacy that is defined by its appearance of being legitimate. It does not matter whether it is staged, as long as the process is conveyed in a convincing manner. In other words, the event should take the form of a trial and its participants should act accordingly. There must be a semblance of judicial independence, but the relationship between power and use of force is separated by a fine line. The performance, or trial proceeding, is legitimate and allows for the legitimation of the exercise of power. In these cases it is the abuse of that power that results in the maladministration of justice.

1 Otto Kirchheimer, *Political Justice* (Princeton University Press 1961).

DOI: 10.4324/9781003405771-3

Early Soviet Agitation Trials

In 1918 Lenin declared that the role of the court was to instil terror and to work towards the aim of socialising the law and, as such, the people.[2] Courts were operationalised as a political weapon. This objective was officially justified and grounded in the prevailing theory of the time, Marxism–Leninism. The new role of the courts is best appreciated in a broader context, namely the way in which trials were perceived by society at large. Before the 1917 Revolution, Russians were chiefly familiar with courts through theatre. It was via this particular art form that the character of future Soviet show trials was shaped and understood. To be sure, fictional trials had themselves evolved in a dramatic way, from socialisation to shaming, from dialogue to terror.[3] The subject matter of these fictional trials would address a public moral concern and their aim was to instil a sense of Soviet-style morality. These early fictional trials of the period were known as agitation trials. The staging of the agitation trials enabled the Bolsheviks to transform the attitudes of people in Soviet society, many of whom were illiterate. Whereas the earliest trials of the revolutionary period were structured in such a way as to encourage dialogue and thus to acquit the fictional defendants, those staged during Stalinist rule relied on humiliation, intimidation, and the collective guilt of all involved.[4] Such spectacles belittled defendant and audience alike. The visual account would be an integral part of this legal discourse. As already mentioned, the spectacle of the dramatised trial would come to represent the 'inverted image of society',[5] whereby authentic social life is replaced with its representation. Gradually the audience came to identify with the trial performances that increasingly superseded real activities and perceptions of law and justice. Photographs served as evidence of the spectacle's authenticity. They also played a role in the transformation of the spectacle into the real. Eventually, following Baudrillard,[6] the line between image and reality disappears, so that no original thing is being represented, but rather a simulacrum, a surface meaning.

These public, dramatised trials have their origins in plays that were staged during the early Soviet period to solve problems experienced inside workers' institutions, namely hooliganism, absenteeism, and lack of interest in cultural conditioning. Theatrical works, such as *The Trial of the Cow*,[7] provided a

2 From Elizabeth Wood, *Performing Justice: Agitation Trials in Early Soviet Russia* (Cornell University Press 2005).
3 Wood, *Performing Justice*.
4 Wood, *Performing Justice*, 1.
5 Guy Debord, *The Society of the Spectacle* (tr. Donald Nicholson-Smith, Black and Red 1970).
6 Jean Baudrillard, *Simulacra and Simulation* (tr. Sheila Faria Glaser, University of Michigan Press 1994).
7 Wood, *Performing Justice*, 2. There has been an interest in visual legal communication within and outside the legal context for some time. No single legal discipline, however, covers all the practices highlighted here. The main research focus lies

blueprint for dramatised trials, and amateur actors and rudimentary props were used. A well-written trial presented the important issues of the day. It was vital for play scripts to demonstrate revolutionary consciousness, and with this end in mind instructions on how to write and stage plays were drafted and taught. At that time, the main focus was on moral and social wrongdoing rather than on crime as such: these performances were educational and entertaining.[8]

Twentieth-century Russian society was obsessed with trials of revolutionaries and political trials, such as those of Alfred Dreyfus, Mendel Beilis, and Oscar Wilde.[9] Discussion at the time pointed to the corrupt nature of the Russian Imperial legal system: 'Open, legal contested trials became the dream of an intelligentsia and indeed an entire nation that had become sick of tsarist arbitrariness and illegality'.[10] This obsession had been further fuelled through the earlier introduction of jury trials in Russia in 1864. In the late 1930s, when he was in exile in Paris, the playwright Nikolai Evreinov wrote *The Steps of Nemesis*, depicting six scenes from Party life in the Soviet Union during 1936 to 1938. Importantly, Evreinov had a background in legal philosophy, and during his studies he began to stage plays. *The Steps of Nemesis* features the defendants of the 1937 show trials and is often cited when comparing theatre to trial proceedings and concurrent public demonstrations.[11]

There was a vested interest in making these trials work. The key to the success of the trials was the personal involvement of political instructors, who were employed by the state to work with society on two levels: educational and entertainment.[12] It was not important that these trials were fictional. Rumour had it that the Red Army, or at any rate a collective political agency of some sort or another, was behind such trials. Because of the existence of jury trials, a culture of trials was easier to entrench in society. This would develop into instructors who would train local counterparts in how to conduct trial proceedings.[13] The Bolsheviks actively publicised the workers' trials and their speeches. According to Lenin, 'the court is an organ of power. The liberals sometimes forget this, but it is a sin for a Marxist to do so … those on trial should carefully consider ways to use the court as a means of agitation'.[14] Significantly, the early years of the agitation trials opened the door to self-criticism and reflection on tsarist trials and ways to involve people in bringing the details

elsewhere, such as history, or visual ethnography, which are invaluable and can be borrowed from – others have done so successfully to renegotiate cultural histories, such as Robert Darnton's *The Great Cat Massacre* (Penguin 1984).

8 Wood, *Performing Justice*, 5–6.

9 Wood, *Performing Justice*, 21–25.

10 Wood, *Performing Justice*, 8.

11 Karl Schlögel, *Moscow, 1937* (Polity 2012), 141.

12 Wood, *Performing Justice*, 8.

13 Agata Fijalkowski, 'Politics, Law and Justice in People's Poland: The Fieldorf File' (2014) 73(1) *Slavic Review* 85–107.

14 Cited in Wood, *Performing Justice*, 23.

to a wider public. This process of self-reflection had not been encouraged in Imperial Russia.

Lenin and others within the Bolshevik leadership recognised from the beginning of their rule that political propaganda had to be made concrete, enemies had to have recognisable faces, and there had to be an engagement with the routines of everyday life. Trial proceedings served as the ideal forum for this. Courts could be used to impart lessons in public morality, practical politics, and self-discipline;[15] scripts could be adapted and improvised, giving the impression that mistakes and retractions were being lived rather than performed.[16] From the start the trials served as a context in which to debate social ideas. Agitation trials from the very outset were thus intended to 'activate' both the participants and the audience. Through their involvement, both groups, it was hoped, would take a more active role in defending the official values of the regime. However, the effect was probably to make audiences increasingly passive. Once it was decided to put on an agitation trial, the audience was captive. As audience members they had to resort to their own play-acting in the form of sham resolutions so they could escape the performance as quickly as possible.[17]

By the late 1920s and early 1930s the use of trials to shame and humiliate defendants had effectively destroyed the humanist impulses of the early revolutionary educators. Instead, defendants were dehumanised. The show trials of this period might convince some foreign observers that they were witnessing real judicial proceedings, but by this time both agitation and show trials had been divested of any compassion or concern to explore real human motivations. Many of the trial photographs included images of the foreign press, an integral feature of the trial's legitimation, as noted earlier. Journalists were photographed observing the proceedings, taking notes, and providing the court with a mask of legitimacy, even when there was no attempt to mete out anything resembling justice. The photographs lent the journalists an air of celebrity, evident in their clothes and body language. They extended the performance of the trial to include everyone in the courtroom, with its parameters drawn wide. Some spectators were taken from the street, seemingly at random. However, they were from selected strata of society, and participated in moulding the depiction of truth[18] and contributing to the dispensing of justice.[19]

15 Wood, *Performing Justice*, 12.
16 Wood, *Performing Justice*, 195.
17 Wood, *Performing Justice*, 207.
18 At the trial of the Albanian writer and dissident Musine Kokalari, school groups were brought in to observe the proceedings. Agata Fijalkowski, 'Musine Kokalari and the Power of Images: Law, Aesthetics and Memory Regimes in the Albanian Experience' (2017) 28(3) *International Journal for the Semiotics of Law* 577–602.
19 Wood, *Performing Justice*, 207.

Trials attracted a large audience, captivated by the sheer drama of the occasion. Spectators were fascinated to see their peers on stage. There seemed to be a prevailing belief in the superior logic and, above all, the superior power of the state, while the judicial officials presiding embraced the idea of a performance in order to enhance a sense of the ubiquity of the state. It was not accidental that the prosecutor Nikolai Krylenko wore hunting clothes in the widely reported Shakhty trial from 1928.[20] During his speeches and cross-examination, he would stalk the courtroom. The prosecutor's tactic would have captured the imagination of many spectators. Krylenko sought to catch his prey in inconsistencies and falsehoods so that he could prove their guilt. This brings to mind Decker's notion of the confession, discussed in Chapter 1.

Elizabeth Wood sets out a convincing argument in her claim that the trial could be perceived as a 'collusive drama'.[21] Courtroom design has its basic functional objectives but it also reflects an institutional ideology, embodied in the public staging of justice. The court as a space is as integral to the trial proceedings as the stage is to a theatre performance. Within the court's physical space, justice is administered, staged, and performed. There are a variety of components, beginning with the decor, furniture, seating arrangement, line of vision, clothes, and various other aspects that have an impact on the eventual performance. The courtroom's design comprises a sign system, through which a society communicates its ideal model of the relationship between participants involved in judicial proceedings.[22] The manner in which the participants in the courtroom drama occupied and owned the space was important.

In early Soviet Russia the participants behaved as if the agitation trial were a 'real' court proceeding, one with fixed rules and an ostensibly uncertain outcome. A collusive drama is reliant on ritual, for it is only through a repeated and gradually enhanced performance that the spectator's attention is captured and the viewer convinced that the illusion is real, 'a given and not a construct'. 'The invisibility of the ritual's origins and its inventors is intrinsic to what the ritual is all about'.[23] The ritual takes on a proactive dimension when the audience becomes an active participant in the proceedings. 'Not only is seeing believing, doing is believing'.[24] Participants were presented with a conflict that

20 Wood, *Performing Justice*, 214.

21 Catherine Bell, *Ritual: Perspectives and Dimensions* (Oxford University Press 1997) 224 and Barbara Myerhoff, 'A Death in Due Time', in John J. MacAloon (ed.), *Rite, Drama, Festival, Spectacle* (Institute for the Study of Human Issues 1984) 149–178. In *Dark Speech: The Performance of Law in Early Ireland* (University of Pennsylvania Press 2007), Robin Chapman Stacey uses Bell's work to consider performance within oral culture in early Ireland.

22 Biyu Du, 'Staging Justice: Courtroom Semiotics and the Judicial Ideology in China' (2016) 29 *International Journal for the Semiotics of Law* 595–614.

23 Bell, *Ritual*, 224, drawing from or referring to Myerhoff, 'A Death in Due Time'. Bell's approach is used in Wood, *Performing Justice*.

24 Bell, *Ritual*, 224; see also Myerhoff, 'A Death in Due Time'.

they then acted out and resolved. It is not hard to see how powerful an impact agitation and show trials must have had on the Soviet imagination.[25]

The trials were originally designed to be educational and entertaining, as study of the agitation trials in early Soviet Russia would seem to indicate. Other famous political trials created a whole trial culture. The 1919–1924 trials were underpinned by a commitment to enlightenment, criticism, and dialogue, while the 1925–1933 trials evinced a stronger preoccupation with eliciting the correct answer. The manifest shortcoming of all such trials was the cultural divide between the educated and the uneducated, and the elites' profound conviction that they had to coax and perhaps even force the general populace to seek a new culture and accept new social norms. While the Bolshevik regime did not create the culture of blame and censure, it had inherited it and never sought to challenge it. In the end, that culture would prove to be its undoing. In a culture of blame individuals are reluctant to take risks or accept responsibility, owing to their fear of criticism, rebuke, or worse. In the face of a threat the natural response is to indulge in recrimination or blame.

The form of the trial attracted people from a wide spectrum of Soviet society who were drawn to the task of fighting illiteracy and to taking power as imaginary judges and lawyers. Stephen Kotkin has written of the process whereby workers learned 'to speak Bolshevik',[26] or, in short, to master a new public political language. The trials deployed this language. Trial scenes had a profound effect on viewers who, in turn, learned new literacy skills. The language accompanied the audience after the performance was over, and went with them to their home. Behind closed doors the language took root; it exerted control over society. Individuals censored themselves as they began to conform to the standards of the model Soviet citizen.

Wood extends this argument from speaking to acting Bolshevik, whereby individuals in positions of authority reinforced compliance and engaged in practices of judging and being judged, and whereby society at large was able to employ a 'dominant form of cultural-aesthetic' mirror that helped it to see itself and to resolve its conflicts. Recalling the above-mentioned notion of an inverted image of society, for every community of any size there is a principal form of ritual or theatre. Political instructors in early Soviet Russia had developed agitation trials as a form that was remarkably context-specific and rooted in local customs and mentalities. This made communication easier. An eyewitness at the Shakhty and the Industrial Party trials from the late 1920s and early 1930s wrote about the nature of the trials, remarking on, for example, the 'calculated melodrama of the proceedings'. Another commented on a 'superb

25 Wood, *Performing Justice*, 214. See also Béla Szász, *Volunteers for the Gallows: Anatomy of a Show-Trial* (tr. Kathleen Szász, Chatto and Windus 1971), and Alexander Dallin and George W. Breslauer, *Political Terror in Communist Systems* (Stanford University Press 1970).

26 As noted by Wood, *Performing Justice*, 10.

drama, bolstered by confessions and documents'; the Shakhty trial was full of the 'circus spirit of the crowds', 'an atmosphere of a carnival', 'a spirit of festival touched with hysteria – a crowd came to see a righteous hanging'.[27] The trial was a 'spectacle of men confessing incredible crimes and embracing death with grandiloquent gestures', 'an ordeal of death', and a 'Roman circus'.[28] These trials provided evidence of a connection with the agitation trials. As in the case of plays staged in theatres, in some of the show trials the Soviet press, radio, newsreels, school announcements, and billboards promoted the trial for weeks and months beforehand. Audiences were given special entrance tickets. The connection between the law and the visual was performativity. The obsession with the contemporary trials of the day was based on the struggle between good and evil, the moment of reckoning.

The power of the performance was melodrama. Peter Brooks identifies stage melodrama as a dominant popular form in the 19th century, when 'realist' novelists created fiction using the rhetoric and excess of melodrama – in particular its secularised conflicts of good and evil, salvation and damnation.[29] Melodrama is an important mode of expression in modern literature and, when staged correctly, can be ideal for staging the dispensing of justice. The melodrama was plain for all to see: villains who had undermined the Soviet order; heroes who had uncovered their treachery; a supreme Soviet state, committed to defending innocent citizens. The indictment was published in the main broadsheets, and it detailed a fantastical set of accusations: an organised network of sabotage and espionage between Moscow, Paris, and Berlin; a plan to destroy all industry; conspiracy and expropriation by foreign agents and operatives. There was also a degree of unpredictability: in other words, would the accused confess publicly and would they be found guilty?

The drama of the trial proceedings was heightened by lighting and staging. The details were put in the hands of technical crews consisting of personnel who had had previous experience staging agitation trials. Ceremony was paramount; guarantees that procedure was apparently being followed were overtly noted. For the spectators, the presence of the international press made the outrageous charges more plausible. Because the Shakhty proceedings were not entirely scripted, improvisation lent the trial a sense of realism. At its core there was political education that advocated class hatred and directed public opinion appropriately.

The technical aspects of the trial were also used in domestic war crimes trials. As noted in the previous chapter, Edmund Stevens, an American journalist covering the 1943 Kharkov war crimes trial for *The New York Times*, recalled

27 Wood, *Performing Justice*, 194.
28 Wood, *Performing Justice*, 214.
29 Peter Brooks, *The Melodramatic Imagination: Balzac, Henry James, Melodrama, and the Mode of Excess* (Yale University Press 1976). I thank Martin Thom for drawing my attention to this work.

the venue – the local theatre – and the way in which its space was used to maximise the effects of lighting and staging. The trial was filmed. Aware though he was that the trial was scripted, and that the spectators were witnessing Kurczewski's notion of legal education and throttling, where there is adherence to order and law but where power is not bound by law, this underpins the way a state operates in its expression of the proletarian dictatorship.[30] By this time, the use of coercion and education[31] was reaching a wider international audience. Stevens noted how the didactic character of the proceedings was successfully conveyed to a packed audience.

The trials were deeply rooted in a hatred of the old regime but also in a self-criticism that was unremittingly negative. By the end of the 1930s virtually the entire first generation of Bolshevik leaders, the so-called Old Bolsheviks, had either died or been arraigned in the Moscow show trials, and then condemned and executed.[32] Educational performances of dramatised trials reveal how productive of new social relations law and the courts could be.

Dramatised trials did not merely repress certain behaviours; they also created new micro-relations of power in the courtroom.[33] Theoretical approaches that address the question of domination, or the creating of new knowledge as a means of control, are important in this assessment of Soviet agitation and show trials. Many of the defendants in the 1937 show trials recognised the setting of their own trial. Already by 1922 they showed solidarity with those marching in the street who called for the 'mad dogs to be shot' in sentencing the defendants before them to death. As Schlögel puts it:

> This fits well with the entire history, in which the dividing line between reality and fiction had been dissolved to the point where it is threatened to jeopardise his life, so much so that it was pure chance whether he ended up as prosecutor or defendant, as judge or as criminal to be executed.[34]

This recalls Jameson's surfeit of surfaces[35] and the lack of depth to any of the legal roles, which did not matter as style was the driving factor, accompanied by its own language and opportunities to read visually.

The image records intense emotional and ethical dramas being played out before different groups of spectators: those at the trial itself and the viewer of the image. The struggles are of good and evil, and their account suggests that the need to confront good and evil, to combat and expel it, is necessary for the social order.[36] 'Man is seen to be, and must recognise himself to be, playing on

30 Kurczewski, *The Resurrection of Rights in Poland*, 44.
31 Kurczewski, *The Resurrection of Rights in Poland*, 44.
32 Wood, *Performing Justice*, 9.
33 Wood, *Performing Justice*, 11.
34 Schlögel, *Moscow, 1937*, 143.
35 Fredric Jameson, *Postmodernism, or, the Cultural Life of Late Capitalism* (Verso 1992).
36 Brooks, *The Melodramatic Imagination*, 12–13.

a theatre that is the point of juncture, and of clash, of imperatives beyond himself that are non-mediated and irreducible'.[37] As Brooks instructs, the very logic of melodrama excludes the middle. In other words, the choice is between the better option of the individual and wider community and a 'retributive, purgative terror'.[38]

Speaking legally relies on qualities of performance, because it taps into affective justice, making the objective experience a personal one related to affective justice and accessing a narrative that concerns good and evil. There is a neat unanimity in the narrative of good versus evil, but it is far from a depiction of a clear divide between the two. Instead we are presented with role reversals. Vladimir Propp, for example, writes about eight broad character types in stories as well as 31 narratemes.[39] For Propp, the relationship between the characters is one of struggle. A good story has a plot that engages the reader because of what is at stake. What was at stake in the specific trial captured in the image? An exploration of this question shows diverging interests at play and the existence of other potential histories.

Cassiday, in her important work on early Soviet courts, identifies Russia's avant-garde tradition at the root of Soviet show trials. Theatre and cinema at that time had the capacity to transform the human spirit via this specific aesthetic lens and tradition. Law was an excellent subject matter with its authority coming from good or evil, or friend or foe, a tension that never dulls for spectators. This discourse complemented the Russian love of fairy tales.[40]

In his study of Russian folklore, Propp discusses the relationship between the characters as one of struggle.[41] All good stories have a plot that engages the reader because of what is at stake. Similarly, Moran's consideration of the television drama series *Judge John Deed*, with an English High Court judge at the centre of the story, could be analysed through the lens of screenwriting.[42] And, consistent with Propp's view, a successful drama series will capture viewers if there is a 'hook'. Cliffhangers and developed character biographies that show the hero/anti-hero as accessible work if the characters believe in what they are doing. The spotlight on the judge succeeds if their world is an integral part of their character biography and the viewers' visual literacy reinserts the world into the life account of the judge and into the cases they are adjudicating. As

37 Brooks, *The Melodramatic Imagination*, 13.
38 Brooks, *The Melodramatic Imagination*, 13.
39 Vladimir Propp, *The Russian Folktale* (tr. Sibelan Forrester, Wayne State University Press 2012).
40 Cassiday, *The Enemy on Trial.*
41 Vladimir Propp, 'Fairy Tale Transformations', reprinted in Brian Richardson, James Phalen, and Peter Rabonowitz (eds), *Narrative Dynamics: Essays on Time, Plot, Closure, and Frames* (Ohio State University Press 2002) 73–93. See also Propp, *The Russian Folktale.*
42 Leslie J. Moran, *Law, Visual Culture and Judges* (Routledge 2021) 103–117 and 118–154.

more viewers participate in the process of watching and following the series, their knowledge will be informed by inclusions and exclusions, with or without their knowledge. Slowly, the viewer becomes part of the judge's imagined community, all with the assistance of the screenwriter.[43]

The general framework of the Soviet trials remained intact, to be exported and applied in other countries, often by Soviet experts who assumed the role of the political instructor in assisting the respective security apparatuses in scripting show trials.[44] Political propaganda thrives on a performance, even if it is nothing but a show, and even if that show is behind closed doors. There are still images to deploy, as well as the intrinsic power of the imagination.

Photography in Russia

Photography had different connotations in tsarist Russia to those with which a Western European audience will be familiar. The flourishing area of photojournalism was attuned to the revolutionary consciousness and served to bring the capacity to document life in all its fascinating detail to the general populace. Lenin himself thus indicated that the camera 'as much as a gun, was an important weapon the Bolsheviks had at their fingertips to secure the revolution'.[45] During the tsarist period, photography was a pursuit of the cultural elite. This would change as photographers became interested in the task of documenting the Russian landscape and territory. As an art, photography was an inclusive career; it was diverse, respectable, and a means of earning a living. For many it was a way to maintain memory across great distances. These ethnographic photographers would in time find themselves working at the very centre of power. Their studios would be a hub of frenetic activity and serve as important training grounds for new apprentices. Photography also required a sense of entrepreneurship and risk-taking.[46] In the Russian empire many Russian photographers opened studios abroad and took advantage of the appetite for photography shared by cultural elites in European cities. The skills they acquired would serve them well in the early days of the Revolution, which was underpinned by a new sense of the future and a greater vision and purpose.

After the 1917 Revolution, images continued to play a role in historical narratives, and later in the visual legal narrative. Lenin is said to have claimed that 'the lens can write history quite well. It's clearer and more understandable. It's a history in snapshots. There isn't a single artist who can come close to touching what a camera can see'.[47] The lens would become an invaluable

43 As discussed in the review of Les Moran's book by Agata Fijalkowski, 'Law, Judges and Visual Culture' (2021) 15 (2) *Law and Humanities* 300–305.
44 Fijalkowski, 'Politics, Law and Justice'.
45 Cited in David Schneer, *Through Soviet Jewish Eyes: Photography, War, and the Holocaust* (Rutgers University Press 2012), 13.
46 Schneer, *Through Soviet Jewish Eyes*, 15.
47 Schneer, *Through Soviet Jewish Eyes*, 20.

means with which to disseminate to society the fact that the court was a political weapon that would in certain circumstances mete out terror. Alongside the development of photography, Soviet criminal legal teams argued about the best way to shape the criminal law according to the new ideological frameworks. Terms of debate shifted and personnel changed, either through purges or more routine replacements. The basic function of the court was fixed in statute, serving as it did as a political weapon. What was captured in the images of it, however, hid diverging legal discourses. Importantly, the spectacle of the trial itself was heightened and its visual account could be fixed or edited by photographers. People could now see who the very latest heroes and villains of the Revolution were.

The Revolution invested considerable energy in publishing, and publishers were eager for more visual materials. With technology providing the means to edit, the ideological context justified the need for an ever greater number of images of society 'in the making'.[48] The Soviet portrait, especially that of Soviet leaders, needed to be imbued with a certain 'holiness'.[49] These first-generation photographers were confronted with significant questions about aesthetics, politics, and ideology. Many were able to make the move from one political context to another, as one set of iconic leaders was replaced by another, the latter then being photographed. The next generation of photographers were involved in another project, namely the creation of Soviet photojournalism. Its institutions operated under the aegis of 'societal propaganda photography',[50] which was published and disseminated across the trades and professions, and in the educational sphere.

The coming together of social, cultural, historical, and political issues in the photographs of this period make them an important source of information about the manner in which visual accounts developed, and how they were viewed and experienced by the audience and the image makers.[51] As noted in the Introduction, Walter Benjamin sought to advance our understanding of the symbolic structuring of space in his discussion regarding the 'now-time' (*Jetztzeit*). 'The dialectical image is an image that emerges suddenly, in a flash'. This notion of the image as a 'flash' (*ein Aufblitzendes*) and the corresponding notion of historical experience as the discharge of an explosive force – the explosive force of here-now, blasting open 'the continuum of history' – is one of the concepts for which Benjamin is perhaps best known. For Benjamin, the period of reproduction of images affects the 'aura' of the artwork in question. Benjamin's here-now adds another dimension to this discussion about images. In addition to its temporal nature, the relation of the Then and Now is also dialectical, possessing an

48 Schneer, *Through Soviet Jewish Eyes*, 25.
49 Schneer, *Through Soviet Jewish Eyes*, 22.
50 Schneer, *Through Soviet Jewish Eyes*.
51 Penny Tinkler, *Using Photographs in Social and Historical Research* (Sage 2013) 90.

imagistic, or explanatory nature.[52] The tension between the productive conflict of opposites is most clearly demonstrated in the photograph. This specific relationship arose with technological advances, which in fact shook up the way we think about time and photography. Time took on an aspect of linearity, of speed, once cityscapes acquired large boulevards, railways were developed, and time zones were created. Photography was part of modernisation, which reinvented our relationship with time and took law and justice with it; it reproduced the dispensation of justice accordingly and shaped legal photography and legal photojournalism.

This visual turn in Soviet Russia refers to a shift in emphasis in the humanities and social sciences towards an increasing concern with the importance of the visible. It embraces visuality as a socially constructed experience as well as what makes social experience possible. The visual is not solely about what can be seen by the eye as part of the phenomenal world, but it also concerns the social organisation, partition, and administration of looking. This concept of the visual is a powerful reply to the alleged transparency of images and argues that visual turn represents a critique of realism across media and disciplines.[53] The political project of visual culture is deeply historical, because it revisions conventional narratives by showing that the difference between whom we see and whom we do not see is linked to the differences between the historical past, some of which has been given circulation and some of which have not.[54] Why do some images become intelligible and others remain unintelligible for a long time? Benjamin exposes the distinction between seeing and knowing that ought to be constantly interrogated.[55] Within history writing, this entails a consideration of visual documents not simply as an illustration of a fact, but as a historiographical tool to mobilise the story told – or untold – by archival sources that themselves construct specific discourses and narratives.

Finally, the technological development of the camera introduced an important dimension to the power relations between the Soviet photographers energised by the Revolution and the authorities. Photographs are taken, brokered, and published with a specific interpretation or meaning in mind – and the Soviets at this time were savvy brokers of images. But to read these images is also to be aware of the decisions that underpin the processes of brokering, as well as the complicated layers of attitudes and behaviours that are informed by social and cultural contexts. There are many actors in a legal propaganda machine. Each decision signifies another layer in cultural representation as the

52 Benjamin, 'On the Concept of History', in Walter Benjamin, *Selected Writings, Volume 4, 1938–1940* (tr. Eiland, Howard and Kevin McLaughlin, Harvard University Press 1999) 389–400, 395.

53 Francesco Ventrella, 'Visual Turn', in James Wright (ed.), *International Encyclopedia of the Social and Behavorial Sciences*, vol. 25 (2nd edn, Elsevier 2015) 207–213.

54 Irit Rogoff, 'Studying Visual Culture', in Nicholas Mirzoeff (ed.), *The Visual Culture Reader* (Routledge 2002) 24–36.

55 Benjamin, 'On the Concept of History'.

image is reproduced and transformed. For law and justice, the concept of the enemy was shaped internally or by law, and externally or by the trial. The affected communities, or those targeted by the dissemination of the image, arguably would be represented in these images, but also not. The meaning of these images is entangled in their reproduction and transformation.[56] The production of knowledge about the enemy hiding within society sustained the narrative about justice and the performativity of the law.[57]

Speaking Legally

In the previous sections we saw how speaking Bolshevik was transformed into acting Bolshevik through the spectacle of the trial, both dramatised and later as a show. This transformation was facilitated by the visual, in the form of theatre plays and photography. The material and cultural components would come to interact across ideological lines. Importantly, the viewer, or member of the audience, could cross a line that was not previously accessible to her, made possible by the political project that encouraged the participation and contribution of society. Aesthetics mattered, and second-generation Soviet photographers understood that edits and variations to the image would affect the political consciousness of the spectator. The materiality of the print of the photo mattered; its reproduction and transformation would allow for the dissemination of the image imbued with the relevant message about law and justice. When in the 1930s the project changed from educational to punitive, to brute domination and power, so too did the *punctum* in photographs capturing the law in action become amplified. Though not necessarily explained by the image maker's intervention, the relationships that were determined by power relations and performance will become important when looking at law's *punctum* in the case studies.

Concluding Remarks

Visual accounts accompanied the master Soviet legal narratives. Soviet legal propaganda made effective use of the courts, whether it be for rehearsals or at the very least a cautionary tale for the spectator about the consequences of straying from the goal of being a model Soviet citizen, or falling into imperialist hands.[58] In this way, legal photography and legal photojournalism was very much present.

56 Zeynep Devrim Gürsel, *Image Brokers: Visualising World News in the Age of Digital Circulation* (University of California Press 2016) 10.

57 John Tagg, *The Burden of Representation: Essays on Photographies and Histories* (Macmillan 1988).

58 Anna Lukina, 'The Soviet Court as a Propaganda Instrument II: The Semenchuk Case, 1936', AUTHLANGUAGE, 21 September 2017, https://thelanguageofauthoritarianregimes.wordpress.com/2017/09/21/the-soviet-court-as-a-propaganda-instrument-the-semenchuk-case-1936/ (accessed 25 July 2022).

Leon Trotsky, in *Literature and Revolution* (1924), saw propaganda as a form of education to bring political consciousness to the workers. As set out above, this awareness on the part of the Bolsheviks made seizing power a procurement that included the acquisition of meaning. In other words, the political void created by the Revolution required a new way of defining the past, present, and future. Legal propaganda was used to establish Bolshevik legitimacy and control public discourse in order to transform societal attitudes. This was done through the introduction of new stories and imagery.[59] As the next chapters will demonstrate, the show trials revealed the enemy within, confirming Stalin's suspicions regarding such domestic traitors and subversives. At the same time, the enemy as depicted in the photographs and circulated among the public shaped societal views about law and justice in unforeseen ways. Looking at the image, we experience the 'already having been of that which is yet to come', or 'the paradox of an instant that endures without a future'[60] to be found within the evolving practice of legal photography and legal photojournalism.

This chapter has discussed visualising law in Soviet Russia, from the early days of the Soviet Union to the immediate, post-Second World War era. It considered this with reference to Wood's work in this area within the context of the agitation trials analysed through an anthropological lens, identifying the significance of ritual and enactment of moral codes in a public venue. The success of this rested with collusion, and the ability to communicate roles. Alternatively, other writers consider these trials from the point of view of drama and show the cooperation and collaboration of the legal and theatre communities in staging moral dramas to get closer toward the goals of the political project. Both communities depended on the authorities for their professions' survival, and both saw an increased reliance on their work, rather than devolution, as predicted initially with the withering away of the law.

Under Stalinism, the law's role in unmasking counter-revolutionary elements was a part of everyday life. Political justice supplied a veneer of legitimacy, while Stalinist justice provided the grounds for using the law as a political weapon to mete out punishment, a punishment most accurately reflected in the notion of a simultaneous throttling and educative process. The narrative should not end there. The photographers came from backgrounds that were afforded a new role in a political project that revolutionised Soviet Russia. They studied with the best in their profession, and their approach was adopted elsewhere, outside Soviet Russia, and held in high regard.

59 Lonny Harrison, 'Doctor Zhivago as a Response to the Weaponization of Soviet Literature and Mass Culture', AUTHLANGUAGE, 23 August 2017, https://thelanguageofauthoritarianregimes.wordpress.com/2017/08/23/2268/ (accessed 25 July 2022).

60 Lindsay Smith, 'The Wont of Photography, or the Pleasure of Mimesis', in Luisa Calè and Patrizia Bello (eds), *Illustrations, Optics and Objects in Nineteenth-Century Literary and Visual Cultures* (Palgrave 2010) 65–86.

The Soviet chapter in photography's history of visualising law and justice is highly significant. It would be acknowledged internationally, not least at the Nuremberg trials. This visual legal model was later transferred to the communist satellite states. Chapter 3 will discuss the dispensation of justice in the first of our case studies, Albania, to set out common features that will inform our understanding of the way that visualising law was operationalised and of legal photography and legal photojournalism.

Chapter 3

Law, Visual Culture, and the Show Trial in Albania

The previous chapters considered the Soviet experience, which is relevant to this first case study of Albania, not only because of the political, social, and cultural context and link, but also because of the connection to the use of visual propaganda to disseminate political messages. As in Soviet Russia, the Albanian experience with the visual was deployed in the communist period, with its image makers participating in the efforts, inter alia, to define and redefine the 'enemy' of the time. And as in the other case studies under scrutiny in this book, visual exposure by photojournalism and legal photography can be part of what makes or breaks the veneer of legitimacy of a regime.

Albania is a unique subject for study because it is a 'photographer's state'. Albanian communist authorities controlled the organisation of the production of photographs, and the meaning that was attached to the specific kind of photograph (portrait or family, for example). Visual culture was fundamental to Enver Hoxha's plans concerning the manner in which the political project was brought to wider society[1] through the use of law.

This chapter focuses on three main issues. First, it will provide a historical overview of key events of the 20th century in Albania. Second, the chapter will consider the show trials that took place in the early years of communist rule, with a closer look at the 1946 'Trial of Political Dissidents' and its most well-known defendant of the 37 on trial, the writer Musine Kokalari. It will develop an account of her life and her trial because Kokalari, the photograph of her, and her trial venue are evidence of the relationship between law and visual culture, and they contribute to the discourse in a meaningful way. Third, in contrast to the other case studies, the chapter will offer a slightly more extensive discussion about the significance of photography in Albania, owing to its rich history. Of course, photography has an important history in East Germany

1 This included the electrification project of 1960, which declared itself as bringing electricity to all Albanians by 1985, including to its dangerous, mountainous terrain. Electrification was declared complete in 1970. The enterprise sparked a mass production of postcards of Albanians working on aspects of this remarkably dangerous endeavour. See *Enver's Bulb – A Short History of Albania's Electrification* (directed by Björn Reinhardt and Eckehard Pistrick 2018).

DOI: 10.4324/9781003405771-4

and Poland too. Albania however is a much smaller country, and its networks and archival materials more accessible, making the study of this question more profound and relevant as to how law and visual culture are inseparable.

The photograph, for example, is a case of both the performativity and the enactment of law: the defendant captured trying to read her court statement to a military tribunal is at the centre of this consideration. The narratives, all of which concern dispensing justice, that emerge from this single image will show how the photograph challenges our visualisation of the enactment of justice. Albania arguably still is a photographer's state, which coexisted with the accelerated version of Hoxha's programme to eliminate political opposition and later any form of independent thinking. Albania has been the focus of important work on this question, and this discussion will engage in particular with Gilles de Rapper's findings. The aesthetic in the photographs, like those of Kokalari, will be considered within the context of the image makers' pre-war training as apprentices in well-known studios. Their training is entangled in the *punctum* of the image, and the photographs capture the viewer in a surprising way, pointing to the sentient dimension of visual epistemology.

In the Albanian case study, material and visual qualities are equally accountable for the 'social salience' acquired by the image.[2] The combination of material culture and the 'visual systems' of the groups producing and using them provides a richer account of the relationship between the law and the visual. There will be numerous contexts in which the image is reproduced and reimagined. Learning more about some of these remarkable image makers provides diverging narratives that informs a wider understanding of the context of dispensing justice in the country. This carried with it the reproduction of different groups of class enemies throughout communist rule. The search for the enemy was relentless, and its authority was dependant on accompanying images. This negotiation and organisation has been discussed in the context of the Soviet Russian experience. To build the Soviet backdrop in the Albanian context, the discussion relies on Elidor Mëhilli's research.[3]

The connection between these points will be demonstrated by showing how 'speaking legally' and law's visual reach reveals what has been overlooked – other individuals' life stories that were affected by the reach of the law as well as those affected by the visual legal propaganda – and what features of the Soviet influence on the individual and the collective can be seen within the legal frame. All these factors inadvertently contributed to building a legal historical narrative on superficial grounds. The contexts of the photographs under scrutiny and in the nature of the show trial cannot but reflect the agitation trials

2 Gabriel Hanganu, '"Photo-Cross": The Political and Devotional Lives of a Romanian Orthodox Photograph', in Elizabeth Edwards and Janice Hart (eds), *Photographs Objects Histories: On the Materiality of Images* (Routledge 2006) 148–165.

3 Elidor Mëhilli, *From Stalin to Mao: Albania and the Socialist World* (Cornell University Press 2017).

or the Soviet trials of the 1930s. At the same time, and as will be shown in the next section, an independent Albania after the First World War might have been short-lived, but during these formative years tangible ideas about nationhood, freedom, and democracy circulated among Albanian intellectuals, which ideas would find expression in many of the photographs of the show trials, demonstrating the incomplete nature of these legal histories that are reproduced and relived since their occurrence. Moreover, inspiration was drawn from contacts, both outside and within the country, with those who brought experiences gained abroad, nurturing a creativity and energy that effected political and social developments.

This chapter argues that Albania is an integral part of the discourse and should be situated more centrally in any analysis of law and justice in this period: its contribution to legal photography and legal photojournalism is vitally important.

Why Albania?

Before we explore the way that visual propaganda developed in the country, it is worthwhile setting the backdrop of key historical events that are relevant to this discussion.

It has been noted that '[t]he Albanians remain in many respects the little known and little understood people … a nation of people still unable to defend their interests and to make their wishes heard'.[4] At the start of the 1900s, Albania's political culture was extremely underdeveloped, with little experience of democracy, opposition, or debate. However, it would be an error to see Albania as not having links with its neighbours and the wider world.[5] During this period, Albanian politics was characterised by intrigue and tension between Bishop Fan Noli, who led the Democratic or Popular Party with Luigj Gurakuqi, and Ahmed Zogu, who was a member for some time.[6] Noli was a liberal and saw himself as representing Albanian national interests. However, he did not connect with the political elite of the country; he had spent many years abroad, which is where his interest in Albanian nationalism grew.[7] Noli represented Albania in 1920 on at least two occasions in Geneva to argue for the country's admission to the League of Nations. A break between Noli, who

4 Arshi Pipa, *Albanian Stalinism: Ideo-political Aspects* (Columbia University Press 1990) 51.
5 Noel Malcolm, *Rebels, Believers, Survivors: Studies in the History of the Albanians* (Oxford University Press 2020).
6 Marianne Vickers, *The Albanians: A Modern History* (I.B. Tauris 2008) 101.
7 Robert Austin, 'Fan Noli, Albania and the Soviet Union' (1996) 30(2) *East European Quarterly* 153–169; Robert Clegg Austin, *Founding a Balkan State: Albania's Experiment with Democracy* (University of Toronto Press 2012); Mëhilli, *From Stalin to Mao*.

represented a pro-European vision, and Zogu, who was the face of the 'old order', was inevitable.

During its nascent years Albania could not move away from regional divisions in a society where state power was viewed as being in Tirana, rather than elsewhere in Albania.[8] Moreover, regions perceived the Tirana administration as a tribe, rather than representatives of a nation. In their view, the Tirana government was trying to destroy the liberty of the people just as previous rulers, such as the Romans, Ottomans, Austrians, Italians, Serbs, or Greeks, had tried to do.[9] Eventually Zogu won. After occupying several key governmental posts, he was able to eliminate the individuals that threatened him most and somehow retain power with the slimmest of margins.[10] In 1924 Noli assumed the post of prime minister; he envisaged an overhaul of agriculture, law, and general administration of the country – his rule lasted six months. Zogu was elected president of the newly created republic in 1925, and he continued to eliminate any opposition. In 1928 he renamed himself Zog and proclaimed himself Zog I, King of Albania. The move was tolerated by the Italians, who used this opportunity to manipulate Zog for their own interests.[11] The country was heavily financially dependent on Italy; in fact Italy succeeded in near total hegemony over Albania in the 1930s.[12] Zog allowed the country to become an Italian protectorate under Mussolini in 1938 and during the Second World War, during which time the country was overrun by various occupying powers.

In 1944, with the end of the Second World War near, the National Liberation Front, under the guidance of the future communist leader Enver Hoxha, consolidated its power with the assistance of execution squads that eliminated opposition members. It should be noted that during the 1920s Albania was the only country in the region without a communist party. The National Liberation Front was a home-grown internal party whose emergence occurred during tumultuous times, and from 1942 onwards it attempted to establish a foothold in the regions. The arrangement between the National Front (*Balli Kombëtar*), the anti-communist national resistance movement, did not last long.[13] With the support of the Allies, the partisans liberated the

8 Vickers, *The Albanians*, 102.

9 Rose Wilder Lane, *The Peaks of Shala* (Chapman and Dodd 1924) 62, as cited in Vickers, *The Albanians*, 103, fn. 8. Lane (1886–1968) was the daughter of American writer Laura Ingalls Wilder. She was a freelance journalist and became enamoured with Albania. She adopted her orphaned translator and guide Rexh Mehta, who served in the Albanian government but was later imprisoned by the Italian fascists and then Albanian communists. For more on Lane, see http://www.albanianphotography.net/wilder-lane/ (accessed 14 September 2021).

10 Vickers, *The Albanians*, 104–110.

11 Vickers, *The Albanians*, 124. See also Edith Durham, in a letter to a friend, noted in Vickers, *The Albanians*, 124, fn. 12.

12 Vickers, *The Albanians*, 132.

13 For more details about the 1943 Mukje agreement, see Vickers, *The Albanians*, 151–153.

country from Axis forces.[14] The British had a sustained interest in Albania, on which the Yugoslavs kept a close eye.[15] The Albanians may have been aided by the British (in terms of military equipment and finance), but they were guided by the Yugoslavs ideologically and politically. In 1944 Hoxha began to set up his government, using the Yugoslav government as a blueprint for state-building, such as the constitution. Albania was ravaged by war and would face serious challenges to repairing its economy, which presented a repeat situation of dependence, this time on Yugoslav political support. At the core of the strategies to develop the country Hoxha always had in mind keeping control as a means to combat any hint of opposition, crushing it with a quick blow. The years 1943 to 1945 were critical in the forging of a post-Second World War Albanian identity.[16]

In his November 1944 interview with *The New York Times*, Hoxha outlined his objectives for the country, in which points 5, 9, and 10 of the plan are of relevance:

> 5. A commission has already been set up to decide just who are war criminals.
> 9. Albania is seeking a close alliance with Marshal Tito's Yugoslavia, since we are bound together now with the Yugoslav blood ties.
> 10. Formation of the Albanian Telegraph Agency to disseminate news of the country to the rest of the world.[17]

A loose legal framework began to be constructed to deal with opponents to the regime under a veneer of legality. With point 10 in mind, the Albanian authorities needed to learn how to 'speak legally'; Albanian communism came to be highly centralised and the communists dominated nearly all aspects of everyday life. It was influenced by Yugoslav and Soviet authorities[18], who provided the tools for 'speaking legally' and assisted the successful and focused drive to eliminate intellectuals, which began early on in 1943 by targeting members of *Balli Kombëtar* and Zogists, then later in a newly created people's republic with the first in a series of trials that caught the imagination of society with the help of visual propaganda. The key instrument of power was the vast

14 Vickers, *The Albanians*, 159. Note that the Partisan Army comprised young people, and of the 70,000 partisan fighters, 6,000 were women. Vickers, *The Albanians*, 160.

15 Vickers, *The Albanians*, 153–159.

16 Bernd J. Fischer, *Albania 1943–1945: A View Through Western Documents* (Albanian Institute of International Studies 2014).

17 Owen Pearson, *Albania in Occupation and War: From Fascism to Communism 1940–1945*, Vol. 2 (The Centre for Albanian Studies in association with I.B. Tauris 2005) 415.

18 In May 1944 Koçi Xoxe writes to Dušan Mugoša, 'our whole movement feels the need greater than ever for your experience', in Pearson, *Albania in Occupation and War*, Vol. 2, 344.

secret police network was created in 1943 and for a while headed by Koçi Xoxe. It would later come to be known as the Sigurimi.

Meanwhile, Hoxha unsuccessfully tried to improve relations with the West and obtain recognition for his government. Following the 1946 purge of Sejfulla Malëshova, former Minister of Culture and Propaganda and the leader of the Party faction, advocated a moderate form of communism in foreign and domestic policy.[19] This point will be revisited later. Albania's relations with the West deteriorated. Albania's application to join UN was also rejected, although it did eventually join in December 1955. In July 1946 signed the Treaty of Friendship, Cooperation, and Mutual Aid with Yugoslavia. Yugoslav influence over Albania's political party and government increased considerably between 1945 and 1948, with Yugoslavia coming to dominate political, economic, military, and cultural life. In 1948 Yugoslavia's expulsion from the Cominform gave Hoxha the opportunity to reverse this situation, and Albania became the first in communist Europe to condemn Yugoslavia. The treaty of friendship with Yugoslavia was broken off, Yugoslav advisers were forced out of Albania, and Koçi Xoxe, now the Minister of Internal Affairs and head of the secret police, was tried and executed, along with hundreds of other so-called 'Titoists'. As a result of these changes, Albania became a fully fledged member of the Soviet sphere of influence, playing a key role in Stalin's strategy of isolating Yugoslavia. In 1949 Albania joined the Council for Mutual Economic Assistance, or Comecon, and proceeded with a programme of rapid, Soviet-style, centralised economic development. In other words, Albania escaped its status as a Yugoslav satellite state, which meant a reversal in legality as well.

To be sure, the time frame in question in this book might be narrow, but it is rich. And, as correctly argued by Mëhilli, in relation to features of Soviet influence, the country's experience was shaped by the terms of its reception of communism and, as we shall see, its use of visual propaganda. Both of these points were informed by the strong links that Albania had to the outside world, before Hoxha's regime closed itself off, with a resulting profound effect on Albanian society. Albanian intellectuals in exile wrote that the country

> could perhaps pardon communism many crimes, but not that of having deprived her of her sons' energy of mind and spirit, a nation's most valuable capital. And when one further considers that Albania is not a nation with an abundance of intellectuals, one can more sensibly evaluate her loss.[20]

Many in the new ruling circle were suspicious of the 'older intellectuals'. Unlike its communist counterparts, such as Poland or Czechoslovakia, it would

19 Vickers, *The Albanians*, 167–168.
20 Pipa, *Albanian Stalinism*, 25.

become difficult for dissidents to draw on support networks not just within the communist bloc but from the West as well.[21]

Speaking Legally

The nature of Stalinist justice would become apparent when the close involvement of Soviet officials in legal education, judicial training, and the drafting of laws, as well as in the application of key decrees in Albania, was revealed. One victim of Stalinist justice observes the following, with respect to the relevance of a trial:

> The whole indicates the part. The bar of history throws light on the trial in court. The court that testifies to the state of the world gives meaning to the testimony of the individual. And vice versa. The individual testimony enhances the picture of the court's procedure which prepares a certain *settling of accounts* with society. The legal trial allows the concealed mechanism of the historical trial to appear. The part reveals the inner structure of the whole.[22]

In other words, there are layers of meaning attached to a proceeding, all of which are contained in a photograph of it. Archival material provides evidence for further analysis of the involvement of specific judicial officials, particularly in the six main political trials, which will be discussed in the next section. These narratives about the Stalinist period are not dissimilar to other communist accounts in that the Albanian case – as do all the case studies under scrutiny here – reveals political motives, legal manoeuvrings, and broader considerations surrounding the case and trial. The political strategy was characterised by the settling of accounts through the perversion of the law.

A couple of features of these trials are therefore important for understanding the wider implications of the Albanian context. First, there were many victims of Stalinist justice at the hands of those who worked behind the scenes. These collaborators, working in the secret police, were drafted to make sure that the agreed Albanian version of communism was accepted. Second, it is important to remember that these judicial crimes were committed at a time when the international law community was discussing the nature of justice and charges brought against judges at Nuremberg proceedings in 1947.[23] In fact, one of the most

21 Robert C. Austin and Jonathan Ellison, 'Albania', in Lavinia Stan (ed.), *Transitional Justice in Eastern Europe and the Former Soviet Union* (Routledge 2008) 176–199, 179.

22 Eugene Loebl, *Sentenced and Tried: Stalinist Purges in Czechoslovakia* (tr. Maurice Michael, Elek Books 1969), 259, emphasis in original.

23 See discussion in Agata Fijalkowski, 'Politics, Law and Justice in People's Poland: The Fieldorf File' (2014) 73(1) *Slavic Review* 85–107.

compelling narratives to dominate Albanian legal discourse in the post-1989 period concerns the settling of accounts in judicial crimes. Ironically, although key elements of this crime have been set out, it is a concept that is very hard to defend in court. The matter was taken out of the prosecution's hands with the death of key perpetrators. Partial justice was achieved by confirming the identities of those who were involved in the decisions leading up to the defendants' imprisonment and exile or execution, with the assistance of images from this collection.

So while it seems clear that to spectators, then and now, what was captured by the camera was a miscarriage of justice, the notion of 'speaking legally' can be analysed further when the image's own biography is investigated.

Bricks Talk

As noted in the Introduction, bricks and mortar are alive with narratives. Visual culture extends to materiality and the meanings contained within a specific artefact, broadly understood. This includes stone, which is relevant to protagonist of this chapter in several ways, from her childhood to her imprisonment and exile. Architecture has never been idle: buildings are appropriated by use and by perception, or, as Benjamin asserts, 'rather, by touch and sight'.[24] An examination of the images taken at one venue shows how the nature of justice is found within its walls, and shows, too, how the performativity of the law takes on different guises of justice.

Figure 3.1 shows a shopping centre in Tirana.[25] It has a ground floor of cafés, bars, and restaurants. An escalator takes you up to the second floor, where you find numerous bars and a few shops. The shopping centre is called Gallery Tirana, Former Cinema 17 November Complex. This is the closest thing to a commemorative plaque. While it is true that the venue used to be a cinema – the Rex Cinema, and later the Cinema 17 November – it is less well known that it also functioned as a venue for trials carried out during communist rule in the period 1946–1951. It was during this time that Enver Hoxha consolidated his power over the populace.[26]

The choice of venue was not random. To select the cinema is to appreciate its performative value:

24 Walter Benjamin, 'The Work of Art in the Age of Mechanical Reproduction', in Walter Benjamin (ed.), *Illuminations* (tr. Harry Zohn, Fontana 1973) 219–253.

25 For an exploration of concrete in present-day Albania, see Smoki Musaraj, 'Temporalities of Concrete in the Communist and Postcommunist Cities', in Nataša Gregorič and Smoki Musaraj (eds), *Remitting, Restoring and Building Contemporary Albania* (Palgrave 2021) 105–129.

26 Tomor Aliko, *Genocide of the Intellectual Elite of the Albanian Nation under the Communist Terror* (Shtypur ne Shtypshkronjen 'Maluka' 2007) 17.

Figure 3.1 Gallery Tirana shopping centre, Tirana, Albania, May 2015
Credit: Agata Fijalkowski.

Performance is innate to humans and ubiquitous in our social interactions. Humans are socialised from childhood ... to imitate, to pretend, to role play, to ritualise and to storytell. It is thus a simple transition to act on our

> performative impulses by developing artistically rendered work that reflects our dramatic nature.[27]

Loudspeakers transmitted the proceedings across the city; the audience comprised the national and international press, as well as spectators with the appearance of having been randomly selected from the streets and schools. These were events not to be missed for the general public – exactly the effect that politicians desired. They formed an important part of propaganda that supported the nascent regime in its quest to root out the enemy from within society. Even though no further information about the trials is available to the public entering the shopping centre, the space is far from static. Space does not let us forget. The 'real' meaning of places demonstrates that we have a sense of place and a fixed identity in the middle of this movement and change. It is more constructive to look at space as a progressive sense of place that recognises that the character of the place is linked to places beyond. In other words, space is best understood socially. Our relationship with space is one that can provoke powerful affective responses to its qualities, designs, or aesthetic assemblages.[28] It is the socialisation of human beings that sets out the groundwork for the relationship with aspects of the material; it concerns the process of making sense of interactions between time and space. This happens as individuals learn to recognise discrete objects and attach significance to them, and is, in fact, inseparable from the embodied or contained experiences of these materialities.[29]

Space itself has a history in Western experience: the network of relations between the sites and society that helps to define the space. In every culture places exist that are formed in the very founding of society. At the same time there are counter-sites that can be understood as 'a kind of effectively enacted utopia in which the real sites that can be found within the culture are simultaneously represented, contested, and inverted, or heterotopias'.[30]

Heterotopia is an effective way to discuss space, as spaces are often linked to slices of time, such as museums or libraries where time never stops building up or topping up. Heterotopias seem to be pure openings but also hide curious exclusions. The way in which spaces relate to other sites assists understanding of materialities by the manner in which they suspect, neutralise, or invert the set of relations that they happen to designate, mirror, or reflect.[31] The inversion of

27 Johnny Saldana, 2008, as cited in Lynn Butler-Kisber, *Qualitative Inquiry: Thematic, Narrative and Arts-informed Perspectives* (Sage 2010) 138.
28 Krisztina Fehérváry, *Politics in Color and Concrete: Socialist Materialities and the Middle Class in Hungary* (Indiana University Press 2013).
29 Fehérváry, *Politics in Color and Concrete*, 19.
30 Michel Foucault, 'Of Other Spaces: Utopias and Heterotopias' (tr. Jay Miskowiec, *Architecture/Mouvement/Continuité*, October 1984), https://web.mit.edu/allanmc/www/foucault1.pdf (accessed 13 October 2021), 3.
31 Fehérváry, *Politics in Color and Concrete*, 19.

time and space that we find in our appreciation of materialities leads us to a set of moments, or what Bachelard refers to as vertical time: the complex instant that gathers and concentrates many simultaneities at once.[32] In this way, our socialisation with materialities can enrich our experience of the law, whereby law has been temporally, or in some other manner, limited in reaching justice by addressing egregious violations of human rights. In another way, these encounters result in finding alternative solutions to the dominant legal historical discourses.[33] There is a certain responsibility that brick has in terms of making accessible the story we are searching for, as in photographs and the way that they are displayed.[34]

The stories embedded in the shopping centre's brick that forms part of the discussion in this chapter concerns one of Albania's most important writers of the 20th century. These discourses are incomplete and do not add anything meaningful to our knowledge of Albanian legal history or the wider consideration of the operationalisation of Stalinist justice.

Before the Rex Cinema (Figure 3.2) became a venue for show trials, it served as a forum for entertainment during the Second World War and when the country was occupied by Italy (1939–1943).[35] The former Italian ambassador to Albania, Francesco Jacomoni di San Savino, who took on the post as Lieutenant General in Tirana, is pictured at the cinema's opening in Figure 3.3. Jacomoni would later be tried for war crimes.[36]

The trial of Francesco Jacomoni took place before the High Court in Rome in 1945. It is ironic that the man behind the regime supporting the construction of cinemas in the Italianate style in Tirana would himself be brought up on charges of 'having committed acts which conspicuously supported the Fascist regime'.[37] This narrative is part of the contemporary narrative of the Tirana shopping complex and also the wider discourses about Albania in the aftermath

32 Richard Kearney, 'Bachelard and the Epiphanic Instant' (2008) 52 *Philosophy Today* 38–45.

33 Maria Elander, 'Images of Victims: The ECCC and the Cambodian Genocide Museum', in Desmond Manderson (ed.), *Law and the Visual: Representations, Technologies and Critique* (University of Toronto 2018) 210–228, 215. See also Vikki Bell, 'The Haunted Nomos: Activist-Artists and the (Im)possible Politics of Memory in Transitional Argentina' (2009) 52(2) *Cultural Politics* 149–178; Interview with then Albanian Ambassador to the UK, H.E. Mal Berisha, London, 19 August 2014.

34 Elander, 'Images of Victims', 215 and Bell, 'The Haunted Nomos'.

35 For a look at the main characteristics of Italian economic and landscape modernisation in Albania, see Enriketa Pandelejmoni, 'Italian Fascist Modernisation and Colonial Landscape in Albania 1925–1943', (2021) *Perspectivas –Journal of Political Science* 43–56.

36 Pearson, *Albania in Occupation and War*, Vol. 2, 423.

37 Jacomoni startled the court by saying that it was impossible to proceed with the case against him without charging the Italian monarchy. He continued to lay blame on Mussolini and Count Ciano, the Italian Foreign Minister 1936–1943. See Pearson, *Albania in Occupation and War*, Vol. 2, 423–425.

Figure 3.2 Rex Cinema, Tirana, Albania, 1940
Credit: CSA, Photographic Archive of Istituto Luce, image no. 2924.

Figure 3.3 Francesco Jacomoni di San Savino at the inauguration of the Rex Cinema building, Tirana, Albania, 1940
Credit: CSA, Photographic Archive of Istituto Luce, image no. 2928.

of the Second World War. Part of the 'optimism'[38] of post-war construction efforts was 'the revolutionary appeal of a far-reaching social project of remaking individuals by redesigning their environment',[39] but rethinking these things will carry with it the original object's history. The account is captive and at any moment freed, much like the narratives contained in images that Benjamin's notion of 'Here and Now' addresses so well – the historical discourse in question is never entirely completed or finished. The Rex Cinema, built by a fascist regime, contains the fight against fascism, in its trials of Albanian political elites and intellectuals in parallel with the trial of Jacomoni in Rome.

There are specific trials to note that are tied to the mortar of the Rex Cinema. The first trial of political elites was that of the 'Great Albanian Leaders', which took place in Tirana in March and April 1945. Sixty defendants from the government were charged with treason. The prosecutor in that case, Bedri Spahiu, claimed that he felt 'ashamed being in the role of the prosecutor in this trial'.[40] At the same time, quasi-judicial measures were taking place against so-called war criminals. Eighteen Albanians were executed following a

38 Mëhilli, *From Stalin to Mao*, 3–4.
39 Mëhilli, *From Stalin to Mao*, 3–4.
40 Aliko, *Genocide of the Intellectual Elite of the Albanian Nation*, 17.

death sentence rendered by a tribunal on 17 November 1944. Among the victims was Bahri Omari, Hoxha's brother-in-law, one of the leaders of *Balli Kombëtar.*[41] Arrests of war criminals continued at a rapid pace, and the definition of the enemy was expanding quickly.[42] On 23 December 1944, Law 21, 'On saboteurs against the people's power and war, on those who harbour war criminals and any of those pursued by the law, on those who know the whereabouts of such individuals and do not report', came into force. This was followed by Law 41, 'On the organisation and functioning of military courts', on 23 January 1945.[43]

The second trial, conducted from June to August 1946, of the 'Albanian Opposition', was the first involving political dissidents.[44] The political and ideological character of the criminal law provisions were confirmed by the nature of the trial: proceedings were held at the Rex Cinema in Tirana with a carefully hand-picked audience and media, as depicted in Figure 3.4, where the prosecutor's speech expressed contempt and revulsion at the opposition's activities. Reports of the proceedings were transmitted throughout the city. Audiences were specifically chosen; often individuals were forced off the street to watch.[45] Each judicial official's role was vitally important to the trial: 'So the shocking truth about a judicial hearing … is that the judge has the freedom to be fully present in all his or her human aspects'.[46] Outside reports state that '[e]yewitnesses at the trial attributed to torture the behaviour of the accused in their easy submission to all of the charges'.[47] This trial is discussed further later in this chapter.

The third trial, against the so-called 'Saboteurs of the Maliq Marshes', was held in November 1946. The draining of the Maliq swamp was meant to be an outstanding example of the *Rindërtim* (Reconstruction) period.[48] The trial concerned the actions of several scientists who were accused of conspiring to

41 Hoxha's sister pleaded with her brother for forgiveness. See Dashnor Kaloçi, 'The Official Letter of Enver's Sister', Memorie.al, https://memorie.al/en/the-official-letter-of-envers-sister-please-with-the-broken-heart-of-a-woman-for-the-forgiveness-of-her-husband-bahri-have-mercy-on-her-in-exchange-for-the-capital-punishment/ (accessed 13 July 2022). See also Pearson, *Albania in Occupation and War*, Vol. 2, 435; Robert Elsie, '1945: The Albanian Treason Trial', Texts and Documents of Albanian History, at http://www.albanianhistory.net/1945_Albanian-Treason-Trial/index.html (accessed 6 September 2022).

42 Pearson, *Albania in Occupation and War*, Vol. 2, entry 16 July 1945, 456. The clergy were widely targeted throughout 1945: see entry 464–465.

43 These laws were reported in the Official Gazette, *Gazeta Zyrtare i Dhejtor 1944* and in the *Gazeta Zyrtare i Dhejtor 1945*. Collection at the Albanian Central Archive, Fond Gazeta Zyrtare. Translated by Florian Agalli.

44 Reported outside Albania. 'The trial began at a cinema …' Pearson, *Albania in Occupation and War*, Vol. 3, 42, 51.

45 Interview with Mal Berisha, London, 19 August 2014.

46 Pearson, *Albania in Occupation and War*, Vol. 3, 51.

47 Pearson, *Albania in Occupation and War*, Vol. 3, 51.

48 Mëhilli, *From Stalin to Mao*, 34.

TIRANË PRILL 1945
273 GJYQI SPECIAL. POPULLI BRENDA NË SALLËN E GJY-
KIMIT

Figure 3.4 Spectators at the 'Great Albanian Leaders' trial, Tirana, Albania, April 1945
Credit: ATSH, image no. 273.

TIRANË NËNDOR 1946
2178 GJYQI I SABOTATORËVE TË MALIQIT. ABDIL
SHAKA DHE ZELIKA MANO PËRPARA TRUPIT GJY-
KUES.

Figure 3.5 Married couple, defendants in the 'Saboteurs of the Maliq Marshes' trial, Tirana, Albania, November 1946
Credit: ATSH, image no. 2178.

sabotage the Maliq swamp drainage project north of Korça. Figure 3.5 shows two defendants from that trial, a married couple, both scientists. The project employed some 8,000 people, who worked were described as voluntary workers and were unpaid. They lived in conditions of poverty and squalor. This (mis)management attracted the attention of the authorities, and after a worker complained to the trade union, the decision was taken by officials to intervene. Yugoslav experts blamed Italian specialists for the slow progress of the Albanians working on the project.[49] The Albanian authorities invented facts connected to Harry Fulz of the US Mission, who allegedly advised the scientists to sabotage their work. These connections were described as treason. Secret telegrams sent by the US representative to Albania to the US Secretary of State describe the defendants' plight and the horrific torture they underwent in detail, as well as the 'fantastic' nature of the charges, such as throwing soil from one side of the ditch to the other, or putting wet earth on dry beds of soil.[50] Further allegations were made that Fultz gave gold sovereigns as bribes.[51] The list of Albanian and American saboteurs and collaborators was wide and resulted in the withdrawal of the US mission from Tirana. The concept of 'the enemy' was expanding.

Some events of 1947 were linked to the circumstances of the Maliq Marshes trial. January 1947 saw religious leaders, this time Franciscan, arrested and charged with concealing weapons and ammunition on church property.[52] By May, the authorities had moved to distance themselves from certain officials, such as Malëshova.[53] Importantly, Lake Maliq was used as a prisoner labour camp for priests charged with treason.[54] The trial against the Technical School in Tirana, in which treason was alleged on the part of the American and British missions, was held from 18 to 20 September.[55] Again, the connection with Harry Fulz was critical, as he was described as being at the heart of the move to instigate an armed uprising against the Hoxha regime. Links were made with convicted war criminals to support the case of treason based on fabricated charges and in which certain individuals accused of the crimes allegedly 'asked to be interrogated a second time because in [their] previous interrogation [they] did not tell the whole truth, being ashamed to admit [their] treachery in front of the people'.[56]

49 Mëhilli, *From Stalin to Mao*, 52–53. The Maliq swamp would later have a labour camp attached to it. Arshi Pipa used cigarette paper as a diary to record acts of cruelty that occurred there. Mëhilli, *From Stalin to Mao*, 53.
50 Pearson, *Albania in Occupation and War*, Vol. 3, 112–113.
51 Pearson, *Albania in Occupation and War*, Vol. 3, 113.
52 Pearson, *Albania in Occupation and War*, Vol. 3, 139.
53 As noted earlier in the chapter. Pearson, *Albania in Occupation and War*, Vol. 3, 181.
54 Pearson, *Albania in Occupation and War*, Vol. 3, 188.
55 Pearson, *Albania in Occupation and War*, Vol. 3, 220–226.
56 Pearson, *Albania in Occupation and War*, Vol. 3, 226.

The fourth trial, or the 'Second Opposition Trial', of 24 individuals, ten of whom were government officials, began in September 1947 and ran until October. Links between the deputies, *Balli Kombëtar* and *Legaliteti* (right-wing, pro-monarchists), were made by the prosecutor, Josif Pashko, who argued that in 'the course of this trial it has been exposed that every organisation and every criminal activity against our People's Power were conducted and financed directly by the Anglo-American imperialists, chiefly by the Americans'.[57] The trial was followed by more arrests of persons suspected of having links with individuals abroad. Disappearances and quasi-judicial executions characterised this time.[58] Meanwhile the correspondent for *The New York Times* set out details concerning Albania's recovery from war owing to Yugoslav financial support that paid for two-thirds of the country's state budget.[59]

The remit of this chapter does not permit further elaboration but it is worthwhile to note that the repression continued and 1948 marked the arrest of Koçi Xoxe and charges of treason levied against the Roman Catholic clergy,[60] with some Roman Catholic Church property converted into theatres, cafés, or dancing halls: 'holy items were sold in public places or profanely used'.[61] Xoxe and his associate Pandi Kristo were accused of Trotskyism and being enemies of the state and people, as well as acting as agents for Yugoslav Trotskyists. Their 'devious' actions were recounted at the first Congress of the Albanian Party.[62] The terror and repression continued, Xoxe's trial was in May 1949, presided over by Hoxha. The prosecutor was Bedri Spahiu. Charges were lodged against Xoxe and five of his associates.[63] Xoxe was accused of trying to seize power in Albania on instructions from Tito. As reported by the *New Times of Moscow*:

> Koçi Xoxe is a shifty little man who combined the brutality of a wolf with the cowardice of a jackal. He wormed his way into the Ministry of the Interior and the Central Committee of the Party. He flooded the country with sleuths of Tito, helped the latter organise their economic invasion of Albania, and violated foreign trade monopoly and the sovereign rights of the Republic.[64]

Xoxe and the five other accused were executed by firing squad in June. During 1950 the net was cast wide in terms of catching the enemy, with many

57 Pearson, *Albania in Occupation and War*, Vol. 3, 227–228.
58 Pearson, *Albania in Occupation and War*, Vol. 3, 230.
59 Pearson, *Albania in Occupation and War*, Vol. 3, 230.
60 Pearson, *Albania in Occupation and War*, Vol. 3, 272–274.
61 Pearson, *Albania in Occupation and War*, Vol. 3, 323.
62 Pearson, *Albania in Occupation and War*, Vol. 3, 305–310.
63 Pandi Kristo, Nesti Kerenxhi, Kristo Themelko, Vaskë Koleci, and Zoi Themeli. Pearson, *Albania in Occupation and War*, Vol. 3, 343.
64 Pearson, *Albania in Occupation and War*, Vol. 3, 344.

foreigners charged and found guilty of treason, receiving coverage by the international press (see Figures 3.6 and 3.7).[65] The enemy was continuously negotiated and organised. Many of those tried were Yugoslav citizens; such events pointed to the further deterioration of Albanian–Yugoslav relations.

In 1951 events became intense. On 19 February a bomb exploded outside the Soviet embassy in Tirana. Celebrations were taking place at that time to mark the country's 34th anniversary. Shortly after, on 26 February, an emergency decree was issued. The decree set out wide parameters and concerned capital crime: 'On the prosecution and trial of activities of terrorist organisations and terrorist acts against representatives of the people's authorities, and of political and other organisations of the Albanian People's Republic.'[66] Twenty-two individuals were executed without trial for the attack on the Soviet embassy. The charges comprised conspiracy with international foreign spies, making them members of a terrorist organisation.

On 10 October 1951 a sixth trial of Western-trained espionage and sabotage agents charged 14 defendants with having links to international organisations, now deemed to be part of the wider international espionage network. The authorities actively publicised the trial that took place in the Cinema 17 November in Tirana.[67] The accused were charged with an attempt to overthrow the state. The prosecutor, Sotir Qirjqi, referred to a network of international organisations.[68] Those captured were alleged to have been trained in parachute jumping, topography, subversive warfare, and techniques of sabotage by American, British, and former Nazi officers in West German camps. Qirjqi's aggressive and at times violent speeches hit headlines outside Albania for an unsuspecting American and British public. What the Americans and British did not know was that many details in the charges were accurate.[69]

In 1954 several other show trials took place. For example, on 6 April the trial of the last group of Albanian parachutists was seen as the 'great show trial'.[70] Radio Tirana provided detailed accounts of their activities, all of which were described as being subversive. One of those convicted was 'to suffer death by the cord'.[71]

The show trials did not end there, but the series of six major trials ensured that an already exhausted post-Second World War society was made subservient to the state via a roaming and ever-changing concept of 'the enemy'. Any independence exercised by individuals would be crushed the moment it

65 The May 1950 trial concerned the paramilitary operation 'Operation Valuable', see Albert Lulushi, *Operation Valuable Fiend* (Arcade Publishing 2014).
66 Pearson, *Albania in Occupation and War*, Vol. 3, 420–421.
67 Pearson, *Albania in Occupation and War*, Vol. 3, 435–436.
68 Pearson, *Albania in Occupation and War*, Vol. 3, 435.
69 As per Lord Bethell, in his *The Great Betrayal* (1984). Quoted in Pearson, *Albania in Occupation and War*, Vol. 3, 436.
70 Pearson, *Albania in Occupation and War*, Vol. 3, 477.
71 Pearson, *Albania in Occupation and War*, Vol. 3, 477.

Figure 3.6 Defendant accused of anti-state activity, May 1950
Credit: ATSH, image no. 8639.

emerged. Witnesses and survivors of these trials describe them as the genocide of intellectuals.[72] The defendants in these trials represented the groups that came under suspicion, corresponding to wider events and political forces that influenced the Albanian authorities' choice of enemy and its depiction in a wider social message. At this time the country had high levels of illiteracy, making the visual message that much more valuable.[73] There is much that the wider English-speaking audience does not know when viewing these images. The narratives of these photographs concerning the dispensing of justice can inform an alternative understanding and approach towards the past and where it is located in the present. It starts with the narratives that explain context and the presence of another agent who never left the scene.

Mëhilli identifies two themes that run through narratives of Yugoslav and Soviet influence in communist Europe in the aftermath of the Second World War that assist our understanding of the accounts within the bricks and mortar

72 Aliko, *Genocide of the Intellectual Elite of the Albanian Nation.*
73 I thank Elidor Mëhilli for drawing my attention to this point. See 'Albania: History and Background', *Education Encyclopedia*, https://education.stateuniversity.com/pages/10/Albania-HISTORY-BACKGROUND.html (accessed 23 October 2022).

Figure 3.7 International press, May 1950 trial
Credit: ATSH, image no. 8638.

from a wider perspective: captivity and failure.[74] The communist-led partisan forces – who were young and inexperienced, but energetic and bold – first insisted on broad anti-fascist collaboration. They effectively framed their opponents as Nazi collaborators. This procession of foreign influences that included 'Mussolini's Balkan entanglements, Nazi occupation, and Yugoslav wartime tactical advice – brought the Communist Party to power but left Albania under Yugoslav patronage'.[75] The Party argued that it was on the right side of history, but it was also aware of its dependence on external forces it could not control. For this reason the Party sided with Stalin in 1948, thus freeing itself from the Yugoslav grip. Lacking experience, Albanian authorities looked for guidance from the Soviets, where they saw in a strong dictatorship the promise of national independence (against Yugoslavia and Greece).[76] Soviet development aid was meant to move the country out of poverty, and Albanian officials used the language of solidarity to obtain credit and defer repayment. This time, however, as noted by Mëhilli, the country's new political elite could exploit the resources of the Soviet empire while upholding national

74 Mëhilli, *From Stalin to Mao*, 5.
75 Mëhilli, *From Stalin to Mao*, 3–4.
76 Mëhilli, *From Stalin to Mao*, 5.

independence. Because Albania embraced Stalinism long after 1956, most analyses of the Cold War ignore the role that it played in Albania for most of its communist history.[77] The Soviet Union was 'a violent experiment in an avowedly non-capitalist modernity', as Stephen Kotkin has put it, 'and in an avowedly non-colonial colonialism'.[78]

Viewing these processes as being interconnected highlights continuities that are not captured in conventional Cold War narratives.[79] Some writers have identified key examples, such as the post-Second World War period when Albanian authorities sought to build socialism by relying on Italian engineers who were stuck in the country after the war: 'The onset of Communist rule was paradoxical: mobilisation to build socialism in a country possessing few workers; a language of enlightenment in the context of predominant illiteracy; radical rejection of the past while recycling Italian Fascist blueprints.'[80] Images prompted progress; it was an illusion, but postcards exchanged during this period were visually read to allow the individual to enjoy this illusion as real.[81]

After the Stalin–Tito break in 1948, Albania transformed itself from a Yugoslav satellite to becoming Stalin's ally and 'it was here that Eastern Europe's show trials of the 1950s had their bloody prelude'.[82] The next section considers one of the defendants in the second of the key trials from this period more closely.

The 'Albanian Opposition' Trial: Musine Kokalari

The previous sections identified key features in the early years of Albanian communist rule that facilitated the creation of courts to deal with war criminals and traitors. There were six trials that were held alongside purges during the period 1945–1951. These trials successfully consolidated the dictatorship and its power over the general populace. As noted above, special military courts were set up shortly after the country was liberated by the National Liberation Movement. The movement quickly organised quasi-judicial trials to eliminate political opposition. The main driver of this was Hoxha's close associate Koçi Xoxe, mentioned in the previous section, who headed the Sigurimi and later became Minister of the Interior. Eventually Xoxe himself was declared an enemy of the people in a secret trial in 1949. He was very popular, which many writers point to as the main reasons for arresting, torturing, and executing him on the pretext that he was a Titoist.[83]

77 Mëhilli, *From Stalin to Mao*, 6.
78 Mëhilli, *From Stalin to Mao*, 7.
79 Mëhilli, *From Stalin to Mao*, 14.
80 Mëhilli, *From Stalin to Mao*, 7.
81 I have a collection of postcards from this period that are photographs of Albanians taking part in different stages of working on larger industrial projects, as in note 1.
82 Mëhilli, *From Stalin to Mao*, 14.
83 Vickers, *The Albanians*, 167–168.

It is fitting to turn to one of the most highly publicised trials at that time, which involves a return to the Rex Cinema. This section will discuss the account of one defendant in the 'The Political Dissidents' trial in particular, that of Musine Kokalari. The image of Kokalari before the military court has been reproduced and disseminated widely, in 1946 and again in the post-communist period. This has affected her family, who observe '[t]here is a picture of her during the trial and from that picture one can see her attitude during the trial. By just seeing her eyes one can understand what kind of woman she was.'[84]

Musine Kokalari was born in 1917 in Adana, Turkey. Her father was a High Court judge there. Her family decided to return to their southern Albanian roots in 1920. They settled in Gjirokastër, a place that would have a hold over Kokalari and her imagination her entire life. Her childhood in Gjirokastër was filled with the fairy tales and folklore of the region. She attended school in Tirana. Her brother Vesim owned the Venus bookstore and worked closely with the main publishing houses in the capital; the *Mesagjeritë shqiptare* (a publishing house) was owned by another brother, Mumtaz.[85]

The Kokalaris were a family of intellectuals. At least two of Kokalari's brothers were active in politics, and both participated in literary life, of which Kokalari was also a part. At this time, as discussed above, Albania was undergoing a transformation from being under Ottoman Rule to an autonomous nation. The Kokalaris envisaged the country would follow a progressive path, and they moved in circles that read and discussed the ideas of thinkers like Sami Fräsheri, who represented the National Renaissance Movement. Kokalari would go on to complete her studies in Literature at La Sapienza, University of Rome, in 1941. The subject of her thesis was Naim Fräsheri as the pioneer of modern Albanian literature. When she was 24 she published *As My Grandmother Tells Me* (*Siç me thotë nënua plakë*), signalling her entry into society as a writer. In that book she celebrates the local Gjirokastëran dialect and sets out a critique of the patriarchal society by which the Albanian woman was confined. Other works include *How Life Swayed* (*Sa u-tunt jeta*) and *Around the Hearth* (*Rreth Vatrë*), both published in 1944. She was very much tied to Gjirokastër, as seen in the image of Kokalari dressed in the local costume in Figure 3.8. She was anti-fascist and anti-nationalist.[86]

84 Personal correspondence with Linda Kokalari, 12 June 2013.

85 Alina Wagner, *Musine Kokalari and Social Democracy in Albania* (Friedrich Ebert Stiftung 2016), https://library.fes.de/pdf-files/bueros/albanien/13145.pdf (accessed 13 July 2022). See also Musine Kokalari, https://musinekokalari.org/en/ (accessed 13 July 2022).

86 Kokalari kept a diary during her studies in Rome. She wrote *My University Life* (*La mia vita universitaria*) in Italian in her final and fourth year at university. Bavjola Shatro Gami, 'A Stranger in Rome: Musine Kokalari and Her Memoir La mia vita universitaria in Twentieth Century Albanian Literature' (2022) 30(1) *Mediterranean Studies* 76–107. Kokalari's memoir was published by Viella in 2016.

Figure 3.8 Musine Kokalari in local costume, date unknown
Credit: musinekokalari.org.

Kokalari's literary achievements earned her an invitation to join the prestigious Albanian League of Writers and Artists. Her publications were unique because of the use of the local vernacular and reference to the prevailing customs of the region. According to her great-niece, 'Musine was ahead of her time and the place she lived in. To this day in Albania I cannot think of anyone to be compared to her.'[87]

Events would unfold that would forever change the course of her life. The year 1944 also saw Kokalari arrested and released after the execution of her two brothers, Mumtaz and Vesim. One brother remained. The terrible fate of her siblings hit her hard and she decided to set aside her first love – writing – for politics. She was associated with the Social Democratic Party (*Partia Socialdemokrate e Shqipërisë*) and wrote for its paper *Zëri i lirisë* (The Voice of Freedom). Kokalari was open about wanting to find justice for the murder of her brothers. Towards the end of the Second World War Kokalari opened a bookstore and was invited to join the Albanian League of Writers and Artists, an organisation that was set up in October 1945 and headed by Sejfulla Malëshova. She was arrested on 17 January 1946. During this time the authorities turned on Malëshova and Kokalari, and her political activities would be affected by the next wave of purges. Before her arrest she sent a letter to the Allied Forces and in it called for free elections. Kokalari did this despite her fears of being rearrested. The tenor of the letter to the Allies was one asking for moral support for free elections, the importance of which, and of freedom of expression, was found in the thinking of Rilindja Kombëtare, or Albanian National Awakening, a movement that was strong from the 1870s until 1912. From it arose a tangible sense of Albanian identity in cultural, political, and social aspects, and although it came late to Albania, it is evidence of social democratic principles created in a country that did not have the conditions for them as other countries did. Kokalari finished writing her book *Si lindi Partia Social Demokrate* (How the Social Democratic Party was Born) in secret in 1972; in this personal account there is further information about the founding of the Party and the people involved.[88]

At her trial the judges adopted an especially aggressive stance. '[Musine] is filled with hate against the great victories of the people… everything changes in our country, where a new life is born, but the diabolical soul of Musine Kokalari knows only hate against the people'.[89] According to her great-niece, 'Musine was not afraid at all and that was extraordinary for her age.'[90] Kokalari did not deny her political activities but instead rejected the official position that her values and love for her country should be viewed as criminal. In addition to live broadcasts of the trial, her photograph appeared twice on the covers of the main Albanian broadsheets. It must have made an impression. In the contemporary context, her image becomes especially powerful in discussions about the elimination of intellectuals from Albanian life. In Figure 3.9, the viewer is

87 Personal correspondence with Linda Kokalari, 12 June 2013.

88 Wagner, *Musine Kokalari.*

89 Pjeter Pepa, *The Criminal File of Albania's Communist Dictator* (tr. Vangjel Morcka, Shtepia Botuese Uegen 2003), 117.

90 Referring to both how old she was and the times in which she lived. Personal correspondence with Linda Kokalari, 12 June 2013.

drawn to her wearing the mourning veil; her veil and her stare set a scene of mystery. Only when we learn the narrative do we begin to engage with the image speaking legally. Her focus on the court almost transcends the photograph, bringing us into her gaze. Kokalari is responding to the court's indictment of her crimes. Kokalari herself is speaking legally, to the court, to us, even though she was not allowed to present her defence in its entirety. Her uncompromising attitude towards freedom of expression and association was made known. While Kokalari was defending her view of the development of democracy in Albania, someone hysterically shouted from the trial venue: 'String her up!', after which the presiding judge asked: 'Did you hear what people want for you, the accused?!' Kokalari responded immediately: 'One day they will say the same for you, your honour!'[91]

The authorities worked hard to mobilise the population against the defendant in any trial, as they targeted specific segments of society; many people were swept away with the emotion. Mal Berisha reports an event at a trial of a very popular priest (Dom Shtjefën Kurti's trial): 'They [the authorities] did all they could to fuel negative feelings. Schoolchildren were forced to attend trials in between lessons'[92] In Kokalari's case, people tried to rip her hair out as she left the building.[93]

Kokalari was given the floor after the prosecution rested its case. She read out her defence but was interrupted by the court because it was felt that what she was saying did not relate to the charges. As what she was saying was beside the point, she was ordered to be silent; her written defence would be attached to the file.[94] Her final words at the trial made reference to Sami Fräsheri: 'I am a disciple of the renowned Sami Fräsheri and with me you want to condemn renaissance.'[95]

The court sentenced Kokalari to 20 years imprisonment in one of the most brutal labour camps, located in northern Albania. The authorities tried to ban and destroy all her works, but part of her work was saved.[96] For example, her memoir and other writings were preserved at the National Library in Tirana. This experience must have been unbearable. Kokalari asked for pardon in 1957, but her request was turned down by the Ministry of the Interior, which instructed the Supreme Court not to grant pardon on the grounds that

91 Personal correspondence with Linda Kokalari, 12 June 2013. Pepa., *The Criminal File of Albania's Communist Dictator*, 117.

92 Interview with Mal Berisha, London, 19 August 2014.

93 Personal correspondence with Linda Kokalari, 12 June 2013.

94 With funding and help from colleagues at in the theatre, film, television, and interactive media department at York University, UK, to mark her centenary I produced the short film 'An Unsung Hero: Musine Kokalari (2017)' in which Musine was able to complete her court statement. See https://youtu.be/3e-i6vIBq0s (accessed 12 March 2023).

95 Pepa, *The Criminal File of Albania's Communist Dictator*, 118.

96 I thank Dr Bavjola Shatro Gami for drawing my attention to this point.

Figure 3.9 Musine Kokalari at the 'Albanian Opposition' trial, Tirana, Albania, June 1946
Credit: ATSH, image no. 1551.

Kokalari was not fit to re-enter society (this was after 11 years behind bars). After 16 years of incarceration, Kokalari was released and exiled for a period to Rrëshen, a city in the district of Mirdita, where she was forced to work as a manual labourer and forbidden to write. Kokalari joked that she was a 'mortar specialist'. She was kept under surveillance for the rest of her life. 'During work, she was what they [Sigurimi] wanted her to be. But after work, she was what she wanted to be: well-dressed, beautiful, and with a book in her hands'.[97] One needs to keep in mind the time and place we are referring to: Rrëshen at that time. When she fell ill with cancer, she was refused a hospital bed and she died in August 1983. In 1993 the then Albanian president Sali Berisha declared Kokalari, together with several other Albanians, a 'Martyr for Democracy'. In Saimir Kumbaro's 2012 documentary *The Martyrs*, the Albanian writer Ismail Kadare remarks that:

> [She] was a distinguished martyr of freedom. She is the first to have formulated in a lapidary manner the idea of pluralism in Albania. She defended herself at the trial, where among other things she said: 'It is not necessary to be a communist to love Albania'.[98]

The way in which Kokalari lived her life demonstrates her commitment to the vision she and her colleagues shared of a future Albanian state, a demonstration of her love for Albania.

Rich narratives stem from court transcripts like those of Kokalari's trial. Legal judgments are as much a property of feelings as of intellectual understandings.[99] The 1946 trial transcript can also be a particular kind of memorial device that is shared by a segment of Albanian society, such as political prisoners. The transcript offers itself up for interpretation and while it may 'freeze' the record, it cannot govern its own interpretation. The transcript provides insights into the nature of the proceedings, the lawyers' opening and closing arguments, and the responses provided in the cross-examination.[100] It is art, broadly understood, that overcomes the law's limitations and confines, such as Kokalari's trial in June 1946. Art brings the spectator closer to Kokalari's story and to stories of her contemporaries. This is because the transcript of Kokalari's trial is brought to life through her image. Her image is read like a document, extending also to her court statement. The spectator can see beyond the notion of 'speaking legally' by deploying visual literacy that invites readings of silences and exclusions. Through excavation we attain a new understanding of law's crucial role in knitting together our past, present, and future that can be attained through the recognition that several mnemonical regimes operate alongside each other.

In order to understand law's role, it is essential to look at these exclusions. Law cannot maintain a separate discourse from the circumstances of human life. Juridical imagery amplifies legal arguments, which then take on a sentient dimension, and which is non-verbal. Legal principles can also be effectively expressed by visual means which have capacity to tell a story of their own:

97 Personal correspondence with Linda Kokalari, 12 June 2013.
98 *The Martyrs* (Saimir Kumbaro 2012).
99 Julia J.A. Shaw, *Law and the Passions: Why Emotions Matter for Justice* (GlassHouse Books 2019).
100 Austin Sarat, 'Rhetoric and Remembrance: Trials, Transcription, and the Politics of Critical Reading' (1999) 23(4) *Legal Studies Forum* 355–378.

> I recall when she [Nexhmije, Enver Hoxha's wife] used to advocate the waging of the class war by saying 'In conformity with the degree of guilt, the dictatorship of the proletariat will have to ruthlessly exclude one person from the ranks and keep him under strict control, imprison yet another, condemn still others to two or three years' imprisonment, and others to 10–20 years, or else to be executed by the firing squad as enemies of the people'. Naturally, such crucial matters are discussed between husband and wife … In his memoirs the dictator himself wrote that 'I always speak with Nexhmije about any matters of that sort'.[101]

When we excavate, we are confronted with a discovery. The representations are not fixed once and for all. At one and the same time the subject of an image is both a criminal and a hero/heroine and the object of manipulation of those in power. CIA documents disclose the harrowing details of another writer and publicist, Qemal Dracini (1922–1947), during his final days of interrogation:

> Professor Qemal Dracini arrested in Tirana saw once on the walls of the Court of the Defence of the People the following words: 'Today 18th September 1946, I am tortured, whipped, electric current from eight o'clock in the evening until one o'clock in the morning. I am writing with my flowing blood and with a nail I found. Signed Miss Musine Kokalari.' The professor, after being tortured, decided to kill himself by cutting his veins.[102]

Kokalari's image is also felt. In terms of what this image 'wants' is its 'presentiment of fate', or the duration of the photograph, found at the core of the defendant's image, which is released as her image travels across different zones of space and time and is viewed. Kokalari herself would appreciate the fine line between hero and villain.

Excavation has been discussed, but not yet the significance of silence. Kokalari's image can also be understood within the context of silence. Writing about Walter Benjamin's period of not writing after learning of, and in response to, his best friend's suicide, Felman considers that what happens in between is far from a break or hiatus. Benjamin himself has underscored that which remains unheard, unheeded in the critically repetitive mechanical reproduction of his work: 'that element in a translation which goes beyond transmittal of subject matter'.[103] Felman convincingly argues that this silence is actually a recitation of an unrecorded history. She draws on milestones in

101 Pepa, *The Criminal File of Albania's Communist Dictator*, 119.
102 Enriketa Pandelejmoni, https://twitter.com/EnriketaPapa/status/1475129360336228353/photo/1 (accessed 27 September 2022).
103 Shoshana Felman, 'Benjamin's Silence' (1999) 25(2) *Critical Inquiry* 201–234, 201.

Benjamin's life to interweave the life account with the unrecorded event and Benjamin as a thinker.[104] Kokalari was not allowed to give her court statement in full, was rendered silent by the court, and later as punishment during her exile as an author. Yet her life account and subsequent silence has rendered this silence as significant, and the 'imperative to tell' later, supported by observers of her movements in Rrëshen. Kokalari herself saw her imposed silence as having meaning that went beyond her sentence. Her stance, captured in the image, underscores the unheard.

Kokalari's image serves as an example of the meaning of space and the power of images in relation to the limitations of the law. Her life account is one of the most poignant of the 20th century. Hers is a story of ambition (as a writer and political voice), repression (by the dictatorial regime), tragedy (her imprisonment and exile), and legacy (of hope, in keeping her story, and other stories, alive[105]). However, it is important to note that while her image is a significant part of the Albanian discourse about its communist past and communist terror, it does not promote a meaningful discourse about responses to the crimes of the dictatorship, nor any meaningful discourse about Kokalari herself and her contribution to the developments and discussions about the political direction of Albania during her youth, before the dictatorship, when there were possibilities. This is because Kokalari's account is shared by and is part of fragmented narratives and diverging discourses. In 1993 the Albanian president declared several Albanians, including Musine Kokalari, to be 'Martyrs for Democracy'.[106] Schools have been renamed after Kokalari. But there is little substance to these initiatives, with hardly any contextualisation of intellectual, political, historical, and biographical context; likewise, there is no reflection of the textualisation of Kokalari's life account. '[T]he very tension between textualisation and contextualisation – might yield new avenues of insight, both into the texts at stake and into their context'.[107]

It is worthwhile reminding ourselves that law is also an important space, or venue, in which we return to the past and deal with the past, which might also involve a confrontation with the past.[108] Law derives from and is channelled through the normative practices of society. Encounters with art are also normative encounters. They raise questions about the past and challenge its narratives. In fact, art can provide important alternative and complementary solutions in certain places and for specific segments of society. Different aesthetic practices can highlight the roles that justice plays and document crimes that legal proceedings are not able to for a variety of reasons: this is done in an

104 Felman, 'Benjamin's Silence'.

105 Fijalkowski, 'Musine Kokalari and the Power of Images'.

106 Fijalkowski, 'Musine Kokalari and the Power of Images', 588–589.

107 Shoshana Felman and Dori Laub, *Testimony: Crises of Witnessing in Literature, Psychoanalysis, and History* (Routledge 1992) xv.

108 Bell, 'The Haunted Nomos', and by the same author, *The Art of Post-dictatorship: Ethics and Aesthetics in Transitional Argentina* (Routledge 2014) 5–15.

effort to also restore dignity to the victim. A photograph can certainly assume this role. As reiterated in Bell's work on images,[109] law becomes jurisgenerative, embracing creativity through these normative encounters. This neglected feature of law can reveal ways in which the image may have a vital part to play in restoring the dignity of victims, as well as in the transition from dictatorship to democracy.[110] The engagement with space and images are normative encounters that derive from the wider body politic. The narratives that emerge from the selected examples challenge the discourses about the Albanian communist past and identify the lack of cohesion in storytelling, a cohesion that paradoxically is intact in the materiality itself. The image reactivates its object in the particular situation of the observer. In the absence of an archive imperative that 'tells all', as noted in the previous section, Kokalari's image becomes a heterotopic site for some segments of Albanian society that acts as an ideal record of the past. However, as Foucault further instructs, heterotopic sites are often created following attempts to construct spaces; they are other sites, an answer to the messiness that surrounds them, a heterotopia of 'compensation'.[111]

As discussed above, the other notable trials were conducted in the same vein as Kokalari's, although they may have stressed other themes of Western espionage that coincided with other show trials, such as the Rajk trial, discussed earlier. They were all public events, with law as the key performance and participants playing a key role in its enactment.

This section has considered the key show trials that consolidated communist rule in Albania. The trials are interconnected to wider discourses about the performativity of Stalinist show trials. This discussion has illuminated the performativity of the law and the enactment of the law before a military court. It has considered the performativity of the law more broadly to include the way that our ideas about justice can be shaped by a venue. It introduced the brokers, the Soviet and Yugoslav teachers who taught the key players who worked most closely with Hoxha about negotiation and organisation of the enemy. Their authority was supported by images. These images, however, also captured affective justice in action, seen in the emotions depicted in the defendants' faces, or their body language before the makeshift court, and the behaviour and gestures of the prosecutors. Because of Albania's relatively small size, the impact of visual propaganda was quick. It effected the construction or destruction of the personal biography of particular significance in a 'photographer's state', as we shall see in the next section.

109 Bell, *The Art of Post-dictatorship*, 5–15.
110 Bell, *The Art of Post-dictatorship*, 5–15.
111 Michel Foucault, 'Of Other Spaces: Utopias and Heterotopias' (tr. Jay Miskowiec, *Architecture/Mouvement/Continuité*, October 1984) 8, https://web.mit.edu/allanmc/www/foucault1.pdf (accessed 13 October 2021).

Visual Culture

Research into visual communist Albania is warranted. One of the most prominent writers in this area is Gilles de Rapper, who has drawn attention to the fact that countless photographs were produced during the communist period in Albania.[112] The purpose of these collections was to create archives as well as to preserve the memory of places, people, and times 'in which and by which the new type of society wanted by the authorities was realised'.[113] Photographers were tasked with recording and documenting the 'construction of socialism'.[114] Significantly, it was also, for some of these individuals, the opportunity to create photographic memories; how much this extends to coverage of show trials by state photographers can be debated. As pointed out by Rapper:

> as a technical process related to industrialisation, photography has a significant relationship to modernisation. It also has the property to fix particular moments (in Albanian, as in other languages, the verb *fiksoj* is frequently used to describe the activity of the photographers) whose serialisation gives an idea, an 'evidence', of the time passing by and, in this case, of the progress made.[115]

The captions for pairs of images in key journals of the communist era used 'before' and 'after', or 'yesterday' and 'today' to demarcate the societal change driven by the political project.

As we learn more about the history of photography in Albania it becomes apparent that 'the communist period occupies a marginal and neglected place: photography is said to have had an instrumental status in the hands of political power and thus to be of little value compared to that which had been produced during the previous period'.[116] Yet we know from previous discussions that photography was popular in Soviet Russia. This is one of the reasons behind family photography, whose diffusion during the communist period is unprecedented; largely reserved for the urban middle and upper classes until the

112 Gilles de Rapper, 'Photography and Remembrance. Questioning the Visual Legacy of Communist Albania', in Jonila Godole and Idrit Idrizi (eds), *Between Apathy and Nostalgia: Private and Public Recollections of Communism in Contemporary Albania* (IDMC 2019) 103–119, 103. See also Gilles de Rapper and Anouk Durand, 'Family Photographs in socialist Albania: State Photography and the Private Sphere', in Eckehard Pistrick, Nicola Scaldaferri, and Gretel Schwörer (eds), *Audiovisual Media and Identity Issues in Southeastern Europe* (Cambridge Scholars Publishing 2011) 210–229; Gilles de Rapper, 'Photographs and *Régime d'historicité*: Past, Present, and Future in Two Photographic Albums on Communist Albania', in Nataša Gregorič and Smoki Musaraj (eds), *Remitting, Restoring and Building Contemporary Albania* (Palgrave 2021) 51–73.

113 Rapper, 'Photography and Remembrance', 104.

114 Rapper, 'Photography and Remembrance', 104.

115 Rapper, 'Photography and Remembrance', 104.

116 Rapper, 'Photography and Remembrance', 104.

Second World War, the family function of photography became accessible to a very large part of the population, including in remote rural areas, owing to the establishment of the so-called 'public service' photography in the 1960s.[117] Rapper and Durand remind us that photography stimulates speech, commentary, storytelling, and recollection, and that a narrative based on photography is often a collective one.[118]

Albania had several famous studios at which photographers trained as apprentices. One of the most established, if not the first, is the Marubi Studio in Shkodra. In the mid-19th century the city was an important economic and commercial centre, if not the most important in the Balkan region. It was here that Pjetër Marubi (or Marrubi) set up business after fleeing the political struggles in Italy. Marubi was an astute businessman; he soon realised that there was a gap in the market since photography had not yet reached Albania, and he sought to channel his own professional work as an architect, painter, and sculptor in this direction.[119] Roque Khodeli, one of his agricultural assistants, and members of his family would serve as Marubi's apprentices. Photography arrived in Albania around 1864–1865.

Marubi would send his apprentices to Trieste to work in the studio of Sébastianutti, his colleague and fellow photographer. Trieste was the gateway to the Austro-Hungarian empire and much innovative work was carried out here by photographers.[120] Marubi's work continued for three generations. Kel (Michael) Marubi, Roque's second son, was the most accomplished in the family. Kel recorded a cross-section of the Albanian people and settings of the era, when borders were not fixed and life was in flux. Everyone was caught in his camera. But above all Kel was a first-class portrait photographer.

Kel was the first to photograph Shote Galica (1895–1927), the celebrated female fighter;[121] at that time she was referred to as the 'Albanian Joan of Arc'

117 Rapper and Durand, 'Family Photographs in Socialist Albania', 210–229. Very few families do not possess at least a few photographs of diverse origins: photographic souvenirs taken by 'nature' photographers (*fotografët e natyrës*), wedding photographs, identity photographs, school photographs or 'emulation' photographs (*fotografi e emulacionit*). Photographs seem to respond to a need to keep souvenirs (*kujtim*), as evidenced by the frequency of the mention, printed or handwritten, of the word 'souvenir' on the prints.

118 Rapper and Durand, 'Family Photographs in Socialist Albania', 210–229. Rapper continues his exploration of photo albums in 'Photographs and *Régime d'historicité*'.

119 Luçjan Bedeni, 'Marubi Archive: Changing the History of Photography in Albania', *Post: Notes on Art in a Global Context*, 25 September 2019, https://post.moma.org/marubi-archive-changing-the-history-of-photography-in-albania/ (accessed 4 November 2022).

120 Tereza Çuni, 'Marubi: The Moving Backdrop' (2020), *European Heritage Days: Journées européennes du patrimoine*, https://www.europeanheritagedays.com/story/49569/Marubi-The-moving-backdrop (accessed 4 November 2022).

121 'Women from the Marubi Archive' exhibition at the Marubi Museum (Shkodër, Albania) 8 May 2016–19 January 2017, https://www.marubi.gov.al/exhibitions/temporary/women-from-the-marubi-archive (accessed 4 November 2022).

by the then French Consul. It must be recalled that at this time, throughout the Ottoman empire, photography was forbidden as being against Islamic principles. But this did not prevent the rich and liberal thinkers having their portraits taken. Kel was commissioned by King Nicholas of Montenegro to photograph the court.

The last decade of the 19th century saw a series of photographic studies spring up throughout the country. Kel's son worked with French photographers and the Lumière Company in Paris.[122] Kel Marubi died in 1940, when the country was in the midst of the misery of war and occupation (Italian until 1943). The Marubi Studio would become a state enterprise, linked with other former photographic businesses. In 1970 Kel's son Gegë donated his and his family's archives to the state: this collection contained the work of the Marubi Studio and three other photographers.[123]

Kolë Idromeno also came from Shkodra. He was a painter who gained experience in Venice. He too opened a studio in the city. Kritaq Sotiri was born in Korça and during his time in the US presented himself to the Steckel studio in Los Angeles. He opened a studio in New York but shortly after returned to Albania.[124] He was joined by another painter and colleague of Idromeno, Vangjush Mio. Sotiri belonged to the pictorialist movement, or pure photography, which was established in Vienna in 1896 in response to the rules imposed by the jury of the Royal Photographic Society in London. Two other studios were set up by Petro, a travelling photographer, and Kristaq Sulidhi. Vani Buda, a possibly less well-known photographer, opened a studio in Korça.

It can be argued that, following the establishment of the Marubi Studio in the 19th century, photography has had a long history in Albania. Throughout the dictatorship, photography was understood simply as taking pictures, and it was not a popular practice prior to the opening of privately owned studios by photographers who had trained abroad. It was at this time that photo-reporters, such as Vasil Ristani, emerged. The figure of the amateur photographer did not disappear after the communist takeover. Many Albanian students came back from the Soviet Union in the 1950s with a camera that they used for family

122 'Studio Marubi: Photographs of Albania 1858–1952' exhibition at the Museum of Cultures (Helsinki, Finland) from 5 May 2010–23 January 2011, https://web.archive.org/web/20131002072425/http://www.nba.fi/en/museums/museum_of_cultures/exhibitions/studio_marubi (accessed 4 November 2022).

123 Gilles de Rapper, 'Photography and *Régime d'historicité:* Past, Preseent, and Future in Two Photographic Albums on Communist Albania', in Nataša Gregorič Bon and Smoki Musaraj (eds), *Remitting, Restoring and Rebuilding Contemporary Albania* (Palgrave 2021), 51–73, 63.

124 'The Legacy of Kristaq Sotiri, Master of Photography', (2020) *Invest on Albania*, 28 February 2020, https://invest-in-albania.org/the-legacy-of-kristaq-sotiri-master-of-photography/ (accessed 23 October 2022).

purposes or which they sold to amateurs.[125] Competitions were organised by the state to promote the practice of photography by non-professional photographers, the prize being to train at a magazine's photographic laboratory. These competitions had the hidden agenda of promoting the construction of socialism. Moreover previously privately owned studios were run by the 'People's Photographers', such as Vasil Ristani and Mehmet Kallfa, two of the more prominent state-employed photographers. Ymer Bali (1894–1967) was another photographer who studied his art abroad – in Austria – and other working photographers included Misto Cici and Petro Dhimitri. But it was the Ristani and Kallfa families that dominated photography in the 20th century after their studios were nationalised.

Private owners of cameras, especially outside Tirana, were rare. During the inter-war period cameras would come from Italy, the US, Germany, and Turkey. Strong economic ties with Italy during the reign of Ahmed Zogu (1924–1939) were responsible for the import of many cameras by officers and soldiers, merchants and students. During the war, cameras could be bought from German or Italian soldiers and others, and were the basis of a second-hand market for a few years. The end of Second World War saw restrictions on foreign travel and issues with supplies of photographic paper. Up until the mid-1960s Soviet materials were used, such as the Zorki camera, a copy of the German Leica, whose production started in 1948, or the Beirette, an East German compact. After the break with the Soviets, cameras from China were available.

As the communists consolidated their power, private studios were progressively shut down. The first public studio was opened in Tirana in 1947. The Albanian Telegraphic Agency, or the ATA, set up in December 1944, started to employ professional photographers, such as Vasil Ristani and Mehmet Kallfa, both of whom previously owned studies in Tirana.[126] ATA was to become the main photographic institution, a place where new generations of photographers were trained by older ones who ceased their private activity. This was a time when authorities enrolled several photographers all over the country to realise the first campaign of identity photographs. The new state needed photography for propaganda purposes but also to identify its citizens. As such, photography

125 Barbara Klich-Kurczewska, 'Luxury from the USSR and the GDR? Cameras and Photographic Equipment as Official and Unofficial Objects of Trade in the People's Republic of Poland', in Marek Maszczak (ed.), *Polski sprzęt fotograficzny z lat 1954–1995 w zbiorach Muzeum Historii Fotografii w Krakowie* [Polish Photographic Equipment from 1954–1995 in the Collection of the Museum of the History of Photography in Kraków] (Kraków 2006) 12–47.

126 Gilles de Rapper, 'Fotografia shqiptare në kohën ekpeditës Stockmann-Sokoli dhe pas saj. Jehonat e së shkuarës – Zerat e së ardhmes' [Albanian Photography at the Time of the Stockmann-Sokoli Expedition and Beyond. Echoes of the Past, Voice of the Future], October 2013, https://halshs.archives-ouvertes.fr/halshs-00879559/document (accessed 4 November 2022).

was seen as a political instrument that had to be kept under strict control. In 1945 and 1946 the new state passed laws that heavily taxed all private activities; many photographers, craftsmen, and merchants were forced to join a public studio or find a job at a state institution. Strict organisation resulted in a strong subjective feeling of hierarchy between photographers. Professional photographers did not form one single group. There was a contrast between those who worked in state institutions and those who worked in cooperatives. The first were better trained and worked using high-quality equipment and material; the others generally had a limited knowledge of photography and had to work with poor-quality equipment. Outside Tirana everyone complained about lack of materials.

Professional photographers would have gained valuable experience during their respective apprenticeships. Another important factor, as noted briefly above, pertains to the developments in the Ottoman empire. Even though religious belief did not support taking photographs, the art of photography blossomed and developed at a rapid rate, resulting in the creation of studios, such as Effendi (Efendi), that would exert their influence on developments in Albania.[127] Photography first appeared in Turkey in the 1850s, and later the first studio was opened by a German chemist, Rabach, in Beyazit. This studio became a school for young people. In 1855 the 'Abdualah Brothers' or Abdullah Frères took over the studio and converted to Islam. This rapid progress allowed them to expand to Cairo and Istanbul. Another acclaimed photographer was Phebus Efendi, who organised courses at the palace of Sultan Abdulhamid II and became a popular figure. The use of photography for profit and trade was achieved mostly by ethnic minorities living in the empire, such as Armenians, Jews, and Greeks, and the use of photography for different purposes was limited to those minorities. By the end of the 19th century the pupils of Abdullah Frères were continuing the traditions of their masters and took photography out of the palace and into daily life, initiating the tradition of photojournalism.[128] It was at Studio Resna that many young photographers trained until 1924, and this fed the movement towards Westernisation and renovation in the region. These influences can be seen in the work of the Marubi Studio.

Another studio of prominence was the Photo Studio Kallfa in Tirana. Mehmet Kallfa was most likely the photographer at Musine Kokalari's trial in 1946, discussed earlier in this chapter.[129] He worked for the ATA from 1944 to 1957. The Kallfa archive comprises key moments in Albanian history. The

127 Stephen Sheehi, *The Arab Imago: A Social History of Portrait Photography, 1860–1910* (Princeton University Press 2016) 1–26.

128 Ekrem Buğra Ekinci, 'The Abdullah Brothers: Pioneers of Photography in the Late Ottoman Period', 6 May 2016, *Daily Sabah*, https://www.dailysabah.com/feature/2016/05/06/the-abdullah-brothers-pioneers-of-photography-in-the-late-ottoman-period (accessed 4 November 2022).

129 Interview with Gani Xhengo, Tirana, 13 May 2015.

socio-economic life that was photographed was an important for the Hoxha regime in promoting the successes of the communist regime. The camera was a vital tool of documentation and control, and became an important part of the discussion about the composition of the enemy.

In the 'photographer's state' of Albania, authorities controlled the very way in which photographs were produced. Photography was thus fundamental to Hoxha's plan of massification and the manner in which the political project was brought to the people. This included the electrification project of 1960, which declared that it would bring electricity to all Albanians by 1985,[130] including to mountainous and difficult to reach areas. Electrification was declared complete in 1970. This endeavour entailed the mass production of postcards of Albanians working on various aspects of this exceedingly hazardous project.[131] Most photographs in circulation informed collective memory and featured contrasting narratives so far as personal successes or losses were concerned.

The photographic collections of the ATA draw our attention to the visual fabrication of the memory of the construction of socialism. Photography, as the politics of representation, is interlinked with its role and relationship to other forms of representation. Albanian photography from that period 'implied a plurality of agents and institutions and took place within political, ideological, moral and technical constraints that must be reconstructed to explain how a particular photograph was produced at a given moment, and how it reached us'.[132] This was seen in the discussion about Musine Kokalari above. Kokalari's image from 1946 continues to travel, pointing to its materiality and who it interacts with on its journey.[133] Importantly, the album of images of the show trial results in us speaking legally as we aim to reconstruct a narrative in the absence of full information. In this approach we engage with affective justice, which invokes a variety of feelings and memory.[134] Likewise, each image 'is the result of a device that imposes a vision; this vision is not transparent or naturally recorded by the camera, rather it is produced by an apparatus'.[135]

As noted previously, the connection with Stalinism and the Soviet approaches to ruling the state never really disappeared. The Soviets brought their history and experience, and the scale of their influence is 'best understood at both the local and transnational levels since, over time, developments in some

130 See the film *Enver's Bulb – A Short History of Albania's Electrification* (directed by Björn Reinhardt and Eckehard Pistrick, 2018). Also this image: https://twitter.com/albaniauntold/status/1300160881423155200?s=12 (accessed 27 September 2022).

131 *Enver's Bulb*.

132 Rapper and Durand, 'Family Photographs in Socialist Albania', 210–229.

133 Rapper and Durand, 'Family Photographs in Socialist Albania', 210–229.

134 Rapper and Durand, 'Family Photographs in Socialist Albania', 210–229.

135 Rapper noting John Tagg, *The Burden of Representation* (1988). Rapper, 'Photography and Remembrance', 104.

parts of the socialist world affected other parts'.[136] With the Soviet Union as a 'distant mighty patron', individuals also came to view themselves differently.[137] Albania earned 'a certain value within the geography of post-war socialism. It becomes necessary, therefore, to think of strategies of discovery, with their intended and unintended outcomes, and how beliefs were tested by transnational encounters'.[138] In Albania, the Soviet dimension to things was viewed as one about style and as much about making a public statement, where all successes and failures were confronted in a 'public fashion',[139] where 'conspicuous boards specifying daily activity and plan fulfilment, placards showing individual and collective pledges (sometimes addressed directly to Hoxha as Komandant), and places of honour reserved for displaying the photographs and names of members of the top-performing brigades',[140] all comprising visual propaganda across the country. The photographs show us the power of space, found in the selected courtroom setting – spacious cinema venues that provided room for large, hand-picked audiences The events were bespoke: tailor-made for wider society. Mëhilli sets out the nature of Soviet-inspired architecture – one of grandeur – seen in the gates to mills, workers' clubs, and film studios. These aesthetics guided and shaped societal relations and organisation, language and communication, and the movement and transition between a person who could be a hero or villain within a very short space of time. And while this discussion focuses on a specific time period, it is important to note that the Albanian account extends beyond Soviet influences, and that the Soviet influence itself continued throughout communist Albanian rule.[141]

A new socialist world came about not because the imposition of Soviet policy succeeded everywhere, or because it succeeded on its own terms. Rather, a new socialist world emerged because it became possible to see oneself through a socialist lens.[142] As Mëhilli aptly notes, before there had been any Soviet invasion of Budapest, the Sigurimi were targeting 'anti-Soviet activities', presented in the trial that concerned the so-called bombing of the Soviet embassy in Tirana, which heralded a wave of repression, arrests of individuals unrelated to the incident, and the execution of 22 persons on fabricated charges of having prepared an terrorist attack against the Soviets.[143] Stephen Kotkin's notion of Soviet men and women learning to 'speak Bolshevik', as discussed earlier and referred to by scholars examining the Soviet agitation trials, also provides a compelling argument for the self- and social identification that was occurring at this time in Albania. The speaking is facilitated by visual

136 Mëhilli, *From Stalin to Mao*, 56.
137 Mëhilli, *From Stalin to Mao*, 56.
138 Mëhilli, *From Stalin to Mao*, 56.
139 Mëhilli, *From Stalin to Mao*, 111.
140 Mëhilli, *From Stalin to Mao*, 111.
141 Mëhilli, *From Stalin to Mao*.
142 Mëhilli, *From Stalin to Mao*, 56.
143 Mëhilli, *From Stalin to Mao*, 88.

propaganda and the power of images was understood by the image makers, who saw their work as part of the construction of the collective narrative about the construction of socialism.

Concluding Remarks

The discussion in this chapter focused on two issues. It looked at one of the most prominent figures in this group – the class enemy. In fact, these heroes, like Musine Kokalari, form an integral part of the discourses concerning past and future post-dictatorial legal spaces, especially those confronting uncomfortable questions about the past. This predicament has been shared by other states but was never properly addressed in a post-communist Albania. The image of Kokalari performs the act of connecting members of society, by establishing people's sense of belonging to that lost community of a communist Albania or by offering itself as a target for their affects, which might include fear or admiration, or both. This discussion has shown how the materiality of the image has the capacity to reorganise society. In other words, the very act of its appearing results in a 'performative reorganization' of space and/or narrative. The success of the image, based on its capacity to mobilise and to affect an audience, arises from its 'semantic porosity and material capacity' to link different elements together.[144] This occurs on three different levels. Structurally the image acts as a connection between a chain of signifiers, connecting various elements to form a story. Psychologically it provides a material veneer for collective and individual projections. Socially it founds various forms of interaction, display, and circulation: 'It is not a piece of memory, it is a piece instead of memory'.[145] Like a tarot card and its particular image, Kokalari's image 'flashes up' in specific settings and discourses. Tarot cards are used by groups, and are therefore an appropriate reference here, Kokalari being a shared memory for a certain generation of Albanians, a fact that lends poignancy and legitimacy to the cultural participation in the information or the emotion that the photograph conveys, and the *punctum*, or the startling, transfixing element that captures the viewer's eye and provokes an involuntary emotional response and personal reading of the image.[146]

This chapter also considered the dynamics of visual law in Albania. Images taken by state-employed photographers were published in the main broadsheets of the day. This unique characteristic was part of a process designed to engage people, including the legal community, by means of the image makers engaging with the education of the masses that also captured and preserved narratives.

144 Oushakine, 'Performative Objects: How Things Do Things without Words', in Julie A. Buckler, Julie A. Cassiday, and Boris Wolfson (eds), *Russian Performances: Word, Object, Action* (University of Wisconsin Press 2018) 54–63.
145 Oushakine, 'Performative Objects', 56–57.
146 Fijalkowski, 'Musine Kokalari and the Power of Images'.

In *About Looking*, John Berger remarks that 'unlike memory, photographs do not in themselves preserve meaning'.[147] In Albania, however, the photograph possessed a vital material quality because it played an integral part in a family history, which came to be known in the case of those afflicted as a 'bad biography', or a life in which the individual or family was under constant scrutiny by the security services. Catherine Epstein notes that the 'biography is a sitting target; nothing can alter the facts of a life already lived'.[148] A biography refers to the lived experience of the individual and it can also refer to the text or description of the life of an individual.[149] The information about the development of photography in Albania is illustrative. The way in which photography intersected with Albanian society and its role during dictatorial rule is a key dimension of this study. It all begins with the establishment of photographers' studios throughout the country. Their introduction signalled an important cultural exchange that depended on strong social and commercial ties.

A photograph can raise questions about the past that are quite distinct from the written record. The image's *punctum* serves to startle the spectator, whose attention is then drawn to the details of the case, the fate of the condemned, and the subsequent measures of justice meted out. The image is a means to talk about the past through itself, and in its materiality. It conveys a continuous message that subsists, and a consciousness of having been there. The manner in which the photograph is used is in reality propaganda. In this way, photographs from trials served an important purpose for the regime, generating knowledge about the general population and the 'traitors' in its midst. On the other hand, the narratives between past and present are interwoven. The photograph continues to be a part of the propaganda about the country's past. And the focus of my discussion, the photograph of Kokalari from her 1946 trial and Albania's approach to 'remembering the past', reveals a number of lessons. The best example is the official confining of the past to history on the grounds that the populace was complicit in perpetrating it. This in turn silences the role of law. When art engages with law, and law meets art at its apex, as in the case of a photograph, the silences have the potential to become opportunities that can then go on to overcome some of the obstacles to the recounting of certain narratives. Kokalari's hidden legacy points to the importance of making sure that reckoning with the past opens up new avenues of learning about the nature of the dictatorship, and that the process of historicising does not underplay how significant justice is for societies emerging from a dictatorship. Her legacy is revealed in schools naming themselves after her, or the organisation of exhibitions about the genocide of which she was a part. This part of her image is far more developed than the call for accountability for the maladministration

147 John Berger, *About Looking* (Bloomsbury 1980) 55.

148 Catherine Epstein, 'The Politics of Biography: The Case of East German Old Communists' (1999) 128(2) *Daedulus* 1–30, 1.

149 Epstein, 'The Politics of Biography', 1.

of justice in her case, at her trial. This is an especially critical moment for a country that is examining the nature of the Albanian dictatorship.[150]

The danger of addressing the image of Kokalari in this way can be criticised as misappropriation and misrepresentation. Over the years that I have studied the trial and her life, Kokalari has been used as a poster child for feminism in Albania and elsewhere. The peril is that we do not engage with Kokalari herself, or her work, but only superficially. Images facilitate superficial connections.

There is another aspect to performativity that concerns discovery. The narrative of discovery refers to mentioning names that have been hitherto unknown to the wider world, either because they have been overlooked or because they have been rediscovered anew. As Katie da Kuhna Lewin points out, this has occurred recently with respect to feminist projects.[151] The presentation of the accounts of women are superficial and often maintain the dominant status quo rather than challenge or require further engagement with the individual and her remarkable account.[152] Kokalari is not the first Albanian pre-communist female writer or pioneer who opposed a patriarchal society, one that Kokalari knew very well. Kokalari is also not the first female to be put on trial. It is important to engage with her story and bear in mind that hers is a repeated story, one of promise and tragedy; so much more can be done in terms of engaging with her key works, which to date have not been translated into English. A wider perspective and appreciation of the feminist project will benefit the way that we deploy aesthetics and search for a more critical examination of affective justice and the politics of visualising justice, especially an image like that of Kokalari.

The adoption of the analysis of law and aesthetics is key and points to a vital question: namely, the capacity of the law to create affective justice. The answer to 'what's in a face?' is that the subject's face is the story of many 'Musine Kokalaris'.[153] Barbara Halla convincingly writes about the untold stories of Kokalari's contemporaries, and also modern writers like Helen Kadare, who, despite being an acclaimed writer, remains largely marginalised from the literary academy and who has never been assigned to a curriculum reading list, unlike her husband. The literary discourse has no room for writers who engage with topics that are not heroic, as Kokalari did. Halla calls

150 Ilir Kalemij, 'Lustration in Albania: The Past and the Future' (2021), on file with author, https://www.academia.edu/45189580/Lustration_in_Albania_The_past_and_the_future?email_work_card=title. See also Austin and Ellison, 'Albania'.

151 Katie de Kuhna Lewin, 'Discover the Untold Stories of the Pre-Raphaelite Sisters: The Politics of Discovery', (2019) LARB, 17 August 2020, https://lareviewofbooks.org/article/the-politics-of-rediscovery/ (accessed 26 July 2022).

152 Something that I have been guilty of and have tried to reflect on. See Sarah Ahmed, 'Institutional as Usual', Blog, 24 October 2017, https://feministkilljoys.com/2017/10/24/institutional-as-usual/ (accessed 26 July 2022).

153 Interview with the Albanian photographer Ismail Kadare, Paris, 6 October 2014.

for a reframing of the educational and literary agendas to break the silence that has a patriarchal hold over Albanian women writers.[154] These questions will also be a part of the reflection on the protagonists in Chapter 4 on the East German context.

154 Barbara Halla, 'Barren Landscape: Who is Afraid of Albanian Women?', *Asymptote*, 20 February 2019, https://www.asymptotejournal.com/blog/2019/02/20/barren-landscape-who-is-afraid-of-albanian-women/?fbclid=IwAR1Pc8-2EWx1vrNrRemeM8djbpe_gz-McahFWdNcVoVxSIwfOH0LidnhpSY (accessed 10 January 2022).

Chapter 4

Law, Visual Culture, and the Show Trial in East Germany

The narrative arc of this chapter will consider the East German experience through the account of judge and later Minister of Justice Hilde Benjamin (1902–1989). Benjamin is chiefly known for her unwavering commitment to communism, and for the judgments she delivered during the 1950s as a High Court judge in cases concerning capital crimes, judgments that earned her the nickname 'Bloody Hilde' or 'The Red Guillotine'. Benjamin presided over the majority of rulings in political cases against groups accused of espionage and sabotage. But there is another part of her life account that merits attention, and that is her contribution to key East German legal developments. Her life and career are less well known in anglophone scholarship and indeed in wider German legal discourses.

The discussion in this book so far has demonstrated the way an image carries with it vast potential for discovery: this is because it has its own biography. Benjamin's life story itself is entangled in wider discourses about East Germany's particular legal trajectory and is relevant to broader legal discourses. My examination of images of her and other relevant images will allow for movement beyond the ideological confrontations of the past, so as to posit novel connections between contending narratives, the better to understand East Germany and its place in legal discourses and its legacies for the future. The (dis)connection between the German Federal Republic and East German legal approaches to the immediate past, especially in relation to certain legal developments regarding issues such as war crimes, is an awkward and live matter, and the relevant narrative is itself bound up with images.

There is also an important debate to be had about East Germany's contribution to international criminal justice and family law, and Benjamin is at the heart of these issues. In this sense, the East German past is still of great interest and promises to remain so for the foreseeable future. As one writer argues, the assertion that '[a]lthough the legacies of East German socialism will linger for many years in Germany, the German Democratic Republic (GDR) is, as they say, history'[1] is misleading. These legacies should be revisited and reconsidered as East German narratives, and then resituated within the wider German legal discourse. The gaps

1 Corey Ross, *The East German Dictatorship: Problems and Perspectives in the Interpretation of the GDR* (Hodder Arnold 2002) 1.

DOI: 10.4324/9781003405771-5

in analysis of the German legal historical timeline, and the omission of East Germany's contribution to the development of the law, presents an inaccurate picture of the German legal system and such analysis risks having little value. The legal historical account includes oppression as much as innovation, but it is much more complex than that. For many Germans the country's history forms a crucial part of their own biographies and identities. All areas of historical enquiry – especially recent history – are affected by shifting political preoccupations; East German history is by no means exceptional in this regard. The connection between scholarly research into the history of East Germany and the shaping of current political and legal consciousness in the united Germany has been quite explicit and very much in line with the German Federal Republic's tradition of contemporary research as 'political education', which was created after the Second World War.[2] As a result there have been conflicting interpretations of the political identity of East Germany and the united Germany, and their role in the wider world. This is changing. There is new and exciting research on new histories of law and rights in the 20th century, including Germany, that is noted in this chapter.

This chapter will begin by considering the crucial facts about some of the key players and architects of the East German legal framework: the Old Communists. The discussion will identify their key actions in a chronological order to appreciate the context and world in which our protagonist was dispensing justice. Second, it will address the show trials in which Benjamin was involved. It is without doubt that Benjamin's role in these trials was unique. The discussion will then turn to Benjamin's life account. Third, it will set out the dynamics of legal propaganda in visual imagery in East Germany. The success of the show trials relied on state-employed photographers who covered them in depth, and the resulting images were published in the main broadsheets of the day; in later times, selected proceedings were televised.

Of course, the first regime to use modern media was also found in Germany, namely the Third Reich, which used the media to maximise propaganda. It would, for example, broadcast and film marches. Gatherings, such as the Summer Olympics of 1936, were filmed[3] and were a significant part of the production of propaganda, as were the show trials before the People's Court (*Volksgerichtshof*) before the presiding judge Roland Freisler. Freisler was known for his aggressive style, berating each defendant. He was an eager participant in the Nazification of the law, and nearly all the cases that came before him resulted in a guilty verdict and a death sentence.[4] It is noteworthy that Benjamin was in Berlin during this tumultuous period, as was Kirchheimer for a while before he emigrated to Paris in 1933. At this time the Nazification of the law intensified, alongside use of legal propaganda. For East Germany, the

2 See insights in Corey Ross, *The East German Dictatorship: Problems and Perspectives in the Interpretation of the GDR* (Hodder Arnold 2002).

3 Leni Riefenstahl, *Olympia* Part 1: *Festival of Nations* (1938), *Olympia* Part 2: *Festival of Beauty*. Also *Triumph of the Will* (1935).

4 Ingo Müller, *Hitler's Justice: the Courts of the Third Reich* (tr. Deborah Lucas Schneider, Harvard University Press 1991).

reliance on using modern media to disseminate specific messages about the dispensing of justice meant that the legal system could align itself with Andrei Vyshinsky's notion of educating to throttle and throttling to educate. The authorities made use of legal photography and legal photojournalism.

The Architects of the East German Legal Framework

This section, which is not meant to be a comprehensive account, will identify several key actors and their particular contributions to the constitutional framework as a means to provide a backdrop. Their efforts established the state as a legitimate nation with a goal of social change. They also provided state authorities with the means to secure control over the master narrative underpinning the statehood and its populace. Otto Kirchheimer's writings on political justice have a significant connection with East Germany, not least because he kept abreast of developments in his native country in the immediate post-Second World War period. His preoccupation with the rule of law and the Third Reich would in time yield to a concern with regime change in a divided Germany. 'Speaking legally' became integral to East Germany's attempts to establish itself as a legitimate state. Kirchheimer notes that the policy of the East German administration served a dual purpose: speedy integration with other communist-led states and the furthering of social change, paving the way for eventual absorption into the Eastern bloc.[5] East German law had its foundations in the Soviet experience and in Marxist–Leninist–Stalinist ideology. With respect to the criminal law, the main works were by the Soviet jurists Evgeny Pashukanis (representing legal nihilism) and Andrei Vyshinsky (representing the value of formal law).[6] Generally speaking, Pashukanis's works were relevant to the development of the East German social courts,[7] while Vyshinsky's writings and practice came to be relevant to the exposition of the dichotomy between formal legality and state power. How this was depicted in court via the concept of 'speaking legally' and in relation to the visual depiction of the dispensation of justice will be discussed in later sections.

The East German legal framework was dictated by the state constitution from 1949. The constitution drew heavily from the 1919 Weimar document, but East German leaders, like Otto Grotewahl (1894–1964), who wanted to address the Weimar constitution's loopholes, soon came to be instrumental in drafting the 1949 document. Grotewahl was a member of the Socialist Democratic Party for Germany, which he joined in 1925. He experienced first-

5 Otto Kirchheimer, 'The Administration of Justice and the Concept of Legality in East Germany' (1958–1959) 68 *The Yale Law Journal* 705–749, 705, fn. 1. He refers to Harold Berman, 'Soviet Law Reform – Dateline Moscow 1957' (1957) 66(8) *Yale Law Journal* 1191–1215, 1212.

6 Peter C. Caldwell, *Dictatorship, State Planning, and Social Theory in the German Democratic Republic* (Cambridge University Press 2003) 63.

7 Peter W. Spierlich, *The East German Social Courts: Law and Popular Justice in a Marxist-Leninist Society* (Praeger 2007).

hand the discrimination against communists by German authorities, and during the Second World War went underground and worked as part of the resistance. He and Wilhelm Pieck (1876–1960) would emerge as key players in the founding of the East German state. The loopholes identified by Grotewahl were resolved in the 1949 document's basic tenets. These principles concerned social justice and public ownership, collective life, and family, and were a reply to the prominence of civil and political rights in the Weimar constitution. Moreover, constitutional rights to education, vocation, and engagement in political life were set out in East Germany's first constitution. This was a progressive document and it reflected the mood and direction of the state and its underpinning philosophy. To reach this point, however, took some time and there were several obstacles to overcome. The task was taken on by the country's leader, Walter Ulbricht (1893–1973).

Ulbricht was an orthodox staunch Stalinist. Ulbricht founded the Independent Social Democratic Party of Germany (the German communist party) during the Weimar Republic. He studied at the Lenin School in Moscow from 1924 to 1925. With the rise of the Nazi party to power, Ulbricht lived in exile from 1933 to 1937 in Paris and Prague, and then in Moscow from 1937 to 1945. Ulbricht was First Secretary from 1960 to 1973 (succeeded by Eric Honecker) and Chairman of the National Defence Council from 1960 to 1971. His notable contribution to the constitutional innovation of his colleagues was telling: 'It has to look democratic, but we must have everything firmly in our hands'.[8] This was reflected in the events of October 1946 when a referendum was introduced by the Soviets in the Soviet-controlled zone in Berlin. The referendum addressed expropriation by war criminals. This issue was used by the Party leader to campaign on an anti-fascism platform, showing how this group of communists fought for socialism and against fascism,[9] a divergence from the Federal Republic's narrative and, significantly, an important item in the biography of the Old Communists.[10] It was also Ulbricht who fought for developing the theoretical underpinnings of the platform.

The role of the 'Old Communists', who were considered revolutionary, was noted and accounts were exchanged in East Germany. Here, the 'Old Communists' were those individuals who joined the German Communist Party *Kommunistische Partei Deutschlands*, (KPD) before 1933 – the year marking Hitler's rise to power. To join the Party at this time was risky. During the Weimar period (1919–1933) communists were ostracised by the state authorities, a view that was adopted and intensified during the Third Reich. The KPD engaged in anti-fascist activities that included illegal resistance, joining the

8 Ned Richardson-Little, *The Human Rights Dictatorship: Socialism, Global Solidarity and Revolution in East Germany* (Cambridge University Press 2020) 27.

9 Richardson-Little, *The Human Rights Dictatorship*, 29.

10 Catherine Epstein, 'The Politics of Biography: The Case of East German Old Communists' (1999) 128(2) *Daedalus* 1–30, 6.

fight alongside the International Brigades in the Spanish War, and/or suffering incarceration in prisons and construction camps. In short, the Old Communists put their life on the line for their political beliefs. Their lives were genuine and spoke of the physical endurance that turned most of them into 'gritty, hard-edged characters who stopped at nothing to further their political aims'.[11] Their personalities seemed laced with a steel forged from iron political convictions. If nothing else, Old Communists, 'rather like Havel and Mandela, were authentic'.[12] Old Communists occupied the most prominent positions in the East German party and state bureaucracy. They were represented in the Socialist Unity Party *Sozialistische Einheitspartei Deutschlands* (SED), Politburo, and Central Committee. They dominated not only political life, but also cultural life.[13] The communist struggle against fascism was central to communism's claims to legitimacy and provided further impetus to the claim that the triumph over fascism was a defining moment in history. This message was amplified in the show trials during this period. Revolutionary values were promoted actively in the creation of institutions and practices that popularised anti-fascist heroes; the history of the KPD and SED, however, was one of much suffering and great courage, but little heroism.[14]

Ulbricht was assisted by the legal theorist Karl Polak (1905–1963) and the momentum of the post-Second World War German political left that used Soviet templates for inspiration when drafting its vision of human rights. As a result, East Germany emerged as a hybrid, anti-fascist state, with roots in the Weimar Republic but essentially operating as a one-party state. Polak himself studied in Moscow, not being able to continue with his studies as a Jew in Germany. Upon his return to the Soviet occupied zone, he actively contributed to the development of law in East Germany, specifically on constitutional matters, working closely with Ulbricht.

The writings of Hans Klenner, who saw human rights as a pillar of the state, would situate the social and economic order of the state more firmly in the legal framework. The discussion will return to Klenner later. In the aftermath of the Second World War, the founders of East Germany created a specific version of socialist human rights, which began with ideals of socialism and anti-fascism.[15] The particular East German approach to human rights and its accompanying language resulted in a broader understanding of human rights protections among East Germans, who in turn contributed to the advancement of law in ways that are not understood because they do not follow the linear historical narrative.[16]

11 Epstein, 'The Politics of Biography', 6.
12 Epstein, 'The Politics of Biography', 6.
13 Such as Robert Havemann. Epstein, 'The Politics of Biography', 6. Andrea Feth, *Hilde Benjamin – Eine Biographie* (Arno Spitz 1997) 19–29. Personal interview with Dr Andrea Feth, Berlin, 9 July 2017.
14 Epstein, 'The Politics of Biography', 8.
15 Richardson-Little, *The Human Rights Dictatorship*, 5.
16 Richardson-Little, *The Human Rights Dictatorship*, 13.

These architects would come to work on, and contribute to, the operation of a system that was rooted in ideology and that would introduce a distinct imprint that was East German in its operation. The architects succeeded in doing so at least partially, and this can be attributed to the efforts of Benjamin and others as well as visual legal propaganda. Some constitutional features were not distinct, such as the disparity between formal legality and state prerogative. This contradiction was evidenced in many communist systems because, like East Germany, most borrowed from the Soviet model. Klenner demonstrated a commitment to Soviet legal thought when presiding over a number of cases. This was repeated by other judicial officials. For example, in a 1951 speech to members of the Supreme Court and the Office of the Public Prosecutor, Max Fechner (1892–1973), then Minister of Justice of the Soviet Zone, considered the defection of 'crime', which he described as every action endangering the community, even if it is formally legitimate and not subject to punishment.[17] This Soviet approach formed the basis of the strict instruction to judges and prosecutors.[18] It presented officials like Fechner with an additional ideological dimension to their assessment of the actions at the heart of the case.

The idea that a lawyer might have her own opinion about politics had no place in her profession, as Benjamin argued before the International Commission of Jurists in her capacity as Vice-President of the Soviet Zone Supreme Court[19] in 1952. A year later, Klenner argued that '[t]he insight into historical necessity, which the proletarian alone possesses and practices, the unity of politics and economics, is the presupposition of authentic legality (*Gesetzlichkeit*), its only possible content'.[20] Referring to Vyshinsky, Klenner asserted that law had a separate existence from politics and social norms. What was needed, in his view, was a requirement that state actors be bound by law and, as such, this called for a clear hierarchy in laws.[21] As readers may recall, Vyshinsky's view would come to prevail after Stalin had assumed power in 1928, when the consolidation of the Soviet legal system served as a means of transforming society. This did not mean limiting the party and state apparatus that were doing the transforming. Soviet law came to be

17 Author unknown, 'Abolition of the Independence of the Courts', in *Injustice the Regime: Documentary Evidence of the Systematic Violation of Legal Rights in the Soviet Occupied Territory of Germany* (Federal Ministry for All-German Affairs 1952) 71. See also Max Fechner, 'Stalin: der Kämpfer für den Frieden, der große Freund des Deutschen Volkes' [Stalin: The Fighter for Peace, the Great Friend of the German People] (1949) 3(12) *Neue Justiz* 297–299.

18 Agata Fijalkowski, 'Politics, Law and Justice in People's Poland: The Fieldorf File' (2014) 73(1) *Slavic Review* 85–107.

19 'For the Rule of Law', Bulletin of the International Commission of Jurists (1954), https://www.icj.org/wp-content/uploads/1955/03/ICJ-Bulletin-1-1954-eng.pdf (accessed 14 July 2022).

20 Caldwell, *Dictatorship, State Planning, and Social Theory in the German Democratic Republic*, 57.

21 Caldwell, *Dictatorship, State Planning, and Social Theory in the German Democratic Republic*, 89.

marked by a basic contradiction between formal legality and state prerogative.[22] For example, the 1936 Soviet Constitution guaranteed judicial independence. At the same time, however, prerogative state action expanded to include, *inter alia*, the extra-legal aspects of purge trials, whereby those charged were dispatched to large-scale labour camps and other party-controlled institutions that took the matter outside the competence of the courts.[23]

The 1949 GDR Constitution also represented this contradiction. It remained a 'dead letter', apart from the rare occasions when Article 144 was invoked ('all laws that contradict constitutional norms will be nullified'), in 'anti-democratic agitation' cases (Article 6 of the 1949 Constitution). Some East German jurists amplified the importance of formal legality – to their peril because mentioning the Constitution could prove dangerous. This was seen in the case of Fechner, who adhered to the concept of social danger as constructed by Soviet criminal legal theorists, but fell foul of the regime when he called on judges to take into account the right to strike[24] articulated in the Constitution in response to the strike actions undertaken in 1953. Fechner was declared a traitor and sentenced to eight years in jail for this constitutional interpretation.[25] In the authorities' eyes, Fechner's position that there was a concept of constitutional review was a disappointment: there was no such concept. After serving a few years of an eight-year sentence Fechner was amnestied and reinstated in the SED.[26]

Indeed, the Constitution did not function as a set of rules to regulate state action but instead epitomised what had been achieved by the state. The work of its architects relied on the creation of specific bodies within the administration of justice to grant them the authority and legitimacy to 'speak legally'. Such a consistent strategy dictates the way that the viewer sees trials, the law, and the manner in which they understand communism. Because they are not able to ignore its features, or 'unthink' it, a broader reading should try to appreciate that, for many, communism bound those who believed in the project as a collective history, and it meant something.[27]

Benjamin replaced Fechner. In 1954, in her new role as Minister of Justice, she offered an insight into socialist legality when she noted that '[s]ocialist legality is the dialectic[al] unity of strict adherence to the laws and partiality in their application'.[28] The East German Constitution in fact glossed over

22 See Ernst Melsheimer, 'Die Stalinische Verfassung' [The Stalinist Constitution] (1949) 3(12) *Neue Justiz* 299–302.

23 Caldwell, *Dictatorship, State Planning, and Social Theory in the German Democratic Republic*, 62–63.

24 Richardson-Little, *The Human Rights Dictatorship.*

25 Caldwell, *Dictatorship, State Planning, and Social Theory in the German Democratic Republic*, 65–66.

26 Richardson-Little, *The Human Rights Dictatorship.*

27 Dr Anna Hájková's insightful comments about the 1952 Slansky trial in her presentation on 'The Communist Resistance Group on Theresienstadt' at the Weiner Historical Institute, 8 September 2020.

28 As cited in Kritz, *Transitional Justice*, 629, fn. 98.

partiality as a commitment to socialist society in its provisions, namely Articles 86, 87, 90, 97 (provisions dealing with the functions of the People's Chamber). 'It is the meaning of socialism and thus of our country to do everything for the benefit of Man, for the happiness of the people, for the interests of the working class, and all working persons'.[29] This is exemplified in the 'dog of Muehlhausen' case, which demonstrates the way that judicial officials could be fooled by the class enemy, where the quashing of lower court proceedings were accompanied by a reprimand of the local prosecutor and judges. Scrutiny of one's actions in private became public when they meant something politically.[30] Benjamin addressed the moral and legal problems associated with the interpretation of constitutional change in a like fashion. In one case the High Court rejected a charge by a husband against another man who had done bodily harm to the first man's wife, in accordance with Article 195 of the Criminal Code. Article 7 of the Constitution proclaimed equality of the sexes.[31] The High Court threw the case out but without asking the wife whether she wished to pursue a claim and press charges against the man for battery herself. Benjamin held that the decision may have been formally correct but contradicted the substance of the constitutional change with respect to equality of the sexes. Gender equality was her priority; without it, the basic tenets of socialism could not be realised:[32] as noted in her 1958 lecture, 'All decisions regarding the shape of the shared family must be made by the husband and the wife together'.[33] Benjamin admitted that the idea of equality was not yet part of the legal consciousness of East Germans: 'Not only are women granted the same rights as men, but in East Germany they are given the means to realise their rights'.[34] She saw that there were still obstacles to overcome regarding expectations about women's role in society, which she would recognise from tropes perpetuated during the Third Reich.[35] The next section looks at 'speaking legally' more closely.

Speaking Legally in the East German Legal Framework

One of the key moments for the dispensing of justice in East Germany occurred in 1947. Until that point, conferences that were all-German gatherings

29 Central Committee Report to the 8th Congress of the Socialist Unity Party (SED) 5 (Berlin 1971), as cited in Kritz, *Transitional Justice*, 630, fn. 100.
30 High Court Judgment of 29 March 1954, 8 NJ242 (1954) as reported in Kirchheimer, 'The Administration of Justice', fn. 53.
31 East German Minister of Justice, Hilde Benjamin: 'Who Has the Say in the Family?' (1 February 1958), in *Volume 8, Occupation and the Emergence of Two States, 1945–1961*, Germany History in Documents and Images, https://ghdi.ghi-dc.org/pdf/eng/Vol.8_Chap.18_Doc.11_ENG.pdf (accessed 14 July 2022), cited in Kritz, *Transitional Justice*, 630.
32 Personal interview with Andrea Feth.
33 Benjamin: 'Who Has the Say in the Family?'
34 Benjamin: 'Who Has the Say in the Family?'
35 Benjamin: 'Who Has the Say in the Family?' Also personal interview with Andrea Feth.

could take place. At that time, the application of Allied Control Council Law No. 10 and the depoliticisation of the judiciary provoked a heated debate and break between delegates from the West and East.[36] In the Soviet zone, the majority of legal norms from the Weimar and Nazi periods remained in force. Allied Control Council Law No. 10 stripped away the authority of clear Nazi laws, but some issues in criminal and family law remained.[37] East German leaders wished to forge their own path. So, in that vein Allied Control Council Law No. 10 was used to pursue prosecution of crimes against anti-fascists proactively, with East German lawyers such as Benjamin arguing that the prohibition of retrospective justice was 'bourgeois legality' and not proper application of the law. The number of trials subsequently accelerated.

In 1949 a new High Court (*Obersten Gericht*) was set up to coincide with the establishment of the Office of the Attorney General. The inception of both institutions ushered in a period of close oversight of the administration of justice. As early as 1950 various post-war administrative bodies had been dispensed with (that is to say, merged with other state organs) and their function transferred to the Ministry of Justice. This was carried out subsequent to the Law on the Further Democratisation of the Organisation and Working Conditions of Public Bodies in the States of the GDR of 23 July 1952.[38] The High Court and the Office of the Attorney General became the guarantors of the judiciary's intellectual output. They ensured that the courts delivered judgments in harmony with the goals of the administration. It was at the heart of this organisational reform and of the attempt to control the political forces of society – as briefly outlined above – that Benjamin worked. The High Court was an appellate court and considered appeals, protests, and complaints lodged against the decisions of the lower district courts. A feature of Soviet justice as well as of the Third Reich, an extraordinary appeal could be lodged only by either the Attorney General or the President of the High Court. In other words, judicial independence was quite simply non-existent. The High Court was a vital means for ensuring that the judiciary functioned in a satisfactory manner. It issued directives for the uniform application of the law that outweighed judicial independence, and any exercise of constitutional interpretation would not be tolerated unless it could be used to support the state prerogative under the cloak of furthering workers' interests in light of the country's ideological goals. The goal of maintaining state prerogative was clear, and was part of the dominant narrative that was supported by publicising high-profile show trials.

These two bodies increasingly oversaw the direction of legal developments, exerting strict control over judicial appointments and the legal profession as a whole. This in turn would determine the overall shape of the proceedings and

36 Michael Stolleis, *The Law under the Swastika: Studies on Legal History in Nazi Germany* (University of Chicago Press 1998) 179.

37 Stolleis, *The Law under the Swastika*, 179–180.

38 (1952) GBDDR 613, as cited in Kirchheimer, 'The Administration of Justice', 707.

the manner in which they were recorded, both in writing and visually. Where written accounts were concerned, the main law reviews would function as the principal forum for guidance on decision making by judicial officials. At the same time, with the creation of the High Court, law underwent a mediatisation.[39] Such footage is vital to the manner in which law is disseminated according to a process of film production.

The production of criminal law proceedings would be carried out in venues that were vast and could accommodate audiences. Ernst Melsheimer (1897–1960), who trained as a lawyer in Prussia at the beginning of the 20th century, developed his courtroom skills in a way that amplified his aggressive, verbal attacks in court.[40] Melsheimer relished his role as Attorney General, a post he assumed in 1949 and held until his death in 1960. As Chief Prosecutor he adopted tactics that would, in hindsight, go beyond what was permissible in an adversarial process. Of course, only select cases were scripted, while other cases were conducted in secret, such as the Waldheim trials discussed later in this chapter. But even the most secret proceedings could never remain completely confidential.[41] The point was to influence public opinion about the law and what was retained in people's imagination. More often than not the dominant image associated with the dispensing of justice was that of Benjamin or Melsheimer, earning them the reputation of *furchtbaren Juristen* (lawyers to fear).[42] The visual turn towards law would for its part cover, but also extend beyond, the legal community, the intention in this regard being to promote what was then known as 'acting Bolshevik'.[43] If the constitution offered judges scope to work independently, it also obliged them to 'unreservedly stand for the goals of the GDR'.[44] The judge was not recognised as an arbiter between parties.

This point, alongside others, were made by Kirchheimer, who notes that East Germany occupies a rather atypical place, one of an expanding legality, a

39 Klaus Marxen, 'Die Mediatisierung des Rechts als Gegenstand der juristischen Zeitgeschichte' [The Mediatisation of Law as an Object of Contemporary Legal History], in Klaus Marxen and Annett Weineke (eds), *Inszenierungen des Rechts: Schauprozesse, Medienprozesse und Prozessfilme in der DDR* [Staging of the Law: Show Trials, Media Trials, and Trial Films in the GDR] (Berliner Wissenschafts-Verlag 2006) 19–36, 19.

40 Annette Weinke, 'Von den frühen Schauprozessen des "verschärften Klassenkampfes" zur fernsehkompatiblen Rechtsberatung der Honecker-Ära' [From Early Show Trials of the Intensified Class Struggle to the Television-Compatible Legal Advice Trials of the Honecker Era], in Klaus Marxen and Anneke Weinke (eds), *Inszenierungen des Rechts: Schauprozesse, Medienprozesse und Prozessfilme in der DDR* [Staging of the Law: Show Trials, Media Trials, and Trial Films in the GDR] (Berliner Wissenschafts-Verlag 2006) 37–80, 60. Stolleis, *The Law under the Swastika*.

41 Hodos, *Show Trials*.

42 Weinke, 'Von den frühen Schauprozessen des "verschärften Klassenkampfes"' [From Early Show Trials of the Intensified Class Struggle], 60.

43 Echoes of Stephen Kotkin, *Stalin: Waiting for Hitler, 1929–1941* (Penguin 2018).

44 Kirchheimer, 'The Administration of Justice', 713, fn. 30.

development made possible by the fact that 'a totalitarian system of government which operates by despotic methods in politics can create a legal order which operates with considerable stability and independence in matters considered non-political'.[45] For example, the 1950 trial against Jehovah's Witnesses addressed this group's religious freedom, which found its limit in actions that undermined the state, such as creating maps for missionaries that showed where fire stations, police stations, and post offices were. These activities were viewed as espionage and resulted in a series of trials before the High Court.

The Ministry of Justice went out of its way not to refer to the defendants as political prisoners, as 'Today no one of taken into custody for his opinions', according to Fechner. 'Prisoners of this kind are not "political prisoners" but criminals.'[46] This position echoes that of the sort of evidence produced in show trials that links the action to 'assistance to an espionage organisation of an imperialist power'.[47] The Jehovah's Witnesses trials were part of the discourse at that time concerning East Germany's location in the preservation of peace in Europe. The main law journals went to great lengths to explain how actions of the organisation had crossed a line from being peaceful to warmongering, further supported by a statement made by Melsheimer, then Prosecutor General, who defined the Jehovah's Witness not as a religious organisation but as a criminal one.

The veneer of legitimacy was important both at home and abroad. Much as in the case for the Soviet Union, the authorities were keen to show that in their country the administration of justice was a transparent and legitimate process that went even further in engaging ordinary citizens than was the case in the West. Unlike the Soviet Union, however, East Germany was a new state faced with the challenges that necessarily accompany any polity's efforts to establish its authority on firm foundations.[48] In this setting, there were no show trials of leaders. Instead, there was a series of trials of ordinary East Germans throughout the communist period. The regime pursued a harsh line and firmly

45 Kirchheimer, 'The Administration of Justice', 705, fn. 1. He refers to Berman, 'Soviet Law Reform', 1212.

46 The punishment applied in the case was based on Article 6 (anti-democratic agitation) and the criminal code. Article 6 extends to espionage, which Benjamin wrote about: See Hilde Benjamin, 'Das Oberste Gericht des Deutschen Demokratischen Republik im Kampf gegen Spionage und Sabotage' [The Supreme Court of the German Democratic Republic in the Fight against Espionage and Sabotage] (1952) 6(6) *Neue Justiz* (1952) 222–245. Article 41 provides for complete freedom of religion but during the trial no questions about religion were permitted. Verdict against Gebert et al., *Injustice the Regime*, 28 and also Verdict against Twarz et al., *Injustice the Regime*, 30.The position of the state was not new – persecution of Jehovah's Witnesses has occurred throughout Europe and has been readdressed by the European Court of Human Rights.

47 Oppression of the freedom of conscience and religion, in *Injustice the Regime*, 21–22.

48 Kirchheimer, 'The Administration of Justice'.

entrenched its political agenda at these trials. To do so successfully, it needed leadership and unwavering commitment to the ideology and one individual had these qualities. The next section will consider one of the most important people in the East German legal framework.

Hilde Benjamin (1902–1989)

This section discusses Benjamin's life account. It will then consider her role in select trials, with the Herwegen–Dessau trials being a critical moment in her career. The role that Benjamin played in relation to legal developments in international criminal law, family law, and gender equality will be addressed before reflecting on the narratives surrounding her place in a wider German legal historical discourse.

East Germany was not the only communist state to register the impact of such societal forces. Nor is Benjamin unique in her determination to see a political vision for the country realised. However, unlike her communist colleagues she was never purged, and therefore continued to wield influence until the day she died. She succeeded in this by trusting only a few people, including her bodyguard and driver, and her housekeeper.[49] Benjamin lived her life under the constant threat of assassination – by one of her party colleagues or by one of her victims. Her bourgeois upbringing, her legal training, and her gender were all viewed with suspicion by her colleagues.[50] In other words, her biography, albeit Old Communist, was constantly questioned and manipulated by her peers.[51] Yet as an Old Communist she was 'first and foremost a disciplined Communist'.[52] Loyalty to the party was paramount. Her commitment to the party's political project, and active effort to promote gender equality as part of social change within the ideological context, was ongoing.

Benjamin, known for her trademark 'Heidi' braids, provides the spectator with images rich in narrative connotations, but equally misleading and problematic. She is shown in Figures 4.1 and 4.2.

Benjamin was from an upper-middle-class, Protestant, West Berlin family.[53] She grew up at a time when politics was at the forefront of public debate. Benjamin was a highly skilled lawyer and a committed communist. It is vital to recall that Benjamin was also part of the German audience that was targeted by the Third Reich's propaganda, obsessed as it was with instilling Nazi-style morality. The regime targeted, among others, Jews, communists, Roma, and

49 Andrea Feth, *Hilde Benjamin – Eine Biographie* (Arno Spitz 1997) 233–240. Also personal interview with Andrea Feth.
50 Personal interview with Andrea Feth.
51 Such as Robert Havemann. Epstein, 'The Politics of Biography', 6.
52 Catherine Epstein, 'The Production of "Official Memory" in East Germany: Old Communists and the Dilemma of Memoir-Writing' (1999) 32(2) *Central European History* 182–201, 200.
53 Feth, *Hilde Benjamin*, 19–29.

Figure 4.1 Chief Prosecutor Hilde Benjamin, 1945
Credit: BArch/Berliner Zeitung.

homosexuals. This experience informs our understanding of her professional role in moulding East German society, alongside her tragic personal losses. Her professional mask hides the resentment and revenge that drove her. Eventually

BStU-Kopie

Figure 4.2 Hilde Benjamin in conversation, date unknown
Credit: BArch, Bild MfS-ZAIG-Fo-3322-Bild-0001.

her personal life became indistinguishable from her professional life. Her philosophy was 'you laugh with your friends; you hate your enemies'.[54] Benjamin's perspective was rooted in a past of discrimination and persecution – as a woman, as a person erroneously supposed to be a member of a persecuted minority, and later as the partner of an individual from an eminent Jewish intellectual family, and as a communist. She survived the war, and with legal qualifications obtained in the pre-war period – and by virtue of her staunch ideological commitment – she resolved to do all she could to help establish an East German communist state. Benjamin was one of the first women to study law at the Humboldt University in Berlin.[55] She had experience as defence counsel in the Weimar Republic, later serving as a prosecutor and then as a judge in the newly created East German state (1949–1953), before assuming the post of Minister of Justice (1953–1967).

Her commitment to communism and her experience in Nazi Germany would shape her outlook personally and professionally: in 1926 she married a medical doctor, Georg Benjamin, who was the brother of the philosopher Walter Benjamin and of her friend Dora Benjamin. This friendship was sustained by a strong political commitment and a common vision for the country that was premised on social justice.[56] Georg and Hilde had a son, Michael, in 1932. She completed her law degree at the University of Berlin, now Humboldt University, Heidelberg, and Hamburg in 1927. Also in 1927 she followed her husband into the Communist Party, and in 1928 she became a state prosecutor. Her husband being Jewish barred her from practising law after 1933. He was sent to a concentration camp, subsequently released but then sent to another, Mauthausen, where he died. Benjamin briefly worked for a Soviet trading firm and was later sent to work in a factory. She was further politicised by the writings and activities of Rosa Luxemburg and Karl Liebknecht.[57] The political scene in this period was intensely volatile, with the communists in particular being regarded with suspicion by the regime, as noted above, and the rise of the National Socialist Party.

After the Second World War Benjamin's legal career assumed a strong and clear trajectory. Very few lawyers who had studied during the Weimar period re-entered the legal profession after the war, let alone female lawyers. If they did so, it was owing to a commitment to ideology or out of naked ambition.[58] Benjamin oversaw the selection of a new judicial cohort, having developed a new filter, so to speak, that served to ensure that the judiciary (people's judges or people's prosecutors) was filled with the right kind of judges; that is, politically disposed ones. Benjamin also saw to it that the number of female judicial

54 Personal interview with Andrea Feth.
55 Feth, *Hilde Benjamin*, 31–40.
56 Feth, *Hilde Benjamin*, 19–29. Personal interview with Andrea Feth.
57 Both murdered in 1919. Feth, *Hilde Benjamin*, 19–29. Personal interview with Andrea Feth.
58 Otto Kirchheimer, *Political Justice* (Princeton University Press 1961) 66.

officials increased (a commitment she retained throughout her career). She worked hard: methodically and 'scientifically'.[59]

Similarities in rhetoric and method between Benjamin and Vyshinsky have already been noted. The East German state was a dictatorship, and political repression remained an important component of its political system until the very end. Political repression represented, however, only one aspect of the tension between legal form and state prerogative in the disciplinary architecture of the East German regime. Its plan of discipline was identified with the criminal law, which, the legal theorist Klenner noted, was the key to various particularly significant cases of political justice, such as the 1950 Herwegen–Dessau trial against the representatives of a large energy company that was then being expropriated, in which Benjamin played the central role.

In 1949 Benjamin travelled to Moscow to attend as part of a delegation of jurists. Upon her return she assumed the vice-presidency of the High Court. Kurt Schumann (1908–1989) was president. The cases that she would preside over were proceedings instigated against two main groups: cases concerning sabotage and those concerning Western agents and espionage. In the first years of the High Court's creation proceedings were brought against Nazi criminals.[60]

The Herwegen–Dessau Trial

The Herwegen–Dessau trial resembled Soviet proceedings concerning cases where the crime of speculation was developed and given centre stage. Klenner's interest in the crime of sabotage meant that a simple clerical error or lack of judgement could result in criminal sanctions. It also emphasised the (implied) willingness of some people to take actions that might inadvertently harm the economy rather than being the result of a specific plan or intent. Benjamin was at the heart of the visual imagery and message underpinning the rationale of the trial.

The show trials were public, supported by a well-funded and organised propaganda drive that began in November 1949 when East German broadsheets focused on a group of economic criminals who allegedly caused damage of 100 million Reichsmark.[61] The coverage was consistent and the lead stories were accompanied by photographs of the detainees in their cells. Many of the pictures depicted the detainees in a degrading fashion.[62] The SED party paper *Neues Deutschland* [New Germany] referred to them as guilty. The captions in another publication, the *Neue Illustrierte* [Newly Illustrated], expanded on the actions of the 'rats in a trap', the defendants:

59 As cited in her State Security (Stasi) file, see William T. Vollmann, *Europe Central* (Viking Press 2005) 588.
60 Feth, *Hilde Benjamin*, 80.
61 Feth, *Hilde Benjamin*.
62 'Conti Affair, Affäre Conti', https://second.wiki/wiki/affc3a4re_conti#cite_note-spiegel-22 (accessed 15 July 2022).

1. Leo Herwegen: 'The Inspirer: Former Minister Dr L. Herwegen, who was paid for his help, arrested by the People's Police at the last minute just before fleeing to the West'.
2. Paul Heil: 'Legal forger: Notary Dr Heil, whose declarations of innocence have been refuted, gave most transactions a semblance of "legality"'.
3. Willi Brundert: 'Espionage agent: Dr Brundert, once a lecturer at a British agent school, a man "with connections", who sabotaged the financial situation by deliberate confusion'.
4. Heinrich Scharf: 'Asset slider: Bank director Heinrich Scharf, whose hand injury suggests a suicide attempt, took part in the illegal board meeting'.
5. Leopold Kaatz: 'Main culprit: Trustee of the company, formerly General Director. Dr Leopold Kaatz organised the 100 million Reichsmark theft, but plays clueless'.
6. Ernst Simon: 'Co-conspirator: Lawyer Ernst Simon, who defended himself in a deceitful manner before the examining magistrate'.
7. Ernst Pauli: 'Handyman: Economic Commissioner Pauli supported the misappropriation of assets by issuing a false certificate'.
8. Hermann Müller: 'Organiser: Dipl.-Ing. Müller, trustee of the company assets, broke the trust placed in him and made the fraud possible'.[63]

The coverage was accompanied by a response from the Federal Republic. In addition to its own broadsheets, the Higher Regional Court in Nuremberg issued a ruling about the legality of the situation in its decision of 19 September 1949:

> An expropriation without compensation in the eastern zone cannot be recognised in the western zone because it attacks the basis of state and economic life in the western zones. The expropriated owner can therefore claim as his own property that is transferred to the western zones after the expropriation. According to international law, it is recognised that sovereign acts of a state only have an effect within the sphere of influence of this state. Due to a longer international practice, it is generally assumed that expropriation cannot cover any property that is located outside the expropriation state.[64]

Unsurprisingly this was ignored by the East German authorities.

63 'Conti Affair, Affäre Conti', https://second.wiki/wiki/affc3a4re_conti#cite_note-spiegel-22.
64 'Conti Affair, Affäre Conti', https://second.wiki/wiki/affc3a4re_conti#cite_note-spiegel-22. See Dorothy Ames Jeffess, 'Resolving Rival Claims on East German Property upon German Unification' (1991) 101(2) *The Yale Law Journal* 527–549.

The trial took place in the City Theatre of Dessau. The choice of space was vital:[65] it could accommodate 1,400 spectators.[66] Invitations were organised and planning was controlled by the Office of the Herwegen-Brundert-Prozess, a body comprising employees of the Central Commission for State Control, high officials from the Ministry for State Security, Justice, and the Police, and the Office for Information of the Council of Ministers. Printed entry cards were valid for only one day of the trial and distributed to deserving political figures.

Fritz Lange (1898–1981), later the Minister for Popular Education, oversaw the choreography of the trial in his capacity as head of the Central Control Commission and an office dedicated to the trials. He gave 'stage directions' to the Chief Prosecutor and the judges by mail from the director's box in the theatre.[67] At the gates of the theatre, youth delegations from the Free German Trade Union and the Free German Youth chanted rehearsed slogans. The proceedings were filmed by state television DEFA newsreel cameras. Berlin radio featured special evening broadcasts.

The trial began on 24 April 1950 before the High Court, chaired by Benjamin in her capacity as Vice-President. In the broadsheets of the Federal Republic Benjamin was compared to Roland Freisler,[68] mentioned earlier: Freisler was a judge in the Third Reich who was known for his aggressive questioning and humiliation of defendants.[69] Melsheimer was the Chief Prosecutor. At the start of each session of the trial the defendants were brought before the court in handcuffs. The main charge concerned the support of corporate interests contrary to ministerial duties[70] in violation of Order No. 160 of 3 December 1945 of the Soviet Military Administration of Germany (SMAD).[71] Defendants, physically and psychologically broken by the interrogations, admitted their crimes.

In terms of charges, Brundert's indictment was based chiefly on allegations of being an active British agent and failing to delete the property from the commercial register, which the public prosecutor held against him as a positive act of embezzlement. Müller was charged as being the main culprit in the securities transactions. The main allegations against Kaatz concerned events in the Dessau sugar refinery during the Nazi era. Simon was accused of having illegally appropriated the relevant commercial register excerpts based on old contracts in order to enable the company to be founded. Pauli's crime predated the formal

65 Feth, *Hilde Benjamin*.
66 Feth, *Hilde Benjamin*, 86.
67 'Conti Affair, Affäre Conti', https://second.wiki/wiki/affc3a4re_conti#cite_note-spiegel-22.
68 'Conti Affair, Affäre Conti', https://second.wiki/wiki/affc3a4re_conti#cite_note-spiegel-22.
69 Müller, *Hitler's Justice*.
70 Feth, *Hilde Benjamin*, 86.
71 Feth, *Hilde Benjamin*, 84–86.

expropriation decision. In order to further prove his criminality, the Court charged him with private purchases as an aviation officer during the Second World War. He was said to have made these advantageous purchases in occupied France and Spain under Francisco Franco; among other things were a fur coat, radio, and food. Benjamin theatrically apologised to the French people for the 'injustice' suffered.[72] On the fourth day of the trial, the defendants Heil and Scharf were tried. Benjamin ridiculed Scharf and his suicide attempt. With his excessively submissive behaviour, Scharf played a role that was also often seen in the Stalinist show trials of the Soviet Union in the 1930s.[73] Ironically, the full admission of guilt from a marginal figure would burden these defendants even more. In return, this 'key witness' experienced leniency in sentencing. In his closing remarks, Scharf thanked the authorities for their good treatment.

The fifth and sixth day of the trial were dominated by Melsheimer, who adopted his usual aggressive stance and referred to the defendants as typical criminals and arrogant careerists, and singled out some, such as Pauli, as 'the worst [criminal] I have ever come across'.[74] A flavour of the proceedings is reflected in Melsheimer's three-hour indictment speech that ended with the words:

> The accused have committed tremendous crimes against our democracy, against our economic development and thus against the peace of the German people and the world, and they are extremely guilty ... While for years the masses of our working people have been working hard and successfully every day to rebuild our fatherland and to rebuild our state on a peaceful and democratic basis, these accused have stabbed them in the back in a treacherous and insidious way ... The accused ... who are paid by a small but influential clique of German imperialist warmongers and their Anglo-American backers, must feel the rigours of our democratic legality for their shameful crimes. They must be severely punished.[75]

In the opinion of the trial observers, the pleadings by the defence lawyers did not attract attention and lasted only a few minutes. The verdict was passed on 29 April 1950. Herwegen, Brundert, and Methfessel (who was absent) were sentenced to 15 years' imprisonment, Müller and Kaatz to 12 years, Heil to eight years, Pauli to seven years, and Simon to four years. Scharf, who was repentant, and a key witness were sentenced to two years. In many ways

72 'Conti Affair, Affäre Conti', https://second.wiki/wiki/affc3a4re_conti#cite_note-spiegel-22.

73 'Conti Affair, Affäre Conti', https://second.wiki/wiki/affc3a4re_conti#cite_note-spiegel-22.

74 'Conti Affair, Affäre Conti', https://second.wiki/wiki/affc3a4re_conti#cite_note-spiegel-22.

75 'Conti Affair, Affäre Conti', https://second.wiki/wiki/affc3a4re_conti#cite_note-spiegel-22.

Scharf's behaviour is reminiscent of the way that a defendant who undertakes *samokritika* experiences an epiphany, as found in Cassiday's analysis of show trials via the lends of melodrama. The Office of Information published a 'political education' brochure entitled 'Debunked – the Story of a Huge Fraud Uncovered' that was disseminated through kiosks.

The Soviet authorities monitored the process closely. The Politburo issued a statement concerning the political message that the trials was supposed to convey: '[t]he process must be conducted in such a way that the role of monopoly capital, its work of disintegration with the help of agents for sale and their criminal activities in the German Democratic Republic are clearly revealed'.[76]

The Dessau show trial was successful on several fronts. It consolidated the central power of the Central Control Commission, which extended its remit to include arrests, torture interrogations, coercion of judges, falsification of indictments, and the appointment of politically disposed judges. The Commission developed into an important instrument of political discipline for securing power. Importantly, East German authorities used the process to divert attention from their own mistakes in economic policy: these difficulties could be explained to the public as a result of external attacks. In addition, it served to discipline and educate internally, within the party itself. However, the hoped-for recognition by the 'working masses', whose imagination was not ignited by the propaganda staging to the extent desired, failed to materialise. The Dessau show trial was not the last of its kind; many similar proceedings were held in 1950 – the show trial year – and afterwards. Melsheimer himself pointed to this during his pleadings: 'It won't be the last trial of this kind'.[77]

Overall, the trial was a great theatrical spectacle. The City Theatre of Dessau provided the best venue for a magnificent installation, which was constructed with neon bulbs, creating an almost theatrical effect.[78] The installation was placed on the wall behind the judge's bench and would have made an impression on the audience. Visitors were invited to attend this grand event; it was a select audience. This was an important moment for Benjamin, who was also on show, and who demonstrated her commitment to the cause and law. Benjamin's account in *Neue Justiz* [New Justice] identified the peculiarities of West German legal interpretations, making it the task of the High Court to reveal the extent of the economic sabotage to W. Averell Harriman, a US businessman and diplomat who worked on the Marshall Plan.[79] In 1953

76 'Conti Affair, Affäre Conti', https://second.wiki/wiki/affc3a4re_conti#cite_note-spiegel-22.
77 'Conti Affair, Affäre Conti', https://second.wiki/wiki/affc3a4re_conti#cite_note-spiegel-22.
78 Feth, *Hilde Benjamin*, 86.
79 Hilde Benjamin, 'Zum Dessauer Prozeß' [To the Dessau Trial] (1950) 4(5) *Neue Justiz* 145–148. See also (no author), 'Harriman Denounced in East German Trial', *The New York Times* (29 April 1950).

Benjamin wrote about the reltionship between the law and the press.[80] Praising the Soviet press and reporting in *Pravda*, Benjamin set the tone, stating that '[i]n larger trials, it is advisable to hold a press briefing beforehand and to give the press the main aspects of the case'.[81]

Benjamin's commitment to presiding over political cases continued. For example, she heard the 1950 trial against Jehovah's Witnesses, discussed in the previous section. In 1952 the High Court heard the case against Johann Burianek and Wolfgang Kaiser, with Benjamin presiding. The rulings, such as Burianek's, were published and their importance as key judgments in East German law was advertised in the main East German legal publication *Neue Justiz*.[82] Members of the political opposition group The Struggle against Inhumanity *Kampfgruppe gegen Unmenschlichkeit* were charged and convicted for their membership in this group and anti-state activity. Burianek received a capital sentence for the planned sabotage of a railway line, the first person to receive the death sentence in the new East Germany. The Chief Prosecutor in these trials was Melsheimer. Benjamin's role in these trials earned her the name of 'Bloody Hilde' or 'The Red Guillotine'. Whether or not an alternate sentence would have existed even in 'calmer times', which these were not, is a moot point, as the decision on sentences was not a matter for the court.[83] Referring to *Burianek* and *The Struggle against Humanity* cases, Benjamin recalls the fight against the enemy that other communist states had followed, noting the *Rajk* trial and that the endeavour started earlier elsewhere than it had in East Germany, making the East Germans' search to expose the class enemy of paramount importance.[84] In 1957 Benjamin, rejecting calls for a 'human communism' or 'democratic socialism', reminded judicial officials that Lenin's principles, when it came to the court, were the only guide to follow and that it was vital to defend the legality of the court (Figure 4.3).[85]

Benjamin and Punishing Nazi War Crimes

Benjamin's reputation was shaped by the narrative that was being created by the state that would define it and set it apart from the Federal Republic: its fight against fascism. This was already grounded in a series of proceedings that

80 Hilde Benjamin, 'Über die Zusammenarbeit von Justiz und Presse' [On the Cooperation between the Judiciary and the Press] (1953) 7(19) *Neue Justiz* 605–606.
81 Benjamin, 'Über die Zusammenarbeit von Justiz und Presse', 606.
82 Inside back cover of 1954 8(1) *Neue Justiz* issue.
83 Feth, *Hilde Benjamin*, 106.
84 Hilde Benjamin, 'Die Staatsverbrechen im Zusammenhang mit der wirtschaftlichen und politischen Entwicklung seit 1945' [State Crimes Concerning Economic and Political Development Since 1945] (1954) 8(2) *Neue Justiz* 35–37.
85 Hilde Benjamin, 'Leninische Prinzipien des Gerichts' [Lenin's Principles Concerning the Court] (1957) 11(21) *Neue Justiz* 673–674.

BStU-Kopie

Figure 4.3 Hilde Benjamin, 1955
Credit: BArch, Bild MfS-HA-IX-Fo-1955.

took place over the period 1945–1949, some of which were public. The Waldheim trials concerned thousands of detainees in Soviet internment camps that were run by the NKVD (Soviet state security police). No one had knowledge of these camps until the press disclosed their existence. These special camps were set up by the Soviets between 1945 and 1950 while occupying East Germany; the other occupying powers also but camps to detain Nazi war criminals. They were used to detain individuals who posed a threat to communist rule. Approximately one-third of the 170,000 people detained were tortured, or died because of starvation or disease such as tuberculosis or dysentery.[86] When the camps were handed over to East Germany in 1950, the authorities had the opportunity to screen and punish Nazi collaborators as well as to identify and

86 'The Innocent Victims of Germany's Postwar Soviet Special Camps', DW, https://www.dw.com/en/germany-postwar-soviet-special-camps/a-54759064 (accessed 15 July 2022); Wolfgang Eisert, *The Waldheim Trials. The Stalinist Terror 1950. A Dark Chapter in the GDR Justice System* (Esslingen and Munich 1993); Günther Wieland, *Judicial Punishment of Occupation Crimes*, in Werner Röhr (ed.), *Europe under the Swastika. Analyses, Sources, Registers* (Heidelberg 1996), https://second.wiki/wiki/waldheimer_prozesse (accessed 15 August 2022).

eliminate any political opposition. The trials were a means to bring to book those who had ties with the Nazis, who had hindered the establishment of Stalinism, or who had been rounded up for entirely arbitrary reasons. It should be noted that the internees had already been tried and sentenced by NKVD special courts. Some 3,400 cases were heard as part of the Waldheim trials, with 385 prison sentences of under ten years imposed, 916 sentences of 10–15 years, 1,829 of 15–25 years, 146 life sentences, and 32 death sentences. Sentences were rendered under Allied Control Council Law No. 10.[87] No legal advice was offered. The trials were not open to the public and lasted between 20 and 30 minutes. In many cases family members and/or relatives were not informed of the outcome of the case, and the first news that they would hear would come many years later. Often the defendants and witnesses were carried in on stretchers. Imprisonment would take place in Soviet internment camps (former concentration camps). Survivors could not believe the charges of collaboration with the Nazis.

Benjamin's presence in the audience for cases where she was not presiding was vital to the event and in keeping with the dichotomy that was in the minds of the constitutional drafters, in particular upholding the anti-fascist narrative. Later Benjamin selected and adjudicated cases concerning West Germans convicted of war crimes and crimes against humanity. As such, Benjamin was at the forefront of purging the regime of fascist elements and Nazi collaborators. Her presence embodied what became a defining feature of Germany: the differences between the then Federal Republic of Germany and East Germany. Both countries deployed markedly different narratives where purging their countries of Nazis was concerned. We have seen Benjamin's unique contribution to the criminal legal process by ensuring that reporting showed her presence at each trial.

According to the official 'line' or perception of history in East Germany, legal action in East Germany to punish Nazi crimes was an unmitigated success. The leadership claimed to have proceeded consistently and above all systematically against Nazi criminals, to have taken into account the degree of individual guilt in each case, and to have sought removal of all tainted persons from their official functions. The 1977 publication of *The Brown Book* by the East German authorities documented the re-emergence of former Nazi officials in the Federal German Republic's government. The book was dismissed by the West Germans as propaganda.

The West and East German approaches to their respective constitutions were different,[88] as were their positions on the Nuremberg trials and pursuit of war criminals. Richardson-Little outlines these approaches based on the manner in

87 Moritz Vorbaum, 'An "indispensable component of the elimination of fascism": War Crimes Trials and International Criminal Law in the German Democratic Republic', in Morten Bergsmo, Wui Ling Cheah, and Ping Yi (eds), *Historical Origins of International Criminal Law: Volume 2* (Torkel Opsahl Academic EPublisher 2014) 397–425, 405–408. For sentences without defence or proof of guilt, see Chapter 2.

88 Richardson-Little, *The Human Rights Dictatorship*, 53.

which human rights are acknowledged in the Basic Law and in the East German constitution, but both reacted to the Second World War, with the fight against fascism being more pronounced in East Germany. At the core is the Universal Declaration of Human Rights, but the two approaches diverge on social class. It would be a mistake to dismiss East Germany's legal path as being completely controlled by the Soviets. It was much more complex than that, and East Germany embarked on its own path to forge socialist human rights.[89]

In the Federal Republic, the International Military Tribunal judgments were not recognised, it being a matter of 'German dignity'.[90] Of 106,496 cases opened after 1945 by the Office of the State Judicial Administration for the investigation of Nazi crimes, only 6,495 produced convictions, 157 of which were sentences to life imprisonment.[91] The West German government did not choose to create a central agency to prosecute Nazi criminals; this was left to specific German states (*Länder*), such as North Rhine-Westphalia. Commentators have pointed to political will, or the lack of it, where this question was concerned.[92] Under German law there never has been a special offence for Nazi war crimes; prosecutions are for murder or for aiding and abetting. More generally, the view that the last link in the chain in command would not be charged has changed with information from archives (in post-communist states). German prosecutors have since admitted that

> Accounting for East German injustices has also given us greater insight into how much leeway existed in a dictatorship. In a groundbreaking 1995 decision, the [German] Federal Court of Justice decided, for example, that the stricter standards that West German courts had applied to East German judges should also have been applied to Nazi judges.[93]

Article 135 of the 1949 East German Constitution expressly permitted actions and rules adopted for the 'overcoming of Nazism, Fascism, and militarism, or which are necessary for the prosecution of crimes against humanity'; in

89 Richardson-Little, *The Human Rights Dictatorship*, 54.
90 Ronen Steinke, *The Politics of International Criminal Justice: German Perspectives from Nuremberg to The Hague* (Hart 2012) 50–51.
91 Hans Baade, 'Individual Responsibility', in Cyril E. Back and Richard A. Falk (eds), *The Future of the International Legal Order: The Structure of the International Environment, Volume 4* (Princeton University Press 1972) 291–330.
92 Jan Friedman, 'Interview with Nazi War Crimes Prosecutor: "I have never seen remorse"', *Spiegel Online International*, 10 May 2011, https://www.spiegel.de/international/germany/interview-with-nazi-war-crimes-prosecutor-i-have-never-seen-remorse-a-761639.html (accessed 26 July 2022). See also Christopher R. Browning, 'Adenauer's Bargain', *The New York Review of Books*, 22 December 2022, 69–70, https://www-pressreader-com.leedsbeckett.idm.oclc.org/usa/the-new-york-review-of-books/20221222/282123525515642/textview (accessed 22 December 2022).
93 Friedman, 'Interview with Nazi War Crimes Prosecutor'.

derogation of the rule requiring all criminal prosecutions to be based on non-retroactive statutory norms, East German courts have uniformly regarded the Nuremberg principles as directly applicable in domestic law, as can be seen in several cases. As Richardson-Little argues, these narratives are interwoven with the Cold War.[94] East Germany was keen to send the West a clear message about its thoughts regarding the West German approach, which it viewed as lenient with respect to sentencing in the denazification trials and its general position on retaining former Nazi leaders in relatively high government posts. This ideological shift was wide. All these factors were present in the trials, beginning in 1960 with the Oberländer trial,[95] where the defendant was tried in absentia. The trial took place after Nikita Khrushchev's speech during a state visit to Austria in July 1959. The speech was the start of the propaganda campaign against West Germany; pointing to former Nazis who were still in government, accusations of Nazism were mad.[96] Theodor Oberländer was the West German minister for displaced persons, refugees and victims of war from 1953 to 1960, but he had been a key player in facilitating the Nazi policies of ethnic cleansing in Poland. He was forced to resign after revelations about his past were made, but he remained in parliament to cast his vote with the minority to veto the extension of the statute of limitations for murder later outlined in the 1965 Act. His (and others') support for rejecting this extension effectively hampered West German attempts to prosecute Nazi war criminals, a matter that generated extensive public discussion throughout the 1960s.[97] The East German court sentenced him to life imprisonment for his alleged involvement in the Lviv massacre of 1941. Authors note the temporal connection between Oberländer's trial and other show trials being prepared at the same time in the Soviet Union (see Figure 4.4).[98]

According to Article 5 of the 1949 Constitution, generally recognised principles of international law were binding upon the government and all citizens. In the next high-profile trial from 1963, that of Hans Globke, the High Court indicated:

> The significance of this norm in relation to the internal criminal laws of states, which also uniformly make punishable murder, battery, maltreatment,

94 Richardson-Little, *The Human Rights Dictatorship*, 54.

95 *DDR v. Oberländer* (in absentia) [1961] *Neue Justiz*, Supplement to No. 10.

96 Meelis Maripuu, 'Cold War Show Trials in Estonia: Justice and Propaganda in the Balance', Tõnu Tannberg (ed.), *Behind the Iron Curtain: Soviet Estonia in the Era of the Cold War* (Peter Lang, 2015) 139–196.

97 Caroline Sharples, 'In Pursuit of Justice: Debating the Statute of Limitations for Nazi War Crimes in Britain and West Germany during the 1960s' (2014) 20(3) *Holocaust Studies* 81–108.

98 Maripuu, 'Cold War Show Trials in Estonia', 154. Oberlander was rehabilitated in 1998, owing to lack of evidence: 'The Oberländer case shows that evidence in Soviet show trials cannot be historically reliable'. Maripuu, 'Cold War Show Trials in Estonia', 175.

Figure 4.4 Public presentation of Theodor Oberländer's crimes, East Berlin, 1963
Credit: BArch, Bild MfS-ZAIG-F0-0680-Bild-0061.

> robbery, and the like, lies in the right and duty of states to designate and punish such officially organised mass crimes aimed at the murder of whole peoples, their extermination, exploitation, and enslavement, as crimes under international law, as attacks on peace and the security of peoples, as war crimes and crimes against humanity.[99]

In this case the East German authorities again demonstrated the Federal Republic's leniency towards fascists. Globke was the West German Undersecretary of State (principal aide to Chancellor Konrad Adenauer) and a former official of the Nazi Ministry of the Interior. His trial also took place *in absentia* in 1963 and he was sentenced to life imprisonment for war crimes and crimes against humanity (see Figures 4.5, 4.6, and 4.7). He remained in office for the duration of the Adenauer regime. The coverage of the *Globke* case by East German media was an effective example of the mediatisation of the law,[100] and

99 *DDR v. Globke* (in absentia) (1963) 17 *Neue Justiz* 449, 507.

100 Henning Waage, 'Der Staatsanwalt hatte das Wort. Zur Repräsentation des Gerichts im Fernsehen der DDR' [The Prosecutor Has the Floor. Representing the Court on East German Television], in Klaus Marxen and Anneke Weinke (eds), *Inszenierungen des Rechts: Schauprozesse, Medienprozesse und Prozessfilme in der DDR* [Stagings of the Law: Show Trials, Media Trials, and Trial Films in the GDR] (Berliner Wissenschafts-Verlag 2006) 175–203, 184–192.

Figure 4.5 Hilde Benjamin in the front row and film makers in the background at the 1963 *in absentia* Globke trial, East Berlin
Credit: BArch, Bild 0708/14/1 N/Brüggmann.

of the production of law with the specific intention not only to educate East Germans, but also to contribute to and shape West German narratives about the East German dispensing of justice to Nazi war criminals, which West Germany had failed to do.

The Horst Fischer trial in 1966 was televised. Fischer had been a high-ranking concentration camp doctor at Auschwitz and the Buna/Monowitz camps, and at the IG Farben corporate camp. The manipulation of close-ups of the prosecutor (Melsheimer was replaced by Josef Streit) and the defendant's hands and his signed orders, or watching him in profile answer questions from above, was designed to contrast good and evil, a legitimate dispensing of justice. Fischer's trial occurred at a time when the prosecution of war crimes seemed to be dwindling. He was found guilty of the murder of several thousand people and was sentenced to death. Benjamin watched both trials. Her presence there was photographed and widely disseminated.

The wider context of the prosecution of German war criminals centres on the externalisation of the crimes and viewing the crimes as ones committed by West Germans. The master narrative shows the East German effort to punish

Figure 4.6 Spectators at the *in absentia* 1963 Globke trial, East Berlin
Credit: BArch, Bild B 0709/04/18 N/ Brüggmann.

Nazi crimes was an unmitigated success as an effort to reinforce its founding principle of fighting fascism. East German authorities argued that they had purged all tainted individuals from official posts. As pointed out by several writers, the Ministry for State Security was at the centre of these prosecutions. Their work was guided by the view that identifying any former Nazi war criminals among state officials was prohibited – it went against the 'decreed

Figure 4.7 Hilde Benjamin in conversation at the 1963 *in absentia* Globke trial, East Berlin
Credit: BArch, Bild MfS-HA-IX-Fo-3477.

antifascist perception of history in the GDR'.[101] A blind eye could be turned to a tainted biography if the individual held an important position or could be blackmailed by the Ministry to become an informer. '"We'll decide who's a Nazi", was the way one member of the State Security (Stasi) formulated this monopoly on interpretation of the past'.[102]

101 'Prosecution of Nazi Crimes in the GDR up to the Fischer Trial in 1965', Wollheim Memorial, http://www.wollheim-memorial.de/en/nsstrafverfolgung_in_der_ddr_bis_zum_fischerprozess_1965 (accessed 15 July 2022).

102 The Auschwitz Trial in Frankfurt am Main (1963–1965) in fact resulted in more national and international attention. No equivalent could be produced in East Germany. See'Prosecution of Nazi Crimes in the GDR up to the Fischer Trial in 1965'. Recent research has shown how the Stasi withheld information that would have incriminated German war criminals within its own ranks. See Henry Leide, *Auschwitz und Staatssicherheit: Strafverfolgung, Propaganda und Geheimhaltung in der DDR* [Auschwitz and State Security: Law Enforcement, Propaganda, and Secrecy in the GDR] (Der Bundesbeauftragte für die Unterlagen des Staatssicheritsdienstes der ehemaligen Deutschen Demokratischen Republik. Abteilung Bildung und Forschung [Federal Commissioner for the Records of the State Security Service of the former German Democratic Republic, Department of Education and Research] 2021).

East Germany forged ahead and in 1964 the GDR enacted the Law on the Non-Prescription of Nazi and War Crimes, which in conformity with the existing legal situation provided that crimes against peace and humanity and war crimes committed between 30 January 1933 and 8 May 1945 were not subject to prescription. This was codified in the 1968 Criminal Code. East Germany ratified the 1968 UN Convention on the Non-Applicability of Statutory Limitations to War Crimes and Crimes against Humanity in 1973. Although she stepped down from her post as Minister of Justice in 1967, Benjamin was at the forefront of these developments.[103]

The approaches of both West and East Germany occupied common ground with respect to the politicisation of the key events marking out legal approaches to Nazi crimes. They differed, however, with respect to accountability and justice, and paving the way to a future. The personal accounts of East Germans attest to this difference.[104] There is no one correct approach and the point of externalisation is valid.

Benjamin and Gender Equality

Benjamin proactively challenged the notion of a class struggle with that of the gender divide. She actively mentored female lawyers and judges, and elevated

103 Feth, *Hilde Benjamin*, 125–126.

104 "I was born and grew up in the German Democratic Republic (East Germany). Our schoolbooks dealt extensively with the Nazi period and what it did to the German nation and most of Europe. During the course of their schooling, all pupils were taken at least once to a concentration camp. In West Germany thousands of leading Nazi army officers, judges who had sent Jews and leftists to their deaths, doctors who had experimented on concentration camp victims, politicians, and others were left unscathed and continued in their professions and received generous pensions on retirement. In the GDR the 'victims of fascism' received extra pensions and other privileges in recognition of their suffering". David Silver, 'East Germany Kept Nazi Past in Mind', Letter to the Editor at *The New York Times*, 22 January 1995: 'In West Germany, many former Nazis were put into high-level Government jobs. Nearly all East German leaders had been in the resistance, in camps or exile. East German archives show that 13,000 Nazis and war criminals were tried and given lengthy sentences. In West Germany, only 8,600 war criminals were brought to trial, many of whom received light sentences. According to a former United States prosecutor at the Nuremberg trials who has been trying to bring Nazi judges to trial, not one has yet been prosecuted, and they draw generous pensions'. Donald Bloxham notes '[T]he war-time alliance had turned on its head, and convicted war criminals were an irksome reminder of the time when Germany was the sworn enemy of the "big three"', in 'Punishing German Soldiers during the Cold War: The Case of Erich von Manstein', *Patterns of Prejudice* 33 (1999), 25–45, 42. Bloxham also notes that the British record of letting convicted war criminals free was more questionable than that of the United States. See also Michael J. Bazyler and Frank Tuerkheimer, *The Forgotten Trials of the Holocaust* (New York University Press 2014) 153–157. See also Vorbaum, 'An "Indispensable component of the elimination of fascism"', 414–415.

women to many positions in the administration of justice.[105] Benjamin led the amendments to family law, to better reflect equality between the sexes; after all, the East German Constitution proclaimed total gender equality and rights of women.[106] Her contribution to family law earned her a Chair in the subject at Humboldt University.[107] She also sought to correct the contradiction in socialism that amplified the working class and ruling class, and the inequality between men and women. She tackled the position of women first, making that a priority and envisaging that it would lead to the next step of trying to resolve the inequality between classes. Her approach was shaped by her experience of discrimination, but also by what she observed during the Third Reich and the marginalisation of women from the Bar. Her proactive work would shape the model of the socialist family and household: 'equality of man and woman in society determines their equality in family law' and that 'marriage law does not diminish a woman's rights'.[108] The main legal journal, *Neue Justiz* [New Justice], set out the justifications for this,[109] such as pushing women into dignity via the constitutional right to work. Benjamin's approach was to address the failures of the Weimar period and then modify it through ideology, and the judicial acts from 1952 were modelled on the Soviet example. Early on Benjamin argued that the court was bound by the Allied Control Council's marriage law and that it had to be applied in accordance with an anti-fascist democratic order. In other words, 'when section 48 of the Marriage Act is applied, the substance of marriage in the antifascist, democratic order of the new state must be respected'.[110] According to Article 30 of the Constitution, marriage 'has to support social goals and social ideals'. These goals were considered unachievable in a broken marriage and as a result the perpetuation of a broken marriage could not be morally justified.

Benjamin's 1954 draft of the family law code, although never adopted, was a distinct code based on an East German incorporation of the Soviet model. It scrutinised terms that were deemed bourgeois in an effort to ground their essence through a socialist lens, and to adjust timing of procedures in relation to the presentation of parties and evidence.

Attempts to Engage with Benjamin's Life Story

This chapter has argued that life stories can disrupt linear narratives, including historical ones, in particular when completed by images. The biography and

105 Feth, *Hilde Benjamin*. Personal interview with Andrea Feth.
106 Richardson-Little, *The Human Rights Dictatorship*, 42.
107 Feth, *Hilde Benjamin*, 227–231.
108 Martin Löhning, 'Family Law in the SOZ/GDR I: Stalinism' (2020) 49(2) *Právnehistorické Studie* [Legal Historical Studies] 48–57, 50–51.
109 Hilde Benjamin, 'Einige Bemerkungen zum Entwurf eines Familiengesetzbuches' [Some Remarks on the Draft Family Code] (1954) 8(12) *Neue Justiz* 349–353. On child rights, see Hilde Benjamin, 'Uber die elterliche Gewalt' [On Parental Authority] (1949) 3(4) *Neue Justiz* 81–83.
110 Löhning, 'Family Law in the SOZ/GDR', 52.

how it relates to the question of what it is for and answering the question about why it matters[111] underpins this exploration. The fine line between hero and villain exists in the image of Benjamin. Her life also reflects hard choices. Unlike Musine Kokalari, discussed in Chapter 3, the dominant narrative is of villain, which suits the main discourse about the nature of the East German dispensation of justice and what Benjamin represents.

Benjamin was forced to relocate in 1967 by Ulbricht, when her 'political fanaticism' fell out of favour. Her involvement in developments in the legal system would be revisited after the fall of communism. As noted above, the life stories of the Old Communists were vital to the legitimacy of the Party, yet at the same time no single Old Communist could enjoy an 'independent revolutionary charisma'. The Party was the hero. Moreover, the mercy of the Party's power was also applicable to the 'veteran'.[112]

There was an important reason behind the harsh and hateful descriptions of her role as a judge. At this time, a career as a judge was not seen as a profession for a woman, even though it had been possible for women to become judges in the period 1924 to 1933.[113] This was a kind of misogyny: a woman should not take up roles that are open for men only. This position was supported during the Third Reich, when it was forbidden for women to work as a judge or a lawyer. Significantly, this experience was a recent past for many, meaning that it was still fresh in the minds of the people when Benjamin began her career in East Germany.[114]

Inga Markovits, in her work about socialist lawyers, observes – not dissimilar to Kirchheimer – that East German judges were functionaries rather than watchmen, products of their own society.[115] Markovits should be read alongside Kirchheimer, in that she writes about the ordinary East German judge who had no reason to believe that their work was any less lawyerly or meaningful than a lawyer from the West. Markovits notes that the East German legal profession came to boast more female members than that of the Federal Republic – just over half, the majority of whom were from working-class backgrounds. It was a direct intervention of Benjamin's, making it her story. Benjamin's 1958 lecture marked the change that was to come:

> The task of achieving further progress in the development of the Socialist consciousness in this area belongs – alongside general social education –

111 Hermione Lee, 'What Is Biography?' British Academy, 7 July 2020, https://www.thebritishacademy.ac.uk/blog/what-is-biography/?gclid=CjwKCAjwoMSWBhAdEiwAVJ2ndh_L-Pi2fFStizzqSw6a3X_gKpa1k9iyWLQFCV9ywnqLU5G7PSVoBxoCJMsQAvD_BwE (accessed 15 July 2022).

112 Epstein, 'The Politics of Biography', 15.

113 Personal interview with Andrea Feth.

114 Personal interview with Andrea Feth.

115 Inga Markovits, 'Children of a Lesser God: GDR Lawyers in Post-Socialist Germany' (1996) 94(7) *Michigan Law Review* 2270–2308, 2299.

> above all to our laws. We still have no new family law. The Civil Code from the year 1900 has not been repealed in its entirety. The legal basis for women's equality in the family is provided by Article 30 of our constitution and by the Law on the Protection of Mothers and Children and the Rights of Women. Added to this is the Decree on Marriage and Divorce of November 1955.[116]

Benjamin saw the law as the driver of these changes.

Further historical accounts in German publications raise a number of different questions about Benjamin and the myth-creation surrounding Benjamin:

> On the Invalidenstrasse, just east of where the Wall would soon rise, the Kaiser-Wilhem-Akademie fur die Ausbildung von Militararzten, completed in 1905, nazified in 1933, was now Hilde Benjamin's courthouse, and every morning she arrived at 0800 hours precisely; at 0750 she was joking with the two Rubblefrauen she saw every day on the side of the street; one of them wore goggles and kept her white-dusted hair up in a bun; the other, who was younger, wore a dark skirt which went not far below the knee; at the recess the Red Guillotine frequently saw them sitting on bricks, resting their backs against the brickheap they had built; the Rubblefrau in goggles stared off into space and the Rubblefrau in the skirt read the newspaper. But that was only for a year. The Red Guillotine missed those two women a little. Sometimes in the summer she wandered to the window and gazed westward. She could see the way that the foliage of the Tiergarten paints the summer clouds green. *Her most important trials are known*, runs the legend, *and need not be mentioned further.*[117]

This excerpt goes some way towards immortalising and romanticising Benjamin. It deals in legend, rather than attempting an accurate summation of her legacy and role in advancing gender equality. The trials discussed in this chapter are examples of maladministration of justice and to romanticise her role in that is wrong. It should be noted that the trials did not go uncriticised, on the grounds that their procedures had violated the principles of due process; the subordination of at least some areas of legal decision making to crass political considerations was the subject of overt critique in novels such as Christoph Hein's *Der Tangospieler.*[118]

The danger of addressing Benjamin's image in this way can be criticised as misappropriation and misrepresentation, not entirely alike but echoing some of the points made in the case of Musine Kokalari, discussed in Chapter 3. As viewers, we no longer engage directly with Benjamin herself, or her contributions, including

116 Benjamin: 'Who Has the Say in the Family?'
117 Vollmann, *Europe Central*, 587–588, emphasis in original.
118 Christoph Hein, *Der Tangospieler: Erzählung* (*The Tango Player: Writings from an Unbound Europe*) (Suhrkamp Verlag 2002).

the problematic ones, but only superficially, because images facilitate superficial connections. Benjamin's life story is instructive in the respective way of being in the world at that time.[119] It leaves a legacy that surpasses the life accounts. Performativity concerns discovery, and the narrative of discovery refers to mentioning names that have been hitherto unknown to the wider world.[120] The presentation of the accounts of women are superficial and often maintain the dominant status quo rather than challenge or require further engagement with the individual and her life account.[121] Recently, MDR German television dramatised a series on Hilde Benjamin's life, showing a growing interest that goes beyond the superficial. A wider perspective and appreciation of discovery of the female project will benefit the way we deploy aesthetics and search for a more critical look at affective justice and the politics of visualising justice, especially an image like Benjamin's.[122] These are not easy questions. Rather than looking through rose-tinted lenses, we should see that the ruins and the *Rubblefrau* (rubble women) as an important metaphor for rebuilding, of which Benjamin was an integral and dedicated part, without losing sight of the fact that her story is complex, full of conflict, and an incredibly difficult account.[123]

Visualising Law

As mentioned in the Introduction to this monograph, those researching show trials argue that the proceedings do not merely embody violations of the due process standards of criminal procedure and material evidence. Nor are they simply a tool used by the regime to eliminate political opposition. In fact, very few of those arrested for political crimes made an appearance in public trials. Yet arrests and interrogations continued and became an important component of political discourses, and an integral part of an 'imaginative laboratory' in which the meaning of ideology was challenged and reconstituted.[124] When the

119 Common themes emerge in the analysis of the Mexican artist Frida Kahlo's life. See Gannit Ankori, *Frida Kahlo* (Reaktion Books 2018) 192.

120 Katie de Kuhna Lewin, 'Discover the Untold Stories of the Pre-Raphaelite Sisters: The Politics of Discovery', (2019) LARB, 17 August 2020, https://lareviewofbooks.org/article/the-politics-of-rediscovery/ (accessed 26 July 2022).

121 See Sarah Ahmed, 'Institutional as Usual', Blog, 24 October 2017, https://feministkilljoys.com/2017/10/24/institutional-as-usual/ (accessed 15 July 2022).

122 MDR production of 'Hilde Benjamin – die "Rote Hilde"' [Red Hilde] (2013). See https://www.mdr.de/geschichte/biographie-hilde-benjamin100.html (accessed 15 July 2022).

123 Concerning ruins, for a thoughtful discussion about funambulism in the post-war German landscape, see Yuliya Komska, 'On the Wire Above the Ruins', *Cabinet*, 4 March 2021, https://www.cabinetmagazine.org/kiosk/komska_yuliya_4_march_2021.php (accessed 15 July 2022).

124 Igal Halfin's notion of 'imaginative possibilities' as discussed in Melissa Feinberg, *Curtain of Lies: The Battle over Truth in Stalinist Eastern Europe* (Oxford University Press 2017) 2.

trial was public, or photographed for the record, visual imagery became a critical part of these discourses, serving to include both the viewer and the wider audience. The connection was not so much between state and citizen as between state and audience. Concepts of guilt and belief require us to suspend the sorts of understanding we may have acquired within the context of Western models of justice.[125] When defendants were unmasked as enemies, the audience became complicit in the rewriting of the lives of those affected, whereby a hero could be reduced to the status of villain and the experience of the confession reinforced the public discourses concerning the meaning of ideology. What was captured in the courtroom shows how the testimony reveals larger truths about the nature of justice and knowledge. The victims caught up in a show trial, many of whom are depicted in the photographs in this collection, perished as individuals rather than en masse.[126] It was a demonstration of what were sometimes harsher and sometimes gentler turns to visual law.

Before the creation of the High Court, ordinary trials played a significant role in paving the way for the East German political project that was premised on a new ideological framework, distinct from the West and the past it shared with the West. The visual turn taken with respect to these trials indicated an awareness among the East German authorities that they would serve to legitimate their legal political project (for according to Lenin, law was a political weapon) and justify the need for measures that punished collaboration with the fascists.

It is worthwhile considering a double murder trial that captured the public imagination but also served the political agenda of the East German authorities. Frieda Lehmann's trial was important to the East German authorities: it was ideologically relevant.

Frieda Lehmann was a 34-year-old war widow who worked at the local incandescent lamp factory in Dresden. In December 1946, Lehmann killed a factory co-worker and the co-worker's seven-year-old son. The especially grisly nature of the murder was reflected in the fact that Lehmann had dismembered the bodies of her victims and taken parts of them out of the house in parcels or burned them in the oven. The motive for the murder was established as greed. The prosecution argued that Lehmann wanted to take over the possessions of her friend, the evidence for this being that Lehmann went to her friend's flat to purloin clothes, cutlery, and other valuables after the scene of crime had been cleared. Several items were sold on the black market. An especially gruesome rumour circulated to the effect that the flesh of the victims had been sold at the butcher's shop where Lehmann also worked. The ancillary story of alleged cannibalism further supported the East German authorities'

125 Boris Gorys, 'The Border between Word and Image' (2011) 28(2) *Theory, Culture and Society* 94–108.

126 Gorys, 'The Border between Word and Image'.

Figure 4.8 Frieda Lehmann facing the judicial bench at her 1946 trial in Dresden
Credit: BArch/Bernhard Braun.

claim that the 'moral corruption of National Socialism' was the cause underpinning the bestial nature of the crime. Lehmann was sentenced to death for the two murders.

Her trial was held at the spacious and appropriately named German Hygiene Museum. There is an eerie nature to the venue and the interaction that was occurring between the defendant and the judges, as depicted in Figures 4.8 and 4.9. The public gallery was full. The strange narrative continued well after her execution. Lehmann's bones were put on display in an exhibition that continued until reunification.[127] Was this to support the narrative about East Germany's success in eliminating fascist corruption? It certainly was an unforgettable murder trial, which captured the popular imagination, taking place in the aftermath of a devastating war and providing alternative narratives about law and justice at the same time as trial proceedings were being held at Nuremberg by the Allied powers in the International Military Tribunal. The Frieda

127 Dreharbeiten im Auftrag des ZDF in der Gedenkstätte Münchner Platz Dresden [Film Commissioned by ZDF in the Munich Square Memorial in Dresden], 3 September 2020, https://www.stsg.de/cms/dresden/aktuelles/dreharbeiten-im-auftrag-des-zdf-der-gedenkstaette-muenchner-platz-dresden (accessed 15 July 2022).

Figure 4.9 Frieda Lehmann and the judicial bench discussing evidence at her 1946 trial in Dresden
©BArch/Bernhard Braun.

Lehmann trial was a rehearsal for the consequences of National Socialism. It was also a rehearsal for future trials aimed to entrench the East German legal narrative, control the public discourse, and transform societal attitudes. In many ways the judge was at the centre of this preparation.

There is a driving force that underpins the law's *punctum* and its irruption in the East German case study, which is illustrated in the performance of education and throttling during the trial proceedings, so effectively captured in Lehmann's face, and in the mannerisms of other officials and defendants. Defendants like Lehmann were integral to laying the groundwork for supporting a state narrative of fighting anti-fascists. Her double murder trial was also a political one. As we observed in Chapter 1, if viewed as spectacles, these trials belittled defendants and audiences alike. The visual account would be an integral part of this legal discourse. The spectacle of the dramatised trial would come to represent the 'inverted image of society',[128] whereby authentic social life is replaced with its representation. Gradually the audience came to identify with the trial performances that increasingly

128 Guy Debord, *The Society of the Spectacle* (tr. Donald Nicholson-Smith, Black and Red 1970).

superseded real activities and perceptions of law and justice. Photographs served as evidence of the spectacle's authenticity. They also played a role in the transformation of the spectacle into the real. Benjamin would have participated as a viewer in the dispensing of justice in the Third Reich, and it would affect her directly, personally, and professionally.

Visuality determined whether the requisite political approach to the dispensing of justice fluctuated, so as to seem either grand and aloof, or humble and routine. Where the law was concerned, on any given day the judge and prosecutor might function 'independently',[129] more or less. But on a trial day, their particular role was governed by the unfolding of the case – almost like a plot in a thriller – that was followed closely by its participants and by bystanders. On these days in particular, it was pertinent for the authorities of a newly created state to get the balance between hero/villain and education/throttling right. This ensured that 'normal' working days functioned without the need for vigilance on the part of the authorities because officials were acting appropriately – 'acting Bolshevik', in other words.[130]

As we reflect on Benjamin, we are faced with diverging narratives. Concerning faces in imagery, Sergei Oushakine points out that 'in the process of the propagandistic adoption of the portrait genre, something interesting happened to the portrait itself'.[131] The portrait, in other words, becomes self-referential and moves away from the biographical to sequence and composition. Portrait, broadly understood, can enrich this discourse by taking itself out of the sequence and revisiting it once again. The dispensation of justice lends itself beautifully to the fluidity of these concepts and dichotomies.

Concluding Remarks

The discussion in this chapter focused on two issues. It first considered the dynamics of visual law in East Germany. Images taken by state-employed photographers were published in the main broadsheets of the day. This unique characteristic was part of a process designed to engage people, including the legal community, by means of Vyshinsky's system of educating to throttle and throttling to educate. The spectacle represented law and justice. This was possible because of a dedicated group of elites who worked hard to maintain unity and conformity within the ranks of the judiciary. The chapter then looked at one of the most prominent figures in this group – Hilde Benjamin. It found that post-unification German narratives find it hard to situate Benjamin within the legal historical narrative of Germany. The discourses vary widely, ranging as they do from hard-line critique of her role in political cases to a more

129 Kirchheimer, 'The Administration of Justice and the Concept of Legality in East Germany'.

130 See Chapter 2.

131 Serguei Oushakine, 'Presence without Identification: Vicarious Photography and Postcolonial Figuration in Belarus' (2018) 164 *October* 49–100.

romanticised image of 'The Red Guillotine'. In fact, Benjamin forms an integral part of the discourses concerning past and future post-dictatorial legal spaces, especially those confronting uncomfortable questions about the past. This predicament has been shared by other states but was never properly addressed by a unified Germany.

The (dis)connection between the Federal Republic and East German legal approaches is most apparent in relation to the Nuremberg proceedings and its aftermath. An examination of the East German case in the light of Benjamin's career leads us to weigh up Germany's indirect contribution to international criminal justice (i.e. retrospective justice) and gender equality. The stricter standards that West German courts had applied to East German judges would later become part of a legal discourse that regretted that the approach was not also applied to Nazi judges. History's visual turn is relevant to this legal historical discussion and discourse, which give rise to questions about the process of recognition and of excavation. The excavation of Benjamin's image has divulged a series of discourses that merit attention. As in the Albanian case study, the irruption in our protagonist's image overlaps with the irruptions in the images of the trial venue, the audience and spectators at the trial, the wardrobe, the judicial officials of the military court: the performativity of the law and enactment of the law, *par excellence*. Its undisclosed narrative is biographical, both Benjamin's and the broader German legal historical account of East Germany and the dispensation of justice.

Hilde Benjamin, one of the first women in Germany to study law, grasped early on that her role would be a pioneering one, dedicated as it was to the revolution and to the status of the political criminal. She is unique among her circle in that she retained her post for a long time and managed to stay alive.[132] Benjamin's image offers a more meaningful sense of what these narratives regarding Germany's confrontation with its history of dispensing justice, both in relation to its Nazi past and East German history, might mean. This stems from the image's power to speak legally and its capacity to challenge internal and external discourses about the dispensation of justice. Benjamin's narrative irrupts in the Frieda Lehmann case; the performativity of their powerful stories allows the individual to attach herself to another community and disassociate from a community that is morally corrupt. This is permitted by the image's public presence. It not only speaks legally but it also acts. Similarly, Benjamin's image performs the act of connecting members of society – Germans from the West or the East – by establishing people's belonging to that lost community of a divided Germany or by offering itself as a target for their affects, which might

132 On the importance of political moments and whether women should be considered to be judges, see Natalia Ginzburg and Alba de Céspedes, with an introduction by Ann Goldstein, 'On Women: An Exchange', *The New York Review of Books*, 22 December 2022, 56–57, https://www-pressreader-com.leedsbeckett.idm.oclc.org/search?query=ginzburg&newspapers=9khf&start=22%20Dec%202022&stop=22%20Dec%202022&hideSimilar=true&type=3 (accessed 15 December 2022).

include fear or admiration, or both. This discussion has shown how the materiality of the image has the capacity to reorganise society. In other words, the very act of its appearing results in a 'performative reorganisation' of space and/or narrative.[133]

The success of the image, based on its capacity to mobilise and to affect an audience, arises from its 'semantic porosity and material capacity' to link different elements together.[134] This occurs on three different levels. Structurally the image acts as a connection between a chain of signifiers, connecting various identificatory elements into a story. Psychologically it provides a material veneer for collective and individual projections. Socially it founds various forms of interaction, display, and circulation: 'It is not a piece of memory, it is a piece instead of memory.'[135] Revisiting the visual and life account aims to reinsert Benjamin's life story into this discourse and enrich our understanding about this individual and key moment in the German legal historical narrative.

Chapter 5 will consider the final case study: Poland.

133 Serguei Oushakine, 'Performative Objects: How Things Do Things without Words', in Julie A. Buckler, Julie A. Cassiday, and Boris Wolfson (eds), *Russian Performances: Word, Object, Action* (University of Wisconsin Press 2018) 54–63, 56.
134 Serguei Oushakine, 'Performative Objects: How Things Do Things without Words', in Julie A. Buckler, Julie A. Cassiday, and Boris Wolfson (eds), *Russian Performances: Word, Object, Action* (University of Wisconsin Press 2018) 54–63, 56.
135 Serguei Oushakine, 'Performative Objects: How Things Do Things without Words', in Julie A. Buckler, Julie A. Cassiday, and Boris Wolfson (eds), *Russian Performances: Word, Object, Action* (University of Wisconsin Press 2018) 54–63, 56–57.

Chapter 5

Law, Visual Culture, and the Show Trial in Poland

As we reach our final chapter, it is worthwhile taking stock of what we have examined thus far. Chapter 3 established that the Albanian case study is one of affect: the images are captivating. The viewer is drawn to a certain aesthetic in the photograph, in large part owing to the image makers' pre-Second World War training as apprentices in well-known studios. The photographs are also powerful, resulting in an emotive response by the viewer, because of the venues where justice was dispensed: these places served as both movie theatres and courtrooms, and their space provided room for a large audience. The spectators' faces and reactions to the proceedings are depicted in the well-crafted photographs of the ATA photographers and of the Istituto Luce. Finally, the photographs are compelling because of the subject matter. For example, through the image of Musine Kokalari we are drawn to the figure, and question her appearance and the purpose of her dress, and her position at a large microphone; we unravel her life, her transgressions, and the longevity of her story all because of the image. It is not only her photograph's *punctum* but also the reproduction of her image that continues to shape relevant discourses that point to a trace of history waiting to be identified during the process of its reproduction, dissemination, and consumption. Control over our knowledge of Kokalari's fate continues on the part of the political elite, with the result that accountability for the maladministration of justice has not been realised, and her life story is manipulated and appropriated. In fact, Kokalari represents Albanian women writers, whose work has been marginalised by literary circles and whose voices have yet to be heard. Kokalari's image becomes a heterotopic site for some segments of Albanian society that acts as an ideal record of the past. As discussed, these sites are often created following attempts to construct spaces; they are other sites, an answer to the messiness that surrounds them, a heterotopia of 'compensation'.[1]

1 Michel Foucault, 'Of Other Spaces: Utopias and Heterotopias' (tr. Jay Miskowiec, *Architecture/Mouvement/Continuité*, October 1984), 8, https://web.mit.edu/allanmc/www/foucault1.pdf (accessed 13 October 2021).

DOI: 10.4324/9781003405771-6

Chapter 4 also saw how the driving force underpinning the law's *punctum* and its irruption in the East German case study illustrates the performance of education and throttling during trial proceedings, which is so effectively captured in the images. Its central figure, the judge, was the official chiefly responsible for meting out punishment against counter-revolutionaries and political opponents. The net was cast wide and it succeeded in capturing substantial numbers of people accused of anti-state activities. The image breaks the superficial reading of Hilde Benjamin's life and the East German legal account. Through the image of Benjamin, again we are drawn to the figure, her life, her transgressions, and her life story, all because of the image. Not dissimilar to Kokalari, Benjamin's image is reproduced along with the simple, linear narrative of 'Bloody Hilde' at the centre of the narrative concerning an East German legal system that was described as repressive and one that was not able to contribute to the development of the law in the correct way, as compared to its West German counterpart. The reference to Frieda Lehmann confirms this pattern.

If Albania and East Germany reflect the fine line between hero and villain contained in the images of the chapters' respective protagonists, Poland offers a different record that has both narratives contained in one account of a key figure – the prosecutor Mieczysław Siewierski - who was an important part of the live and visual account of the administration of justice. In Poland we confront a story about a war waged against the judiciary by the Polish authorities controlled by the Stalinist regime. In many ways this period in Poland's history is similar to that of its counterparts, apart from the lack of an international show trial on the scale of the Rajk trial. But Poland did have show trials that were widely publicised, as well as a series of trials that were carried out in secret.

To understand law, visual culture, and the show trial in Poland, we will begin with an examination of the challenges faced by the Polish judiciary in the immediate aftermath of the Second World War. It is at this moment that we can identify common and competing approaches taken by the Polish authorities to reshaping the judge and her milieu. The images show a hidden history of the Polish judiciary. One the one hand we see the misadministration of justice in show trials and on the other a dispensation of justice that produced novel approaches to legal interpretation.

The subject matter is important. The level of mistrust between Polish judicial officials and authorities was negotiated across legal developments that included the creation of special courts and tribunals that required lawyers with legal knowledge to contribute to their operation. Overall, Polish lawyers distanced themselves from political power in order to attain a degree of independence. This approach was, of course, not always successful. This game of cat and mouse could be seen in the legal team of its court set up to try war crimes, the Supreme National Tribunal (*Najwyższy Trybunał Narodowy*, SNT), will be shown. One example is discussed in this chapter, but there are more that merit further attention and research.

Chapter 5 will consider the images of lesser-known individuals pointing to an undiscovered grey area that needs to be brought to the fore and located within dominant discourses about the nature of justice during the period. It will discuss the context of the administration of justice in Poland in the aftermath of the Second World War, with reference to relevant visual imagery. These two topics will be brought together in a brief consideration of the 1944 Majdanek trial. While the Majdanek trial shares the quality of the earlier Soviet trials, it marks the move by Polish authorities towards preparing to 'speak legally' to a wider audience. Applying the visual and accepting the performativity of the law shows how a legal principle comes alive when we can identify the lawyers behind it. The focus will be on the prosecutor Mieczysław Siewierski. Siewierski was prosecutor of the Supreme Court and also of the SNT. He has been specifically selected for this chapter because his life account and career represent the nature of the dispensing justice at this time in Poland. The images discussed in this chapter were chosen because they have so far not been more widely available, and therefore their power has not been appreciated.

At a war crimes trial, a series of relationships are amplified, including law and politics, local justice and reckoning, individual responsibility and collective guilt, making history and performing justice, and legitimation.[2] The importance of this amplification is located in the guilt of the defendant and innocence of the prosecuting authorities, something that will be picked up later in the discussion.[3] These paths were defined by internal and external forces. Indeed, '[t]he Holocaust and the pressures of Sovietisation would make for strange bedfellows. The postwar communist government, commonly known as "People's Poland", theoretically was beholden to no one except its creator, Stalin, and yet was heavily dependent on ideologically unreliable technocrats to maintain the machinery of the state'.[4] To appreciate the Polish context is to accept that the narrative is messy, but not necessarily incoherent, when the common denominator of impartial and independent dispensation of justice is shared. This was a time of opportunity that many Polish lawyers understood to be temporary; decisions had to be made about professional priorities and personal risks. 'People's Poland understood that its own reserve of support in devastated postwar Poland was so shallow that to simply exclude prewar jurists would bring about the complete collapse of the judicial system and its own discreditation'.[5] The internal policy was conveyed by Polish authorities, who tolerated the presence of pre-war judges in their ranks.

2 Gerry Simpson, *Law, War and Crime: War Crimes Trials and the Reinvention of International Law* (Polity 2007) 1.
3 Simpson, *Law, War and Crime*, 88–91.
4 Andrew Kornbluth, *The August Trials: The Holocaust and Postwar Justice in Poland* (Harvard University Press 2021) 6–7.
5 Kornbluth, *The August Trials*, 7.

The Dispensing of Justice and Its Visual Imagery

The dispensation of justice in Poland at this time is generally presented as two distinct matters. First, there is the administration of justice in general terms. The legal basis for this was provided for in the number of decrees passed by the provisional government of that period. This will be discussed in further detail below. Second, there is the administration of justice that comprises far-reaching and not commonly discussed legal interpretations of Polish law that would eventually feed into the development of international criminal law. Both trajectories involved judges and sometimes the same individuals. Of course, running alongside these narratives is the discussion pertaining to the maladministration of justice.

The Polish judiciary – comprising those who survived the Second World War – began to see a change in the way it dispensed justice towards the end of the war and during the key years that followed. The Polish judicial pool was, for all intents and purposes, decimated during the war. This took its toll on many of the survivors, who had to make hard decisions about a future legal career in a different political landscape. Even those who were Marxists during the pre-war period and claimed allegiance to the political-ideological direction that the Polish state was taking were not immune; there was always the suspicion of taint and corruption. The transformation of the judiciary was masterminded by Leon Chajn, who was the chief architect of the post-war Polish legal system. Under his leadership of the PKWN (Polski Komitet Wyzwolenia Narodowego) in 1944 (and from 1945 to 1949 as Undersecretary of State in the Ministry of Justice), a close eye was kept on the judiciary. Meetings with judges were organised periodically.

Most judicial officials saw Chajn as a careerist who was ambitious and not deserving of the post.[6] His presence before the symbol of justice in Figure 5.1 is telling. The scales of justice are particularly prominent in this image of Chajn, and they seem to convey an air of watchfulness that reflects the state of affairs at that time. The statue towers over the audience behind speaker Chajn, reinforcing his message about the dispensing of justice and warning judges to keep in line with the objectives underpinning post-war Poland's new legal framework that favoured a more punitive approach. Chajn was disappointed in what he perceived as lenient sentencing, a message espoused in the creation of an Office for Judicial Oversight (*Departamentu Nadzoru Sądowego*), which accused the judiciary of remaining at the margins, passive, and unwilling to contribute to the political project: a 'medieval guild' (see Figure 5.2).[7] The idea was promoted that all judicial personnel had to be screened carefully as new courts were being instituted in the recaptured regions, and eventually in a post-war Poland. One of the screening tools to be implemented required judicial personnel to reapply for their positions.[8] This process obliged individuals to disclose their previous work experience and placed particular emphasis on their

6 Kornbluth, *The August Trials*, 171.
7 Kornbluth, *The August Trials*, 162.
8 Kornbluth, *The August Trials*, 162.

Figure 5.1 Leon Chajn at a gathering of judicial officials, Wrocław, Poland, 1946
Credit: IPN, fond 1315/25.

activities during the German occupation. Even so, it was clear that qualified judges were few and far between, and that those who had survived would be needed at least for the immediate period to focus on the prosecution of crimes committed by the Germans.

Chajn was dissatisfied with the attitude of the pre-war judges.[9] There was a deep mistrust of the pre-war judicial pool, and as a consequence a vigorous campaign of indoctrination in Marxism–Leninism–Stalinism was initiated. The 'war over the judiciary' had two objectives: to destroy all pre-war tendencies in the decision-making process and to erode the prestige of the judicial profession.[10] The

9 Teresa Torańska, *Them: Stalin's Polish Puppets* (Harper Collins 1987). The Polish version is *Oni* [Them] (Mysl 1986) and discussed in Agata Fijalkowski, *From Old Times to New Europe: The Polish Struggle for Democracy and Constitutionalism* (Ashgate, 2010) 97–101.

10 The notion of the 'war over the judiciary' is developed by Andrzej Rzepliński in *Sądownictwo w Polsce Ludowej: między dyspozycyjnoscia a niezawisłością* [The Judiciary in Poland: Between Disposability and Independence] Oficyna Wydawnicza 'Pokolenie' 1989), discussed in Fijalkowski, *From Old Times to New Europe*, 90–108. Rzeplinski's work – and another book on dispensing justice in 1944–1954 by Maria Turlejska, *Te pokolenia żałobami czarne … Skazani na śmierć i ich sędziowie 1944–1954* [These Generations in Black Mourning Dress … Condemned to

Figure 5.2 Gathering of judicial officials, Wrocław, Poland, 1946
Credit: IPN, fond 1315/33.

authorities appointed judicial candidates who had not satisfied the basic requirements stipulated by the law up to that point, and by creating special schools under the auspices of the Ministry of Justice to train the new judges on aspects of the people's justice.[11] But he need not have worried. As we have seen above, lawyers trained in pre-war Poland contributed to this teaching. At the same time, the Polish dispensation of justice was contributing to the development of international criminal law at the Supreme National Tribunal in such a way as to work against the 'war against the judiciary' campaign. Both narratives were reinforced by Soviet legal propaganda. The communist regime was not yet fully established, and pre-war judicial officials were not all prepared to acquiesce in political indoctrination.

Death and Their Judges] (2nd edn, Aneks 1989) – are analysed by Adam Lityński, 'Obraz sądownicztwa karnego pierwszej dekady Polski Ludowej: Uwagi na marginesie ksiażek Andrzeja Rzeplińskiego i Marii Turleskiej'[The Judiciary and Criminal Law and Justice during the First Decade of the Polish People's Republic: Remarks from the Margins of the Books by Andrzej Rzeplińskiand by Maria Turleska], (1991) 43(1–2) *Czasopismo Prawno-Historyczne* [Legal Historical Journal] 153–170. See also John Mcgiel, '"Frenzy and Ferocity": The Stalinist Judicial System in Poland, 1944–1947, and the Search for Redress', (1994) 1101 *The Carl Beck Papers in Russian and Central European Studies*, 26–33 in particular.

11 Fijalkowski, *From Old Times to New Europe*, 97.

Nonetheless, relations were less confrontational, as communists held the balance of power in Polish–Soviet relations.[12] Lityński notes a significant incident in 1946 that resulted in the arrest of all judges and prosecutors at a gathering in Kielce by the Soviet army.[13] Chajn intervened and saw to the release of 17 judicial officials; the fate of the rest is unknown. The loss of so many judges and prosecutors did not go unnoticed by the authorities. The deadline set out in the Decree of 22 February 1946 concerning the registration and compulsory employment of the administration of justice of individuals qualified to take the position of a judge was extended many times.[14]

Returning to 1944, the promulgation of the Decree of 31 August 1944 (1944 August Decree) was critical. It was a vital piece of legislation passed by the PKWN that was a step towards 'speaking legally'. It stated that anyone who

> assisted the German occupation authorities in the commission of murder of civilians or POWs, or in their mistreatment or persecution, or act[ed] to the detriment of individuals pursued or sought by German occupation authorities for any reason... by denouncing, capturing, or deporting them, is subject to the death penalty, or imprisonment of up to fifteen and no less than three years, or for life.

The 1944 August Decree concerned the punishment of fascist-Hitlerite criminals guilty of the murder and ill-treatment of the civilian population and prisoners of war, and the punishment of traitors to the Polish Nation (as amended by the Decree of 16 February 1945 and later the revised version of the 1944 August Decree was consolidated into a Schedule to the Proclamation of the Minister of Justice of 11 December 1946).[15] It still underwent several key changes until 1948. As Kornbluth notes, the cases brought under the 1944 Decree comprised 32,000 trials for war crimes and collaboration, but represented much more than the Polish judicial response to German crimes.[16]

The first revision of Polish criminal law was the passage of the Military Penal Code of 23 September 1944, which replaced key provisions within the 1932

12 Paulina Gulińska-Jurgiel, 'How to Punish National-Socialist Crimes in Poland', in Paulina Gulińska-Jurgiel, Yvonne Kleinmann, Miloš ⊠ezník, and Dorothea Warneck (eds), *Ends of War: Interdisciplinary Perspectives on Past and New Polish Regions* (Wallstein 2019) 346–370, 355.

13 Lityński, 'Obraz sądownictwa karnego pierwszej dekady Polski Ludowej', 158–159.

14 Lityński, 'Obraz sądownictwa karnego pierwszej dekady Polski Ludowej', 158–159.

15 The revision was published in Dziennik Ustaw, No. 69, item 677. For example, Jerzy Sawicki, Tadeusz Cyprian, and the international lawyer Julian Makowski, among others, contributed to these revisions mainly with a view to align the law with the rulings at Nuremberg. See Kornbluth, *The August Trials*, 165.

16 Kornbluth, *The August Trials*, 7.

Criminal Code.[17] The purpose of the provisions was to protect the new political structure. They were not directed only at soldiers but also extended to civilians, and were very much oriented to target members of the Polish underground movement who had placed themselves in the opposition. The changes were followed by the Decree on State Security of 30 October 1944, an equally repressive piece of legislation which addressed attempts at overthrowing the Polish state, terrorist attacks, subversive activity, and sabotage.[18] Each of the crimes called for the death penalty, which resulted in some controversy as this was not in line with Polish thinking and was opposed by several judges, to the dismay of the authorities.[19] This decree was replaced by another, namely the Decree on Crimes of Dangerous Nature during the Reconstruction of the State.[20] The 1932 Criminal Code was suspended by Article 68 of the Decree of 13 June 1946, known as the 'little Criminal Code'. The first acts to address the judiciary were 15 August 1944 and 12 September 1944, which introduced mix trial courts (professional and lay judges), the latter decree created separate 'special courts', which were to deal with so-called fascist-Nazi crimes,[21] until amendments made to the 1944 August Decree gave District Courts the remit to try these crimes. The Criminal Code also established separate military courts. A 'secret section' of the Supreme Court operated between 1950 and 1954.[22] The Warsaw jail located at Rakowiecka Street (seen in Figure 5.3) served as a location for some of the proceedings at this point.

Despite the fact that these proceedings were held in secret, most Warsaw residents knew about them, which also served as a form of legal propaganda, albeit via

17 Dekret Polskiego Komitetu Wyzwolenia Narodowego z dnia 23 wrzesnia 1944r. Kodeks Karny Wojska Polskiego [Decree of the Polish Committee for National Liberation from 23 September 1944, The Military Criminal Code], Dziennik Ustaw, No. 6, item 27.

18 Decree of the Polish Committee for National Liberation from 30 October 1944 Concerning State Security, Dziennik Ustaw, No. 10, item 50.

19 Kornbluth, *The August Trials*, 96.

20 Decree of the Polish Committee for National Liberation from 13 June 1946 Concerning the 'Little Criminal Code', Dziennik Ustaw, No. 53, item 300.

21 Rozporządzenie Kierowników Resortu Sprawiedliwości i Resortu Bezpieczeństwa Publicznego z dnia 3 października 1944r. w sprawie wykonania Polskiego Komitetu Wyzwolenia Narodowego z dnia 12 września 1944r. o specjanych sadach karnych dla spraw zbrodniarzy faszystowsko-hitlerowskich [Order of the Leaders of the Department of Justice and the Department of Public Safety from 3 October 1944 Concerning the Implementation of the Decree of the Polish Committee for National Liberation from 12 September 1944 Concerning Special Criminal Courts for Fascist-Nazi Crimes], Dziennik Ustaw, No. 7, item 35. Many of the former members of the underground movement were sentenced to death or to harsh punishment in these courts. No appeals could be made; the courts' decisions were final and binding.

22 Adam Strzembosz and Maria Stanowska, *Sędziówie warszawscy w czasie próby, 1981–1988* [Warsaw Judges during Rehearsal, 1981–1988] (IPN 2005).

Figure 5.3 Entrance to the prison at ul. Rakowiecka, Warsaw, Poland, 1946
Credit: AIPN, fond GK-14-3-8-3-1.

a private forum.[23] The proceedings at Rakowiecka Street were brutal, and the rights of the defendant were not given any consideration. For example, in most cases defendants were not given details of what crime they had been accused of, and this was limited to the reading out of the charge by the court; nor were witnesses present, limited, once again, to their testimonies being read out in court.[24]

23 Adam Lityński, 'Administracja, Polityka i Sąd Tajny w Polsce Ludowej' (Administration, Politics, and Secret Courts in People's Poland), (2010) 10 *Roczniki Administracji i Prawa*, 21–37, 32. Also George H. Hodos, *Show Trials: Stalinist Purges in Eastern Europe, 1948–1954* (Praeger 1987).

24 See Katarzyna Maria Piekarska, 'Naruszanie zasady jawności w "sadach tajnych"' (Violation of the Principles of Open Proceedings in the 'Secret Courts') (1995) 27 *Studia Iuridica* 25–41.

Between 1944 and 1946 some 670 death sentences were passed, some one hundred during NKVD-style sham proceedings which violated all principles relating to a right to a fair trial.[25]

The 1944 August Decree looked to the past as much as it looked to the future. This policy of purging was based on false accusations: the underlying aim was to serve the Soviet authorities' goal of ousting political opponents and promoting their own 'social revolution'. This same decree sentenced so-called Polish 'traitors' for 'assisting the enemy'. Most of the legislation that was passed between 1944 and 1945 did not rely on normal legislative techniques, such as statutes and decrees. Instead, many critical matters were decided unofficially, not always by authorised officials, and often remained unpublished, apart from criminal responsibility which was set out in the relevant decrees. It was clear that the enactments that were passed during this period were meant to accelerate the consolidation of communist power. The 1944 August Decree would catch returning members of the Home Army (*Armia Krajowa*, AK) whom Polish authorities viewed suspiciously and felt threatened by, such as the wartime hero General August Emil Fieldorf, who was charged with crimes under the amended the 1944 August Decree and sentenced to death in secret appeal proceedings. He and his peers were victims of this Decree. It is worth noting the Decree of 22 January 1946 concerning the defeat of Poland in September 1939 and the 'fascistisation' of public life, which will be discussed shortly.

The Majdanek Trials

Another series of trials were prepared during this period when the Polish authorities were purging the country of the so-called enemy. The parallel series of trials were war crimes proceedings which were integral to a successful legal historical narrative whose message was strongly anti-fascist and one that would gain momentum with the fashioning of the Nuremberg trials and participation of Polish lawyers in preparing cases for prosecution.

The Majdanek trials were a series of proceedings that were carried out in Poland and Germany. The Majdanek trial held in Poland in 1944 was of exceptional importance to the pursuit of justice for crimes committed by the Germans on Polish soil by Polish authorities. By way of background, the Majdanek camp, built in 1941, was originally a forced labour camp that held Jews. By 1943 Majdanek had expanded to include several sub-camps. It claimed tens of thousands of lives; estimates indicate that 70,000 Jews and 20,000 non-Jews, mostly Poles, were murdered, but unofficial estimates argue that the numbers are much higher. The camp was the first to be liberated by the Allies. It was viewed as the 'pinnacle of nazi industrial killing' before the

25 For recent documents relating to the above-mentioned death sentences, see Jerzy Kochanowski, 'Zabrakło desek' [They Ran out of Desks], 15 November 1997, 46 *Polityka* 80.

liberation of Auschwitz.[26] The Red Army entered Majdanek in July 1944 and found horrific and disturbing clues as to events prior to their arrival, best encapsulated in the remarks of Boris Efimov, the Soviet Jewish caricaturist who was with the Red Army, who reflected 'What kind of human imagination is capable of visualising what happened here in these minutes?'[27] Figure 5.4 depicts a war crimes proceeding before a Soviet military court on Polish territory.

The Majdanek trial offered the pro-Soviet PKWN the chance to assert its legitimacy internally and externally. The proceedings were public and held in Lublin. The findings were primarily witness testimonies and interrogation statements of captured SS functionaries: these materials would be sent to the Soviet delegation at Nuremberg. Defendants were brought into court through palpable scenes of emotion and potential violence, as crowds cried death chants. The presiding judge was Bohdan Zembrzuski; the prosecution lawyers were Jerzy Sawicki and Henryk Cieśluk; the defence lawyers were Wojciech Jarosławski and Kazimierz Krzymowski.[28] The defendants were charged under

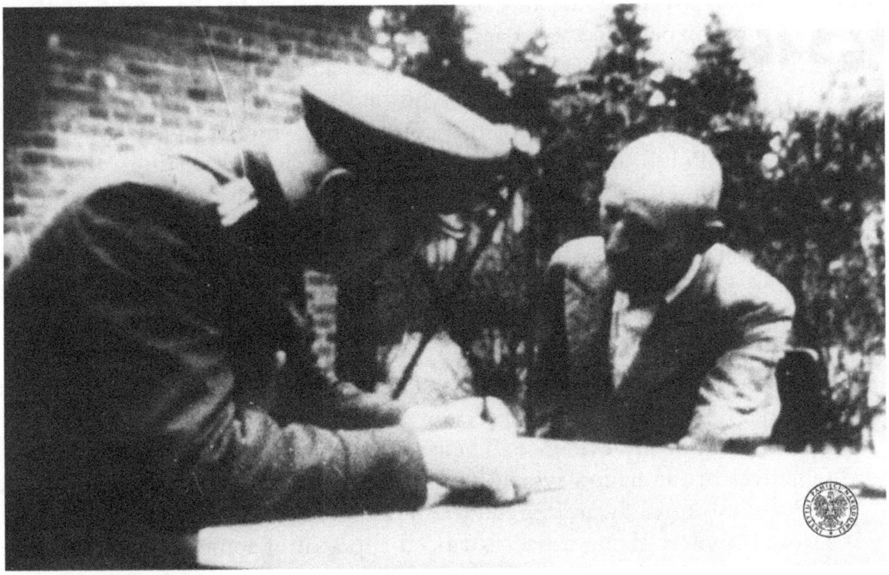

Figure 5.4 War crimes hearings carried out by a Soviet military court on Polish territory near Lublin, 1945
Credit: AIPN, fond GK-14-3-12-1-1.

26 Gabriel Finder and Alexander Prusin, *Justice Behind the Iron Curtain: Nazis on Trial in Communist Poland* (University of Toronto Press 2018) 30.
27 Francine Hirsch, *Soviet Judgment at Nuremberg: A New History of the International Military Tribunal after World War II* (Oxford University Press 2020) 165–166.
28 Finder and Prusin, *Justice Behind the Iron Curtain*, 34.

Article 1 of the 1944 August Decree for participating in torture, mistreatment, and murder of camp inmates, and two functionaries faced additional charges of rape.

There are photographs taken at the Majdanek trial proceedings that are especially powerful owing to close-ups of the spectators, defendants, the bench, and defence counsel. Figure 5.5, showing an unidentified defence counsel's curled hand as he delivers his speech, with the (perhaps) defendant weeping beside him, is emotive. The images are compelling because of the drama, religious symbolism, close-up shots of the Romani victims, and displays of emotion by the victim and legal counsel alike. Prosecutors also explicitly deployed emotion in courtroom settings, etiquette, and protocol, but more often in an implicit fashion.

It would be easy to label this trial as a show trial. Yet the trial itself was a prelude to bigger and better trials and innovation in how to interpret evidence and apply the law to such atrocities. As images of this trial disclose an important connection between the lawyers at the Majdanek trial and the Nuremberg proceedings.[29] This irruption in the images is relevant for the broader international criminal law timeline and draws our attention to the work of these lawyers, whose experiences overlapped and shaped approaches, either directly or indirectly, adding another layer to the Soviet agitation trials discussed earlier in this book. They are another example of the struggle between good and evil, and the moment of reckoning. In this concentric layout of justice, the shared experiences of Polish and Soviet counterparts comes back to the earlier war crimes trials. For example, one of the Soviet prosecutors at the Nuremberg trials, Roman Rudenko, had been the Chief Prosecutor at the Trial of the Sixteen.[30] Polish lawyers at Nuremberg, who also were members of the legal team at the SNT discussed their Soviet counterparts' performances there, in particular

> the force of their arguments [General Rudenko, Colonel Pokorovsky, and Colonel Smirnov] consisted precisely in their straightforward and succinct presentation of the evidence. Their approach was more like that of representatives of the nation which had suffered [at] the hands of the criminals, and [who] now [were] present[ing] an account[,] rather than that of learned lawyers giving a well-balanced appraisal of someone's crimes. The account they had to present was [remarkably wide-ranging] in scope and

29 Jerzy Sawicki, lead prosecutor at the Majdanek trial and later part of the prosecutorial team of the Supreme National Tribunal (*Najwyższy Trybunał Narodowy*, SNT), confirmed the tangible emotional dimension of the law, as cited in Kornbluth, *The August Trials*, 126.

30 Agata Fijalkowski, 'Politics, Law and Justice in People's Poland: the Fieldorf File' (2014) 73(1) *Slavic Review* 85–107. The Trial of the Sixteen was a show trial of 16 members of the Polish Underground, who were accused of illegal activity and tried in Moscow in 1945. See also Hirsch, *Soviet Judgment at Nuremberg*.

Figure 5.5 Defence counsel at the Majdanek trial, Poland, 1944
Credit: IPN, fond L-244/1.

shocking in precision; it could not admit of any legal scholasticisms in view of the overwhelming evidence of facts.[31]

31 Tadeusz Cyprian and Jerzy Sawicki, *Nuremberg in Retrospect: People and Issues of the Trial* (Western Press Agency 1967) 48–49.

At the Majdanek trial, Polish lawyers would allow for the moment of reckoning to come on display, where speeches referred to the 'system of evil' that permeated the Nazis' vision of world order:

> Words are created by humans, but what happened in the camp is inhuman. Words are comprehensible, but what happened here is incomprehensible. Words have their own logic, but what happened here … This is Majdanek! Imagine the powerlessness of mothers, who went to their deaths along with their children. This is Majdanek![32]

The Majdanek trial dispensed justice swiftly, with defendants knowing of the charges only 48 hours before the trial and with limited legal advice.[33] Figure 5.6 shows observers at the Majdanek trial.

The legal framework of the Majdanek trials mirrored the Soviet model in terms of style and performance, notably the 1943 Krasnodar and Kharkov trials. The Majdanek trial also took advantage of the propaganda against Germans, which was consistent and all-pervasive. Daily news bulletins would announce that there were no good Germans, only bad Germans. Political leaders would ask that no mercy be shown to Germans who had escaped justice. Polish society at that time was steeped in a rhetoric of hatred towards Germans. It was in this spirit that the Majdanek trial was conducted. Figure 5.7 shows the judicial bench at the Majdanek trial.

The power of a prosecutorial speech was never more important. Julia Shaw notes that 'a lawyer is always at best more than simply a lawyer, just as the law is never nothing but the law … [t]he words of the law contain more than they say. The texts are not just words. They have *anima*, spirit and that is to be preferred and to be followed'.[34] There is power in display in institutions, 'such as law to incite, induce, or seduce its subjects [which] is only possible because social relations are always subject to sensory experience: consequently aesthetic responses trigger certain emotions which shape our personal and collective notions of beauty, which in turn, can motivate a greater concern for justice'.[35]

32 Finder and Prusin, *Justice Behind the Iron Curtain*, 38.

33 The Nuremberg process changed the way that these trials were conducted, at least with respect to evidence regarding war crimes. Rudenko was quite successful in cross-examination at Nuremberg; Telford Taylor, *The Anatomy of the Nuremberg Trials* (Little, Brown and Company 1992) 346. 'General Rudenko's address was like his physique – squarely built, stocky, tough … His address contained only a few pages on legal issues … and the rest of his long argument dealt with crimes of individual defendants, with a very brief hortatory conclusion': Taylor, *The Anatomy of the Nuremberg Trials*, 499.

34 Julia J. A. Shaw, *Law and the Passions: Why Emotions Matter for Justice* (GlassHouse Books 2019) 17, noting Peter Goodrich, '*Flores quae faciunt coronam* or the Flowers of Common Law', in O. Ben-Dor (ed.), *Law and Art: Ethics and Aesthetics* (Routledge 2011) 259–272, 270–272.

35 Shaw, *Law and the Passions*, 29.

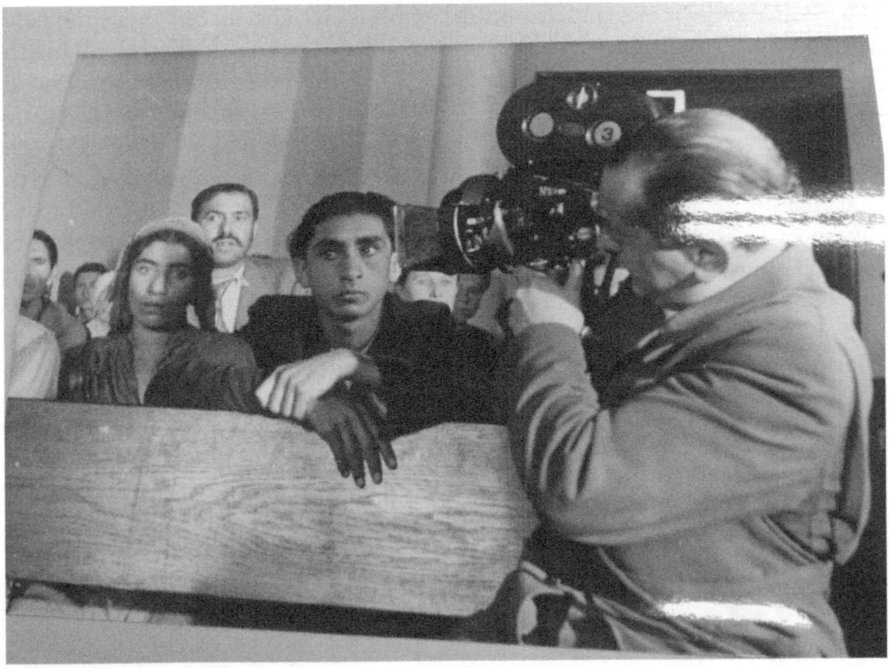

Figure 5.6 Spectators at the Majdanek trial, Poland, 1944
Credit: IPN, fond 2514/12.

Figure 5.7 Special criminal court, Lublin, Poland, 1944
Credit: IPN, fond GK-14-3-10-1-1.

The Polish prosecutors understood the symbolism. The success of a prosecutor rests on her ethos, which is based in turn on the power of rhetoric. Rhetoric 'offers a systematic account of how passions are the property of rational mental activity and rhetoric and rhetoric based on emotion can offer an alternative mode of perception and consciousness'.[36] As noted earlier with regard to the Soviet agitation trials, the moment of reckoning was a pivotal point for the dispensation of justice: 'Man is seen to be, and must recognise himself to be, playing in a theatre that is the point of juncture, and of clash, of imperatives beyond himself that are non-mediated and irreducible'.[37] The choice of the individual and wider community is at stake and felt as a 'retributive, purgative terror'.[38] The members of the National Commission for the Investigation of German-Hitlerite Crimes, like those seen in Figure 5.8, were attuned to these

Figure 5.8 Members of the National Commission for the Investigation of German-Hitlerite Crimes, 1945. Seen here are Investigating Judge Jan Sehn (left), the Polish writer Zofia Nałkowska (middle), Judge N. N. Kornacki (right).
Credit: AIPN, fond Kr-2-20-1-13-1.

36 Shaw, *Law and the Passions*, 13. I thank colleagues at Royal Holloway, namely Christos Kremmydas, Lene Rubinstein, Simone Gigliotti, and Lawrence Newport, organisers of the stimulating Nurnberg 2.0 workshops, for provoking further thoughts about the prosecutors' rhetoric in their speeches at the Nuremberg trials.
37 Peter Brooks, *The Melodramatic Imagination: Balzac, Henry James, Melodrama, and the Mode of Excess* (Yale University Press 1976), 13.
38 Brooks, *The Melodramatic Imagination*, 13.

sentiments. The Commission played an important role in gathering evidence for the prosecutions at Nuremberg and for the national war crimes trials.

The Supreme National Tribunal

The towering scale of justice shown in the previous section was vigilant but also turned a blind eye to some legal developments. This was the case with respect to the Supreme National Tribunal (*Najwyższy Trybunał Narodowy*, SNT).[39] The SNT was created further to an agreement concluded by the Allies to punish all the major war criminals of the European Axis at the International Military Tribunal at Nuremberg, as set out in the Charter of the International Military Tribunal of 8 August 1945. The remaining war criminals were to be judged in the territory of those countries where they had committed their crimes, further to the 1943 Moscow Declaration, which stated that following any armistice with the German government (present or future), German individuals suspected of involvement in wartime atrocities would be sent to those countries for trial and punishment. The SNT brought with it the endless possibilities for legal propaganda. Thus its composition needed to be of highly qualified, well-trained lawyers who would bring legitimacy and credibility to a court that would be scrutinised domestically and internationally. The members of the legal team were photographed and filmed, very much in the spirit of the times, as noted at the Soviet trials and at Nuremberg. At each of these trials photographs were taken and disseminated to a population that was eager for information. The SNT fulfilled the criteria of 'speaking legally'; but restricting its achievement to only that would be a disservice to the team that applied and forged a legal path that would form the legal principles of the prosecution, prohibition, and prevention of genocide.[40] By 1948, the Polish legal team was

39 The Decree of 22 January 1946 set out the remit of the SNT, Dziennik Ustaw, No. 5, item 46.

40 A total of 49 persons were sentenced. In each of the seven trials the focus was on a particular activity of the Nazis, and each was held at venues that corresponded to the crimes in question:

1.The first trial was that of Artur Greiser from 21 June to 7 July 1946 in Poznań. The proceedings centred on the scale of the persecution and suffering of the population of the Greater Poland (*Wielkopolska*) region. The trial proceedings are in the *Law Reports*.

2.The second trial was that of Amon Leopold Göth, the Commandant of the Płaszów camp from 27 August to 5 September 1946 in Kraków. The prosecution focused on the way in which the Nazis had treated the Jewish population of the German-occupied territory, the General Governate (General Government) and the civilian population in the labour camps. As Grzebyk notes, the verdicts in these cases were passed before the final judgment at the IMT. The trial proceedings are in the *Law Reports*.

3.The third trial was that of Ludwig Fischer (Governor of the Warsaw District), Ludwig Leist (section chief in the Office of the Warsaw District and plenipotentiary of the Governor for Warsaw), Josef Meisinger (chief of security police and security accustomed to national publicity. The prosecution was experienced in reaching out to various sources of Polish law to find a basis for the charges. It is worth noting that the trial proceedings themselves were one of four trials that were held in Poland and that are in the *Law Reports.*[41]

The trials also demonstrated that the German invasion of Poland was not a coincidence but the result of an excessively lenient approach adopted by the West towards Germany after the First World War. This is best exemplified in the penultimate war crimes trial, with the pre-war Polish authorities portrayed as inept.[42] These proceedings – the trial of Albert Forster – were held in Gdańsk from 5 to 27 April 1948. As noted throughout this book, the trial venue was of great significance, for the judicial bench and the audience, as seen in Figures 5.9, 5.10, and 5.11, at different proceedings during the time period in question.

Albert Maria Forster (1902–1952) was *Gauleiter* (District Leader) and *Reichsstatthalter* (Governor) of Danzig-West Prussia, the German-annexed territory of occupied Poland.[43] His administration of the territory was under scrutiny for,

service of Warsaw) and Max Damme (section chief in the Headquarters of the Ordnungspolizei) from 17 December 1946 to 24 February 1947 in Warsaw. The proceedings concerned the nature of the rule of the occupying forces in Warsaw and the Warsaw district, and the persecution of the Polish and Jewish population.

4.The Rudolf Höss trial was held in Warsaw from 11 to 29 March 1947. The proceedings focused on the organisation of the concentration camps, including Auschwitz, and on the medical experiments conducted there. The trial proceedings are in the *Law Reports.*

5.At the fifth trial, also known as the Auschwitz trials, some 40 persons were tried. These trials were held from 24 November to 16 December 1947 in Kraków. The prosecution presented evidence in an attempt to show how this camp was a genuine death factory.

6.The Albert Forster trial, held in Gdańsk, from 5 to 27 April 1948, addressed Forster's actions aimed at detaching Danzig (Gdańsk) from Poland. The trial proceedings are in the *Law Reports.*

7.The final SNT trial was that of Josef Bühler, deputy to Hans Frank, which was designed to show that the extermination policy was not limited to Poland. The trial proceedings lasted from 17 June to 5 July 1948.

Grzebyk, 'The Role of the Polish Supreme National Tribunal', 605.

41 Footage from trial can been seen at *Forster Trial.* 1948, British Pathé, https://www.britishpathe.com/video/forster-trial (accessed 28 January 2022). Siewierski is seen at 00.29.

42 As noted by Patrycja Grzebyk, 'The Role of the Polish Supreme National Tribunal in the Development of the Principles of International Criminal Law', in Morten Bergsmo, Wui Ling Cheah, and Ping Yi (eds), *Historical Origins of International Criminal Law: Volume 2* (Torkel Opsahl Academic EPublisher 2014) 603–630, 606. Also see hints of a portrayal of the Polish authorities' pre-war ineptitude in 'Trial of Gauleiter Artur Greiser', *Law Reports of Trials of War Criminals, Selected and Prepared by the United Nations War Crimes Commission*, Volume VII (London, 1948).

43 The Free City of Danzig, now Gdańsk, was a city-state controlled by the League of Nations between 1920 and 1939.

Figure 5.9 Amon Göth trial, Kraków, Poland, 1946
Credit: IPN, fond GK-14-3-22-2-1.

Figure 5.10 District court in Kraków presiding over the trial of 18 members of the Kraków-Płasków concentration camp, Poland, 1948
Credit: AIPN, fond GK-14-3-17-28-1/Stanislaw Dąbrowiecki.

Figure 5.11 Spectators at the Rudolf Höss trial, Warsaw, Poland, 1947
Credit: AIPN, fond GK-14-3-15-12-1.

inter alia, participating in a criminal organisation, deprivation of rights of Poles in Danzig (Gdańsk), persecution and abusing Poles, mass murder, destruction of Polish culture, and Germanisation policies. Forster was presented by the prosecution as the co-author of the plan to gain control over the territory and attack Poland.[44] He was found guilty of war crimes and crimes against peace that were available at the time.

Who Was Mieczysław Siewierski?

Nowhere are the themes of the emotive nature of the crimes, law, and victims more apparent than in the image and life story of Mieczysław Siewierski. Figure 5.12 shows Siewierski delivering his prosecutorial speech in the Artur Greiser trial. In an ironic twist of fate, Siewierski later found himself facing the same charges that he successfully prosecuted up until that point and on an international stage.

Siewierski and his prosecutorial team were behind the success of this trial and the others that preceded it. They brought with them experience and training that encouraged innovation in legal thinking and legal interpretation. Behind the scenes, however, officials viewed several of its members suspiciously and waited for the best moment to arrest him. For Siewierski, the time came in June 1950. The preparation

44 Grzebyk, 'The Role of the Polish Supreme National Tribunal'.

Figure 5.12 Prosecutor Mieczysław Siewierski at the Artur Greiser trial, held at the auditorium of the Adam Mickiewicz University, Poznań, Poland, 1946
Credit: PAP/J. Zyszkowski/Alamy.

of the case against him took two years.[45] To understand why Siewierski caused such unrest on the part of the authorities an account of his life is required.

Siewierski was born on 22 October 1900. He was one of four children. The Siewierski family struggled to make ends meet, but his parents did all they could to make sure that Siewierski was supported in his studies, a point he

45 Elżbieta Romanowska, 'Procesy karne przeciwko dr. Mieczysławowi Siewierskiemu w Polsce w latach 1950–1956' [Criminal Proceedings Carried Out in Poland against Dr Mieczysław Siewierski from 1950 to 1956] (2016) 9 *Z dziejów prawa* [History of Law] 99–130, 104. Details of arrest and charges at IPN, fond BU Wa-III-53291486(4)/19. Siewierski's personal papers are at IPN, fond Wa-BU 660/629. Romanowska has carefully analysed the materials IPN, fond BU 0259/584, in particular Siewierski's lengthy testimony.

made at his interrogation by the security services in 1950.[46] From a young age he demonstrated that he was a bright student; he eagerly pursued a law degree at a time when Poland regained its independence after over a century of rule under partition between three empires. Siewierski found himself in the eye of the storm, with Poland considering which of the five separate legal systems once imposed on its territory would be consulted for developing the Polish criminal code. His studied under Wacław Makowski and worked on the legal commentary to the 1932 Criminal Code with the Supreme Court prosecutor Jerzy Nisenson.[47] It would have been an exciting time to work with such illustrious figures. Wacław Makowski (1880–1942) himself was a Polish politician, lawyer, and scientist. He was one of the authors of the 1932 Criminal Code and of the 1935 Polish Constitution, the so-called April Constitution. Makowski was interested in Soviet criminal law. In fact, he wrote the preface to the Soviet Penal Code (*Kodeks karny Rosji Sowieckiej*) of 1926. Makowski was interested in the connections between Soviet criminal law and the Italian school of positive law. In his work he located Soviet criminal law in Polish jurisprudence; developments in his thinking were cut short by the outbreak of the Second World War.[48] Makowski's background, writings, and time as Minister of Justice that shaped the inter-war Polish leader Josef Piłsudski's arguably authoritarian 'Sanacja' government and the 1935 Polish Constitution would later form the basis of charges against Siewierski.[49] Siewierski managed to complete his PhD in 1948 in Poznań in a very different political climate.

Siewierski was a talented legal academic and prosecutor of the Supreme Court, as well as the SNT. This was acknowledged by his mentors and in the nominations and postings noted above. His solid knowledge of the German language and German law made him the ideal candidate for the SNT legal team. He played a prosecutorial role in six trials at the SNT. In 1946 he acted as a prosecutor in the trial of Arthur Greiser. He is pictured at that trial in Figure 5.12. As lead prosecutor in the Amon Göth trial, Siewierski identified the Jewish victim in their speeches.[50] They also knew

46 Romanowska, 'Procesy karne przeciwko dr. Mieczysławowi Siewierskiemu', 99–130.

47 Romanowska, 'Procesy karne przeciwko dr. Mieczysławowi Siewierskiemu', 99–130, 108. Also Tomasz Grzegorczyk, 'Mieczysław Siewierski (1900–1981)', in Agnieszka Liszewska and Anna Pikulska-Radomska (eds), *70 Lat Wydziału Prawa i Administracji Uniwersytetu Łódzkiego* [Seventy Years of the Faculty of Law and Administration at the University of Łódź] (University of Łódź Press 2015), 173–175, 173.

48 Romanowska, 'Procesy karne przeciwko dr. Mieczysławowi Siewierskiemu'.

49 'Sanacja' refers to the 'moral healing' of the government undertaken by General Jósef Piłsudski when he staged a successful coup in May 1926. The Constitution that was promulgated during Piłsudski's rule is authoritarian in nature in that it grants excessive power to executive. See Grzegorz M. Kowalski, 'The Amendment of August 1926 to the first Polish Constitution of the Second Republic*', (2014) 7 (2) *Krakowskie Studia z Historii Państwa i Prawa*, 317–322.

50 Michael J. Bazyler and Frank Tuerkheimer, *The Forgotten Trials of the Holocaust* (New York University Press 2014) 103.

that any Polish extradition request made to pursue war crimes charges domestically would rely on evidence of proceedings adhering to due process principles.[51] The SNT trials did so, as many observers, several from Nuremberg, attested.

Siewierski was accused of participating in the 'fascistisation' of Poland in violation of Article 1(b) of the Decree of 22 January 1946 concerning the defeat of the Poland in September and the 'fascistisation' of public life, and also for collaborating with the Gestapo in violation of Article 2 of the 1944 August Decree.[52] The former charge was based on his prosecutorial responsibilities at the Supreme Court in Warsaw, and his connections with Makowski and Nisenson. Because of his senior post, it was alleged that he actively took part in the 'Sanacja' campaign to purge communists from the Piłsudski government. Moreover, during the Second World War, Siewierski was a member of the London-based Government (where he was working on how to bring war criminals to justice): both these activities were deemed to be in violation of the 1946 Decree as 'fascistising' public life.[53] In contrast to the transparency of the SNT trials that he had been a part of, Siewierski was charged in a secret criminal legal process. These charges were based on key provisions of the 1944 August Decree that were used to charge war criminals brought before the SNT. The 1944 August and 1946 January Decrees eliminated the principle of *lex retro non agit* by criminalising actions from the pre-war period. The term 'fascistisation' was extended to state officials, putting them on equal footing as nazi war criminals.[54] The evidence for the second charge was tenuous.[55] The 1946 January Decree provided authorities with the power to hold Siewierski without charge. Moreover, control of the case was in the hands of the state security, rather than the SNT.[56] As noted above, the prosecutor was under the radar of the authorities: Jakub Berman, in charge of the state security apparatus at the Ministry of Public Security, had sought to arrest Siewierski for some time; surveillance of the lawyer for the duration of his time as part of the SNT legal team was put in place. This move coincided with the general approach towards former members of the Polish resistance. As mentioned above, the

51 Dieter Schenk, *Albert Forster: Gdański namiestnik Hitlera: Zbrodnie hitlerowskie we Gdańsku i Prusach Zachodnich* [Hitlerite Crimes in Gdańsk and Western Prussia] (Polnord 2002).

52 Mark A. Drumbl, 'The Supreme National Tribunal of Poland and the History of International Criminal Law', in Morten Bergsmo, Wui Ling Cheah, and Ping Yi (eds), *Historical Origins of International Criminal Law: Volume 2* (Torkel Opsahl Academic EPublisher 2014) 563–602, 580.

53 Romanowska, 'Procesy karne przeciwko dr. Mieczysławowi Siewierskiemu', 108, 119.

54 Romanowska, 'Procesy karne przeciwko dr. Mieczysławowi Siewierskiemu', 103.

55 Romanowska, 'Procesy karne przeciwko dr. Mieczysławowi Siewierskiemu', 114–115.

56 Romanowska, 'Procesy karne przeciwko dr. Mieczysławowi Siewierskiemu', 113–114.

main purpose of establishing the secret section in the courts was to eliminate political opposition, that is members of the Polish underground. The use of the term 'fascism' equated pre-war lawyers with so-called Hitlerites. The most flagrant example of this was the trial of Fieldorf and other members of the Polish Home Army,[57] or the journalist and writer Kazimierz Moczarski. Siewierski was imprisoned in the same cell that Forster had occupied.[58] There are no images of Siewierski's own trial.

Siewierski knew that he could be facing a capital sentence. He embarked on appealing the charges, arguing that he was loyal to the Polish People's Republic and did not falter in his commitment to its cause and mission to rebuild the country. 'I fully appreciate the good brought to society by the new state system and the great prospects for the future of the state on the way to socialism, then in socialism already implemented on the basis of the Soviet experience'.[59] He never admitted to the charges. He maintained that between 1926 and 1939 he had undertaken several key positions within the government, with the support of the Polish authorities at the time, because of his experience and professionalism. In his lengthy testimony, Siewierski notes his commitment to prosecuting war crimes, a role that the People's Republic provided him and one that demonstrates his loyalty as well as his awareness of and dedication to the legal approaches now tied to new ways of political and economic thinking.[60] Despite the lack of evidence, the prosecutor recommended five years' imprisonment that was extended to six years by the Supreme Court. In July 1951, after Siewierski's arrest that June, the sister of the Russian revolutionary Feliks Dzerzhinsky appealed to Polish President Bolesław Bierut to close the case against Siewierski, offering strong support of his character and his loyalty to the People's Republic: the appeal was ignored.[61] Amnesty laws reduced the sentence, and with Stalin's death in 1953, after a long wait Siewierski was released and rehabilitated, but not before facing new charges based on connections with members of the Home Army. In 1956, the events of Polish October, also known as the Polish thaw or Gomułka's thaw (after the Polish leader), marked temporary political change, and he was exonerated and fully rehabilitated. After that, he devoted his life to scholarly and research activity, and for years he remained a

57 See Stanisław Marat and Jacek Snopkiewicz, *Zbrodnia, sprawa generala Fieldorfa – 'Nila'* [A Crime, The Case of General Fieldorf – 'Nil'] (Warsaw 1989), as quoted in Piekarska, 'Naruszanie zasady jawności w "sadach tajnych"', 26, n. 1.

58 Joanna Lubecka, 'German Crimes Tried in Poland', in Magnus Brechtken, Władysław Bułhak, and Jürgen Zarusky (eds), *Political and Transitional Justice in Germany, Poland and the Soviet Union in the 1930s and 1950s* (Wallstein Verlag 2019) 210–238, 229. Also Finder and Prusin, *Justice Behind the Iron Curtain*, 130.

59 Romanowska, 'Procesy karne przeciwko dr. Mieczysławowi Siewierskiemu', 113.

60 IPN, fond BU 0259/584, 77.

61 Romanowska, 'Procesy karne przeciwko dr. Mieczysławowi Siewierskiemu', 122.

university professor of criminal law and published extensively on the subject. Siewierski died on 9 October 1981.

The image of Siewierski contains key narratives that all tie into the main questions that arise in this monograph's analysis of images of show trials in Poland. The discussion in this chapter took a sideways look at trial proceedings that do not entirely fit with the previous two case studies. It has done so to illuminate the power of the image and the contention that new histories continue to emerge about the law, legal propaganda, and nature of justice in the aftermath of the Second World War. Show trials needed to operate alongside political trials to fulfil the criteria of speaking legally, which was and continues to be a contentious question.

Siewierski's experience is a vivid example of the dual nature of the Polish dispensation of justice discussed in this chapter. His case also picks up on the point of legitimation in that the life account is one that supports the claim that the law is not linear, but one that oscillates between the past and the future, and takes time to move sideways as well.[62] This oscillation can also occur between the types of trials, whether public or secret, a point driven home by Hodos,[63] who understood the value of the word of mouth in relation to the clandestine kangaroo court, which fed into a sort of visual legal propaganda. Siewierski is not yet fully visible in the international criminal law timeline; yet the Forster trial appears in the *Law Reports*.[64] The alignment with the jurisprudence at Nuremberg is evident. The Forster case continued the SNT position with respect to the responsibility of higher officials and members of a criminal organisation.[65] Forster's position and membership of a criminal group made him responsible for the crime against peace. The SNT found that the occupation and annexation of the Free City of Danzig (Gdańsk) from Poland was the result of lawlessness aggression that was a separate act of aggression and violation of international law when it was illegally incorporated into the Reich.[66] The Forster case identified actions that Siewierski argued were 'comparable to Teutonic crimes'[67] that would later make their way into the UN Convention on the Prevention and Punishment of Genocide, such as the forcibly transferring children to the Third Reich, now found in Article 2 on the Convention. In the prosecutor's view, the 'most primitive, brutal, and glaring

62 Simpson, *Law, War and Crime*.
63 Hodos, *Show Trials*.
64 It also was noted by the International Criminal Tribunal for the Former Yugoslavis in *Krstic*. See Mark A. Drumbl, 'Germans Are the Lords and Poles Are the Servants: The Trial of Artur Greiser in Poland, 1946', in Kevin Heller and Gerry Simpson (eds), *Hidden Histories of War Crimes Trials* (Oxford University Press 2013) 411–429.
65 Grzebyk, 'The Role of the Polish Supreme National Tribunal', 614.
66 Grzebyk, 'The Role of the Polish Supreme National Tribunal', 619.
67 Trial transcript of the Albert Forster trial, 5–6 April 1948, National Archives of Gdańsk, Fond 2384, No. 2311, 23. I thank Julia Reynolds for her assistance in obtaining these materials.

actions were those taken against children'.[68] He described how these children were taken to the Reich to be raised as Germans.[69] The total ban on speaking Polish was identified as one part of the nazi policy to destroy Polish cultural life.[70] As in the *Greiser* case, the prosecutorial position highlighted plan to exterminate Jews and the brutal policy of germanisation that was imposed.[71] During the *Forster* trial, Siewierski indicated that '[m]orality does not permit me to prosecute someone on the grounds that they are German … I prosecute them because they committed a crime'.[72] These are a few examples of how Siewierski and his team were part of the development of these crimes within the wider international criminal legal timeframe.

As noted above, early on Siewierski embraced his dream to pursue legal innovation. He survived the war and sought to continue his legal career. This hope was alluded to at the Forster trial when he noted how 'we are all parties in this process … that sees law as a way to seek justice'.[73] In his own appeal, he somehow managed in extremely difficult circumstances to dig deep and draw on his legal knowledge to fight the charges against him. Siewierski's story is the story of others who were the 'enemy' as seen through the 1944 August Decree. In this discussion, in contrast to the images of Kokalari's trial in Albania and Benjamin presiding over trials in East Germany, this image is not of Siewierski on trial is not visible. The chapter discusses these narratives of invisible show trials via the depiction of this particular prosecutor at the trial proceedings of one of the most important trials of the post-Second World War period.

Concluding Remarks

This chapter has discussed law, visual culture, and the show trial in Poland. It has demonstrated that Soviet visual culture shaped the programme of legal

68 Trial transcript of the Albert Forster trial, 5–6 April 1948, National Archives of Gdańsk, Fond 2384, No. 2311, 26.

69 Trial transcript of the Albert Forster trial, 5–6 April 1948, National Archives of Gdańsk, Fond 2384, No. 2311, 26.

70 Trial transcript of the Albert Forster trial, 5–6 April 1948, National Archives of Gdańsk, Fond 2384, No. 2311, 29.

71 Drumbl engages with Catherine Epstein's work, *The Model Nazi: Arthur Greiser and the Occupation of Western Poland* (Oxford University Press 2010) on Greiser to show deficiencies in the prosecution's case against Greiser because the SNT ignored the tension and rivalry between the two defendants when they were in charge of Danzig (Gdańsk). Drumbl, 'Germans Are the Lords and Poles Are the Servants: The Trial of Artur Greiser in Poland, 1946', 411–429.

72 Elżbieta Romanowska, 'Procesy karne przeciwsko Mieczysławowi Siewierskiemu (1950–1956)' [Criminal Proceedings Carried Out against Mieczysław Siewierski (1950–1956)], *Witryna Historyczna* blog, 3 February 2021, https://www.witrynahistoryczna.pl/artykuly/prokurator-z-pasja-procesy-karne-przeciwko-mieczyslawowi-siewierskiemu-1950-1956/ (last accessed 6 November 2022).

73 Trial transcript of the Albert Forster trial, 5–6 April 1948, National Archives of Gdańsk, Fond 2384, No. 2311, 35.

propaganda in the country, with the assistance of Soviet 'teachers', and while keeping a vigilant eye on the judiciary. The images considered in the Polish experience focus on the symbols of justice, including the judge, who in this case can represent both the hero and the villain while not disrupting the narrative about justice. I assert that visual footage is a source of data that works alongside legal sources. An examination of archival materials that to date have not been widely disseminated and/or analysed will yield vital information about lesser-known lawyers and the law at a critical juncture in history – in the immediate aftermath of the Second World War and at a time when a reassessment of international criminal law and justice was widely debated, even internally in certain formats when cross-border discussions were controlled.[74] As Moran argues, 'judges are too important to be ignored or treated as trivial objects to be briefly glanced at then passed over'.[75] An examination of the lawyers in the Polish case study shows a common denominator in the form of justice, and an exploration set out in a concentric discussion follows the path that its dispensation takes. Its manifestation possesses a sentient quality.

Moreover, the images are affective and carry an important non-verbal meaning that amplifies the relevance of the account of the trials and their participants. A study of visual imagery of these proceedings will inform a better understanding of the role certain actors played in the advancement of international criminal law and the significance of war crimes trials in general. The Polish contribution to the development of legal principles, in international criminal law for example, such as the prosecution and punishment of genocide, lacks study. We can learn much more about the development of the law and show trials, political trials, and international proceedings. More recently, legal academics and legal historians have written about the individuals behind specific legal principles.[76]

The connection between law and visual culture is amplified in war crimes trials because of the subject matter and its emotive dimension, making such trials high-value events where authorities can reinsert their message about law and justice via performativity. The images contain information about the nature of the dispensation of justice; use of trial coverage as a pedagogical tool concerning the ideological context as much as to reinforce the anti-fascist narrative; and law and order or, in other words, control.

The Polish case study offers a different record that emanates from its visual account of the administration of justice. It also challenges the way the show trial is understood, but in relation to two different kinds of trials which come together at the source of law: the 1944 August Decree. In the series of

74 Agata Fijalkowski, '"Tadeusz Cyprian" Photographer and War Crimes Lawyer' (2021) 15(1) *Law and Humanities* 47–83.

75 Leslie J. Moran, *Law, Visual Culture and Judges* (Routledge 2021) 1.

76 Philippe Sands, *East-West Street: On the Origins of Genocide and Crimes Against Humanity* (Weidenfeld and Nicolson 2016) and Hirsch, *Soviet Judgment at Nuremberg*.

relationships that transpires between law and politics, local justice and reckoning, individual responsibility and collective guilt, and making history and performing justice, it is the notion of legitimation that illuminates the fine line between hero and villain. The discussion of the lawyer and prosecutor Mieczysław Siewierski addresses the pertinent problem of discerning the legal historical narratives that his life account represents. More specifically, Siewierski's account can be located with the context of the sentient power emanating from the image. The sensory experience underpins the power of the subject matter and ability for image makers and brokers to control its dissemination.

Conclusion

The consideration in this monograph demonstrates how law and visual culture are partners in an enactment of performativity. Law and images work together to speak through a sensory experience that comes from looking at the enactment of the law. The images reflect normative values and the world around us. As such, law and visual culture are best understood within a social and cultural context. Just as the images are made and disseminated according to stakeholders, their material and cultural dimensions are something that repeatedly challenge our understanding of history. To reach this understanding, we have drawn on the works of, *inter alia*, Barthes, Didi-Huberman, Benjamin, and Cassiday. In this final reflection, it is worthwhile also to look at the work of Desmond Manderson, Chiara Bottici, and Peter Goodrich.

Manderson points out that 'law is making a claim not just through the images but *about* the images, about the legal system's relationship to light and vision, the coming together of its power to illuminate and the illumination of its power'.[1] The force of law through image is amplified through our negotiation of the space in between the individual and social imagination, which Chiara Bottici refers to as 'imaginal'.[2] For Bottici, the imaginal acknowledges the potential that images have to 'communicate ideas and norms, to frame experiences, to constitute relations, to generate the emotions that construct the world we live in'.[3] Legal discourse functions no differently to political discourse, in that images, in addition to being conceptual, are physical and 'possess vital discursive functions that organise normative, aesthetic and legal structures' – a sort of 'living presence'.[4]

Peter Goodrich builds on Bottici's work to discuss 'imaginal law' and identify and locate law's social presence in art, which informs and changes our understanding of juridical practice. This book reinforces the point that law is not a

1 Desmond Manderson (ed.), *Law and the Visual: Representations, Technologies and Critique* (University of Toronto 2018) 5, emphasis in original.
2 Chiara Bottici, *Imaginal Politics* (Columbia University Press 2019).
3 Manderson, *Law and the Visual*, 5.
4 Manderson, *Law and the Visual*, 5.

DOI: 10.4324/9781003405771-7

singular discipline. These works see law's presence all around us; they emphasise that law does not work in a vacuum and that it engages in a dynamic process of imprinting, transforming, and mutating. Bringing law that is at the margins into the light opens possibilities regarding discourses about its presence, as well as its negative and positive effects on our lives and more broadly with respect to justice. It is silent and it is affective.

Chapter 1 addressed Stalinist justice in Central and Eastern Europe in relation key themes relating to the way in which the image irrupts in the three case studies addressed in this monograph. In all the case studies the concept of crime was reworked to conform with the prevailing Soviet legal thinking of the period, which attempted to rework notions of crime and guilt according to wider European discourses of the period. As the thinking progressed, respective amendments were made to criminal code provisions. Importantly, social danger replaced crime, and this opened a broader remit with respect to what could be considered a social danger. This was done in the interest of the working class. In each case study, the law operated as a weapon, visually and physically, as well as a pedagogical lesson, also visually and physically. Both had their roots in the Soviet model.

Chapter 2 explored the way that images can be regarded as a powerful tool both of propaganda and of political justice in the Soviet context. Before the camera became the preferred medium to visually record social and political change, political justice was performed on stage, and later on screen. Visualising law is understood here to include the agitation trials under the rule of Lenin (1917–1924) and of Stalin (1924–1953), and the role of photography in Soviet Russia. While each case study had its own experience with photography and how it was used in legal propaganda, the Soviet model guided the way it was operationalised during this period, allowing for a few particularities to emerge, namely in the photographer's technique showing a distinct feature and brand. Manderson's position on law's reach from within and as part of an image attests to its performative power.[5] The characterisation of the judge in theatre performances changed as the aims of the legal project were reconsidered by the drafters of the law. So, instead of devolution, law played an even more prominent role in public and private life. The pace of its development complemented that of the theatre, which also altered its approach when playwrights and film directors opted for a return to the religious origins of a Greek drama because it was found to be the most effective means to achieve social change.[6]

Chapter 3 established that the Albanian case study is one of affect: the images are captivating. The viewer is drawn to a certain aesthetic in the photograph.[7]

5 Manderson, *Law and the Visual*, 5.

6 Julie A. Cassiday, *The Enemy on Trial: Early Soviet Courts on Stage and Screen* (Northern Illinois University Press 2000) 9.

7 Alison Young, 'From Object to Encounter: Aesthetic Politics and Visual Criminology' (2014) 18(2) *Theoretical Criminology* 159–175; *The Scene of Violence: Cinema,*

As the discussion showed, this was in large part owing to the image makers' pre-war training as apprentices in well-known studios. Albania has been considered the 'photographer's state' for good reason. Several photographers who trained at the Marubi Studio and elsewhere in Albania and abroad, and who survived the Second World War, found work at ATA. It would be hard for them to ignore these experiences or change the way in which they carried out their craft when covering the show trials; their skills were not set aside even during the personal encounter with the subject of the photograph.[8] The photographs are also powerful because of the venues where justice was dispensed: these places served as both movie theatres and courtrooms and their space provided room for a large audience. One of the key venues serves as a wider consideration of the temporarily of image: one-time governor and spectator Jacomoni, pictured attending the Rex Cinema, which was later used as a courtroom, was later tried as a war criminal in Italy. ATA photographers also captured the spectators' faces and reactions to court proceedings. Finally, the photographs are compelling because of the subject matter itself, which naturally gives rise to questions centring on the fate of the defendant. Through the image of the writer Musine Kokalari, we are drawn to the figure and question her appearance, and why she is dressed as she is, and why she is standing in front of a large microphone; we unravel her life, her transgressions, and the longevity of her story, all because of the image and her expression in it. The photograph of Kokalari is an excellent example of how to manoeuvre the space between the *punctum* and the irruption. It is not only her photograph's *punctum* but also the reproduction of her image that continues to shape relevant discourses that point to a trace of history waiting to be identified during the process of its reproduction, dissemination, and consumption. Control over our knowledge of Kokalari's fate continues on the part of the Albanian political elite, including in respect of exhibitions at the national museum and historical institutes dedicated to the memory of communism and political crimes, such as the Institute for the Study of Communist Crimes and Consequences in Albania; the result of which is that accountability for the maladministration of justice has not been realised, and her life story continues to be manipulated, consumed, and appropriated, as if in a vicious cycle. This process is driven by her own image because the space between the individual and social imagination has permitted it to control the legal historical narrative rather than mediate the discourse.[9]

Chapter 4 also saw how the driving force underpinning the law's *punctum* and its irruption in the East German case study illustrates the performance of

Crime, Affect (Routledge Cavendish 2009); *Judging the Image: Art, Value, Law* (Routledge 2005).

8 Maria Elander, 'Images of Victims: The ECCC and the Cambodian Genocide Museum', in Desmond Manderson (ed.), *Law and the Visual: Representations, Technologies and Critique* (University of Toronto 2018) 210–228, 215.

9 Bottici, *Imaginal Politics*, 1–11; Peter Goodrich, 'Vision and Decision'.

education and throttling during the trial proceedings, so effectively captured in the images. Its central figure, the judge, was the official chiefly responsible for meting out punishment against counter-revolutionaries and political opponents. The net was cast wide and it succeeded in capturing substantial numbers of people accused of anti-state activities. The image breaks the superficial reading of Hilde Benjamin's life and the East German legal account. Through the image of Benjamin, again we are drawn to the figure, her life, her transgressions, and her life story, all because of the image. Benjamin's image is reproduced along with the simple, linear narrative of 'Bloody Hilde' at the centre of a narrative concerning an East German legal system that was described as repressive and one that was not able to contribute to the development of the law in the correct way, as compared to its West German counterpart. Benjamin, too, can be released when her contribution to German law is discussed as part of a wider German legal historical discourse. The way in which the viewer visualises law when looking at her image might alter as this change will accommodate the wider context of the social change that gripped East Germany. At the same time, while she was an important part of the repressive nature of the judicial system, it is vital to recognise her life account as complex.

Chapter 5 showed how Poland offered a different record that emanates from its visual account of the administration of justice. It also challenges the way the show trial is understood, but in relation to what kinds of trials? After all, not are all trials political? For Gerry Simpson,[10] in his study of international criminal justice and war crimes trials, it is vital to identify international criminal justice, and within this war crimes trials, as a series of relationships, first, between law and politics, local justice and reckoning, individual responsibility and collective guilt, and making history and performing justice. In making the case, Simpson expands his claims to include the notion of legitimation, in other words that of the guilt of the defendant, and at the same time the innocence of the prosecuting authorities. The discussion of Siewierski addressed the pertinent problem of what the image is the history of, and its physical power and ability to contribute to a better-informed discourse about Poland's role in shaping the international criminal law timeline, and efforts to define war crimes understood broadly and to apply it to specific cases. More specifically Siewierski's account asks the reader and viewer to reflect upon the law's potential as well as its limits.

The three case studies, including the Soviet experience, are better informed when set in their specific social and cultural contexts. Three questions arise in relation to common themes and diverging narratives, which relate to (1) the life story and law's performative power; (2) 'speaking legally' and visual literacy; and (3) dispensation of justice during this period.

10 Gerry Simpson, *Law, War and Crime: War Crimes Trials and the Reinvention of International Law* (Polity 2007).

The Life Story

Two of the three protagonists in the respective chapters are women, and all three are hero/villain. There is a risk of appropriation in all instances. As noted in Chapters 3 and 4, there is another aspect to performativity that concerns discovery. The narrative of discovery refers to mentioning names that have been hitherto unknown to the wider world, either because they have been overlooked or only recently rediscovered. As Katie da Kuhna Lewin points out, this has occurred recently with respect to feminist projects.[11] The presentation of the accounts of women are superficial and often maintain the dominant status quo rather than challenge or require further engagement with the individual and her remarkable account.[12] Kokalari is not the first Albanian pre-communist female writer or pioneer against a patriarchal society, one that Kokalari knew very well. Kokalari is not the first female to be put on trial, as we have seen. It is important to engage with her story and bear in mind that hers is a repeated story, one of promise and tragedy. At the same time so much more can be done in terms of engaging with her key works, which to date have not been translated into English. A wider perspective and appreciation of the female project will benefit the way we deploy aesthetics and search to look more critically at affective justice and the politics of visualising justice, especially an image like that of Kokalari.

Similarly, Benjamin's account calls for further engagement. As researchers we can remind readers about the repressive nature of the East German legal system, but also remind them of a more comprehensive account of legal developments within social and cultural contexts. It becomes far too easy to romanticise Benjamin's biography and sensationalise it by referring to her tactics on the bench as a judge as 'bloody'. Mieczysław Siewierski similarly runs the risk of appropriation. But this is more to do with the way that the Polish dispensation of justice during this period is understood by a wider audience; there is much more to investigate as regards this question in relation to individual lawyers and the development of law, nationally and internationally. Siewierski played a key role in the legitimation of dominant political forces and he paid a high price for this: 'The legitimation effect of trial tends to be a less well-advertised function of war crimes trials but it accounts for at least part of the enthusiasm for such trials'.[13] In Siewierski's case, Polish authorities try 'not only to illuminate the past but also to justify the present'.[14] The three life stories can be viewed via Manderson's approach to images in transition. There is the image of history

11 Katie de Kuhna Lewin, 'Discover the Untold Stories of the Pre-Raphaelite Sisters: The Politics of Discovery', (2019) LARB, 17 August 2020, https://lareviewofbooks.org/article/the-politics-of-rediscovery/ (accessed 26 July 2022).

12 See Sarah Ahmed, 'Institutional as Usual', Blog, 24 October 2017, https://feministkilljoys.com/2017/10/24/institutional-as-usual/ (accessed 15 July 2022).

13 Simpson, *Law, War and Crime*, 91.

14 Simpson, *Law, War and Crime*, 91.

that provides us with both a way of seeing and overlooking, and the image in history that refers to the physical force of visualisation.[15] How these images are made visible will shape history. Consider the representation of Kokalari in the broadsheets, later reproduced in post-communist narratives. Equally think about the post-communist narratives about Benjamin and Siewierski: their stories live at the edge of the (legal) historical discourses.

'Speaking Legally' and How to Understand Visual Meaning

These skills are acquired through culture and materiality of artefacts. Space in the Albanian case study evidences the way that narratives cut across time, starting with the Rex Cinema as a venue to celebrate fascist Italy's gift to Tirana, which is then turned into an anti-fascist push that involved trials of innocent people. These narratives are reconciled as slices of time for present-day consumers of the venue. The law, in the way it is reproduced in images, is also consumed, and refashioned to suit present-day state perspectives on communist rule in Albania, and which acknowledge the maladministration of justice but do little to achieve justice. What is seen in the photographs of the 'Genocide of the Intellectual' is the 'material product of a material apparatus set to work in a specific context'[16] to keep the law out, or at least contained. Kokalari's image, for example, is part of this discourse. Yet there is little information (or confrontation with the image) conveyed with respect to what makes her an intellectual, and why she should be considered as part of the discourse. As a result other stories, of Kokalari's contemporaries, are refused entry into the discourse. As her case shows, the fate of intellectuals was inconsistent: some were executed, others imprisoned, with arbitrary imposition of punishment a characteristic of the regime. As noted above, a more substantial account would show that society (and a wider audience) were denied access to her writings, as the authorities banned her from pursuing a writing career. The harshness of her sentence is but one example of the fate of intellectuals during this time. Kokalari was part of the political opposition; the enemy would soon be another segment of society, such as scientists, priests, and engineers. The irruption in her image, for example, is evidence of intellectual life at a time the country was struggling with its nascent statehood and internal political conflicts.

The narrative concerning Benjamin is similarly controlled in Germany. Benjamin became a lawyer when very few women entered the legal profession. The Second World War interrupted the pace of progressive thinking. Attitudes that were not tolerant of women in such positions remained after the war.

15 Shane Chalmers, 'The Visual Force of Justice in the Making of Liberia', in Desmond Manderson (ed.), *Law and the Visual: Representations, Technologies and Critique* (University of Toronto 2018) 141–157, 142.

16 John Tagg, *The Burden of Representation: Essays on Photographies and Histories* (Macmillan 1988), 3–4.

Benjamin answered these challenges formidably. In Poland, the visual literacy of the domestic trials is now being considered, to learn more about the people who were shaping international criminal law at that time. Siewierski is yet another example of a survivor responding to internal politics in a formidable fashion. In all three cases there exists a tension between the internal and state narratives and even wider global discourses.

Dispensation of Justice during This Period

Researchers continue their work on communist rule and Stalinist justice, and studies show that there is much more to say about this period and the nature of law and justice. Interdisciplinary work is an important step forward to gaining a better understanding of the period. Concerning law, reaching out to non-legal sources is a vital step away from doctrinal approaches that are rooted in binary narratives. It is a bold and natural step when visual culture becomes part of the framework; it offers up a fresh way to look at ongoing discourses. Throughout this discussion, Walter Benjamin's position that history is incomplete rings true in all three case studies. The wider context of visual epistemology lends support to this contention.

In all three examples it was demonstrated that the Soviet model provided the blueprint for the law and the show trial framework. Soviet (and Yugoslav, in the Albanian case) instructors assisted in the setting-up and operationalisation of these trials. Owing to the size of the country and networks, more could be considered in the Albanian context, including details of the backgrounds of the photographers and the venues. In all three cases none of the protagonists have been treated in great depth in the English language. Each had a role to play in the development of their country's legal system and show trial discourses; all three shaped these discourses.

This was possible because of the aesthetic underpinning a trial. As Cassiday notes, the fact that theatre is tied to a public trial after the Soviet Revolution is no accident; they were both part of the larger modernist project that not only commented on life but also worked to reform, redirect, and revolutionise it.[17] The melodrama of the almost near conversion of the defendant was almost embedded in the show trial, with the confession and *samokritika* as key components, because it was both affective and effective. At the same time, Cassidy notes that a point has been missed by writers on Soviet jurisprudence and show trials, namely that the fusion of law and drama goes back to Ancient Greece, when law courts and theatre evolved together.[18] In Soviet Russia, rather than continue on the path to devolving the law and replacing it with political ideology, moves were made to make the bond between law and drama closer, in order to 'effect the greatest social change possible'.[19] The bond between law

17 Cassiday, *The Enemy on Trial*, 5–6.
18 Cassiday, *The Enemy on Trial*, 8.
19 Cassiday, *The Enemy on Trial*, 9.

and drama has always been there, and never went away. It only comes to the public eye in high-profile domestic and international trials, but it is always there. Soviet prosecutors at Nuremberg displayed the kind of rhetoric referred to by Cassiday,[20] a point noted by the Polish delegation observing their speeches.[21] The reliance on the relationship between law and drama served the wider purpose of taking part in the longer-term political project. In the photograph the ambition and the tragedy are played out at the same time.

In this book's case studies we see how the 'law of and in the image' can hide and expose questions of legitimation and authority[22] pertaining to Stalinist rule and how we view defendants, judges, prosecutors, and justice. How these are viewed are connected to the emotive responses at viewing the images, which disturbs as we do not know how to answer what the image wants. Moreover, viewing might involve setting aside our sovereignty and surrendering, inviting an emotive response to look at some images that possesses a form of rhythmic organisation. Visualising law is an active process that can catalyse a conversation about *punctum* and/or an irruption. But it is more than this. The notion of imaginal law is useful. Bottici's work shows how views about what comprises justice and its dispensation is an individual and collective process.

The question remains as to what the image wants. Visualising law in this way requires extra-legal sources and analysis to reveal the nuances of a question that has been well researched but in which there is still much to discover about key players, case law, and critiques of current international legal criminal frameworks, as well as a better recognition of legal biographies that make for a richer history about law under communism. It is neither here nor there; we are in between the spectacle and the frame, which our unconscious reaches out to and connects with; we see, we look, and we try to understand the image's meaning. The sensory experience of its effect is felt long after we have viewed it.

20 Cassiday, *The Enemy on Trial*, 8.
21 Tadeusz Cyprian and Jerzy Sawicki, *Nuremberg in Retrospect: People and Issues of the Trial* (Western Press Agency 1967), 79–132.
22 Manderson, *Law and the Visual*, 5.

Bibliography

Ahmed, Sarah, 'Institutional as Usual', Blog, 24 October 2017, https://feministkilljoys.com/2017/10/24/institutional-as-usual/

Aksenova, Marina, 'Symposium on Art, Aesthetics, and International Justice' (2020) 114 *AJIL Unbound* 103–107

'Albania: History and Background', *Education Encyclopedia*, https://education.stateuniversity.com/pages/10/Albania-HISTORY-BACKGROUND.html

Alexopoulos, Golfo, 'Stalin and the Politics of Kinship: Practices on Collective Punishment, 1920s–1940s' (2008) 50(1) *Comparative Studies in Societies and History* 91–117

Aliko, Tomor, *Genocide of the Intellectual Elite of the Albanian Nation under the Communist Terror* (Shtypur ne Shtypshkronjen 'Maluka' 2007)

Ambler, Eric, *Judgment on Deltchev* (Hodder and Stoughton 1952)

Ankori, Gannit, *Frida Kahlo* (Reaktion Books 2018)

Anon, 'Abolition of the Independence of the Courts', in *Injustice the Regime: Documentary Evidence of the Systematic Violation of Legal Rights in the Soviet Occupied Territory of Germany* (Federal Ministry for All-German Affairs 1952)

Arendt, Hannah, *Eichmann in Jerusalem: A Report on the Banality of Evil* (Penguin 1963)

Austin, Robert, 'Fan Noli, Albania and the Soviet Union' (1996) 30(2) *East European Quarterly* 153–169

Austin, Robert Clegg, *Founding a Balkan State: Albania's Experiment with Democracy* (University of Toronto Press 2012)

Austin, Robert C. and Jonathan Ellison, 'Albania', in Lavinia Stan (ed.), *Transitional Justice in Eastern Europe and the Former Soviet Union* (Routledge 2008) 176–199

Azoulay, Ariella, 'The Darkroom of History' (2005) 10(3) *Angelaki: Journal of the Theoretical Humanities* 57–77

Azoulay, Ariella, 'The Lethal Art of Portraiture' (2015) 8(2) *Photography and Culture* 213–226

Baade, Hans, 'Individual Responsibility', in Cyril E. Back and Richard A. Falk (eds), *The Future of the International Legal Order: The Structure of the International Environment*, Volume 4 (Princeton University Press 1972) 308–345

Barrett, Nina, *The Leopold and Loeb Files: An Intimate Look at One of America's Most Infamous Crimes* (Agate Publishing 2018)

Barthes, Roland, *Camera Lucida: Reflections on Photography* (tr. Richard E. Howard, Vintage 2000)

Baudrillard, Jean, *Simulacra and Simulation* (tr. Sheila Faria Glaser, University of Michigan Press 1994)

Bazyler, Michael J. and Frank Tuerkheimer, *The Forgotten Trials of the Holocaust* (New York University Press 2014)

Becker, Howard, 'Do Photographs Tell the Truth?', in T. Cook and C. Reichardt (eds), *Qualitative and Quantitative Methods in Evaluation Research* (Sage 1979) 99–117

Bedeni, Luçjan, 'Marubi Archive: Changing the History of Photography in Albania', *Post: Notes on Art in a Global Context*, 25 September 2019, https://post.moma.org/marubi-archive-changing-the-history-of-photography-in-albania/

Bell, Catherine, *Ritual: Perspectives and Dimensions* (Oxford University Press 1997)

Bell, Vikki, 'The Haunted Nomos: Activist-Artists and the (Im)possible Politics of Memory in Transitional Argentina' (2009) 52(2) *Cultural Politics* 149–178

Bell, Vikki, *The Art of Post-dictatorship: Ethics and Aesthetics in Transitional Argentina* (Routledge 2014)

Benjamin, Hilde, 'Uber die elterliche Gewalt' [On Parental Authority] (1949) 3(4) *Neue Justiz* 81–83

Benjamin, Hilde, 'Zum Dessauer Prozeß' (1950) 4(5) *Neue Justiz* 145–148

Benjamin, Hilde, 'Das Oberste Gericht des Deutschen Demokratischen Republik im Kampf gegen Spionage und Sabotage' [The Supreme Court of the German Democratic Republic in the Fight against Espionage and Sabotage] (1952) 6(6) *Neue Justiz* (1952) 222–245

Benjamin, Hilde, 'Über die Zusammenarbeit von Justiz und Presse' [On the Cooperation between the Judiciary and the Press] (1953) 7(19) *Neue Justiz* 605–606

Benjamin, Hilde, 'Einige Bemerkungen zum Entwurf eines Familiengesetzbuches' [Some Remarks on the Draft Family Code] (1954) 8(12) *Neue Justiz* 349–353

Benjamin, Hilde, 'Feierliches Gedenken von Andrej Januarjewitsch Wyshinski' [Solemn Commemoration of Andrei Janyevich Vyshinsky] (1954) 8 *Neue Justiz* 678

Benjamin, Hilde, 'Die Staatsverbrechen im Zusammenhang mit der wirtschaftlichen und politischen Entwicklung seit 1945' [State Crimes Concerning Economic and Political Development Since 1945] (1954) 8(2) *Neue Justiz* 35–37

Benjamin, Hilde, 'Leninische Prinzipien des Gerichts' [Lenin's Principles Concerning the Court] (1957) 11(21) *Neue Justiz* 673–674

Benjamin, Hilde, 'Who Has the Say in the Family?' (1 February 1958), in Volume 8, *Occupation and the Emergence of Two States, 1945–1961, Germany History in Documents and Images*, https://ghdi.ghi-dc.org/pdf/eng/Vol.8_Chap.18_Doc.11_ENG.pdf

Benjamin, Hilde and Ernst Melsheimer, 'Zehn Jahre demokratischer Justiz in Deutschland' [Ten Years of Democratic Justice in Germany] (1955) 9 *Neue Justiz* 259–266

Benjamin, Walter, 'The Work of Art in the Age of Mechanical Reproduction', in Walter Benjamin (ed.), *Illuminations* (tr. Harry Zohn, Fontana 1973) 219–253

Benjamin, Walter, 'On the Concept of History', in Walter Benjamin, *Selected Writings, Volume 4, 1938–1940* (tr. Howard Eiland and Kevin McLaughlin, Harvard University Press 1999) 389–400

Berger, John, *About Looking* (Bloomsbury 1980)

Berman, Harold J., 'Principles of Soviet Criminal Law' (1947) 56(5) *The Yale Law Journal* 803–836

Berman, Harold, 'Soviet Law Reform: Dateline Moscow 1957' (1957) 66(8) *Yale Law Journal* 1191–1215, 1212

Boobbyer, Phillip, *The Stalin Era* (Routledge 2000)

Bottici, Chiara, *Imaginal Politics* (Columbia University Press 2019)

Bloxham, Donald, 'Punishing German Soldiers during the Cold War: The Case of Erich von Manstein', *Patterns of Prejudice* 33 (1999), 25–45

Bowen, William J., James J. Duane, and Benson P. Fraser, 'Media Coverage and Public Opinion of the OJ Simpson Trial: Implications for the Criminal Justice System' (1997) 2(2) *Communication Law and Policy* 261–287

Brooks, Peter, *The Melodramatic Imagination: Balzac, Henry James, Melodrama, and the Mode of Excess* (Yale University Press 1976)

Browning, Christopher R., 'Adenauer's Bargain', *The New York Review of Books*, 22 December 2022, 69–70, https://www-pressreader-com.leedsbeckett.idm.oclc.org/usa/the-new-york-review-of-books/20221222/282123525515642/textview

Burke, Peter, *Eyewitnessing: The Uses of Images as Historical Evidence* (Reaktion Books 2001)

Butler, W E., 'Towards an Introduction to Russian Legal Theory' in *Russian Legal Theory* (Dartmouth 1996) xxxv–xxxvii

Butler-Kisber, Lynn, *Qualitative Inquiry: Thematic, Narrative and Arts-Informed Perspectives* (Sage 2010)

Caldwell, Peter C., *Dictatorship, State Planning, and Social Theory in the German Democratic Republic* (Cambridge University Press 2003)

Calvino, Italo, *The Castle of Crossed Destinies* (tr. William Weaver, Vintage 1998)

Cassiday, Julie A., *The Enemy on Trial: Early Soviet Courts on Stage and Screen* (Northern Illinois University Press 2000)

Chalmers, Shane, 'The Visual Force of Justice in the Making of Liberia', in Desmond Manderson (ed.), *Law and the Visual: Representations, Technologies and Critique* (University of Toronto 2018) 141–157

Chicherin, B., *A History of Political Theories* (5 vols, The Macmillan Company1877–1902)

Conquest, Robert, *Stalin: Breaker of Nations* (Penguin 1998)

'Conti Affair, Affäre Conti', https://second.wiki/wiki/affc3a4re_conti

Cover, Robert, 'The Folktales of Justice: Tales of Jurisdiction' (1984–1985) 14 *Capital University Law Review* 179–203, https://openyls.law.yale.edu/bitstream/handle/20.500.13051/2048/The_Folktales_of_Justice.pdf?sequence=2&isAllowed=y

Cyprian, Tadeusz and Jerzy Sawicki, *Nuremberg in Retrospect: People and Issues of the Trial* (Western Press Agency 1967)

Dallin, Alexander and George W. Breslauer, *Political Terror in Communist Systems* (Stanford University Press 1970)

Darnton, Robert, *The Great Cat Massacre* (Penguin 1984)

Dean Carolyn J., 'Atrocity Photographs, Dignity, and Human Vulnerability' (2015) 6(2) *Humanity: An International Journal of Human Rights, Humanitarianism, and Development* 239–264

Debord, Guy, *The Society of the Spectacle* (tr. Donald Nicholson-Smith, Black and Red 1970)

Decker, Stephanie K., 'The Role of Public Confessions in Show Trials: An Analysis of the Moscow Show Trials' (2019) 32(4) *Journal of Historical Sociology* 459–477

Didi-Hubermann Georges, *Confronting Images* (tr. John Goodman, Pennsylvania State University Press 2005)

Douzinas, Costas and Lynda Nead (eds), *Law and the Image: The Authority of Art and the Aesthetics of Law* (University of Chicago Press 1999)

Drumbl, Mark A., 'Germans Are the Lords and Poles Are the Servants: The Trial of Artur Greiser in Poland, 1946', in Kevin Heller and Gerry Simpson (eds), *Hidden Histories of War Crimes Trials* (Oxford University Press 2013) 411–429

Drumbl, Mark A., 'The Supreme National Tribunal of Poland and the History of International Criminal Law', in Morten Bergsmo, Wui Ling Cheah, and Ping Yi (eds), *Historical Origins of International Criminal Law:* Volume 2 (Torkel Opsahl Academic EPublisher 2014) 563–602

Du, Biyu, 'Staging Justice: Courtroom Semiotics and the Judicial Ideology in China' (2016) 29 *International Journal for the Semiotics of Law* 595–614

Duncanson, Kirsty and Emma Henderson (eds), *Courthouse Architecture, Design and Social Justice* (Routledge 2021)

Edwards, Elizabeth, 'Photography and the Material Performance of the Past' (2009) 48 *History and Theory* 130–150

Edwards, Steve, *Photography: A Very Short Introduction* (Oxford University Press 2006)

Eisert, Wolfgang, *The Waldheim Trials. The Stalinist Terror 1950. A Dark Chapter in the GDR Justice System* (Bechtle 1993)

Ekinci, Ekrem Buğra, 'The Abdullah Brothers: Pioneers of Photography in the Late Ottoman Period', *Daily Sabah*, 6May 2016, https://www.dailysabah.com/feature/2016/05/06/the-abdullah-brothers-pioneers-of-photography-in-the-late-ottoman-period

Elander, Maria, 'Images of Victims: The ECCC and the Cambodian Genocide Museum', in Desmond Manderson (ed.), *Law and the Visual: Representations, Technologies and Critique* (University of Toronto 2018) 210–228

Elsie, Robert, '1945: The Albanian Treason Trial', *Texts and Documents of Albanian History*, at http://www.albanianhistory.net/1945_Albanian-Treason-Trial/index.html

'The Epistemology of Visual Thinking in Mathematics', *The Stanford Encyclopedia of Philosophy* (19 February 2020) https://plato.stanford.edu/entries/epistemology-visual-thinking/

Epstein, Catherine, *The Model Nazi: Arthur Greiser and the Occupation of Western Poland* (Oxford University Press 2010)

Epstein, Catherine, 'The Politics of Biography: The Case of East German Old Communists' (1999) 128(2) *Daedulus* 1–30

Epstein, Catherine, 'The Production of "Official Memory" in East Germany: Old Communists and the Dilemma of Memoir-Writing' (1999) 32(2) *Central European History* 182–201

Fechner, Max, 'Stalin: der Kämpfer für den Frieden, der große Freund des Deutschen Volkes' [Stalin: The Fighter for Peace, the Great Friend of the German People] (1949) 3(12) *Neue Justiz* 297–299

Fehérváry, Krisztina, *Politics in Color and Concrete: Socialist Materialities and the Middle Class in Hungary* (Indiana University Press 2013)

Feinberg, Melissa, *Curtain of Lies: The Battle over Truth in Stalinist Eastern Europe* (Oxford University Press 2017)

Felman, Shoshana, 'Benjamin's Silence' (1999) 25(2) *Critical Inquiry* 201–234

Felman, Shoshana, 'Theaters of Justice: Arendt in Jerusalem, the Eichmann Trial, and the Redefinition of Legal Meaning in the Wake of the Holocaust' (2000) 1(2) *Theoretical Inquiries in Law* 466–507

Felman, Shoshana and Dori Laub, *Testimony: Crises of Witnessing in Literature, Psychoanalysis, and History* (Routledge 1992)

Ferrari, Sonia Campaner Miguel, 'Images beyond Representation: Evidence and Depth of Meaning', in Asun López-Varela Azcárate (ed.), *Mind and Matter* (Interchopen 2021)

Feth, Andrea, *Hilde Benjamin – Eine Biographie* (Arno Spitz 1997)

Feyertag, Karoline, 'The Art of Vision and the Ethics of the Gaze: On the Debate on Georges Didi-Humerman's Book *Images in Spite of All*, transversal texts (April 2008), https://transversal.at/transversal/0408/feyertag/en#_ftn17

Field, Hermann and Kate Field, *Trapped in the Cold War: The Ordeal of an American Family* (Stanford University Press 2002)

Figes, Orlando, *The Whisperers: Private Life in Stalinist Russia* (Picador 2007)

Fijalkowski, Agata, *From Old Times to New Europe: The Polish Struggle for Democracy and Constitutionalism* (Ashgate 2010)

Fijalkowski, Agata, 'Politics, Law and Justice in People's Poland: The Fieldorf File' (2014) 73(1) *Slavic Review* 85–107

Fijalkowski, Agata, 'Musine Kokalari and the Power of Images: Law, Aesthetics and Memory Regimes in the Albanian Experience' (2015) 28(3) *International Journal for the Semiotics of Law* 577–602

Fijalkowski, Agata, 'Law, Judges and Visual Culture' (2021) 15(2) *Law and Humanities* 300–305

Fijalkowski, Agata, '"Tadeusz Cyprian" Photographer and War Crimes Lawyer' (2021) 15(1) *Law and Humanities* 47–83

Fijalkowski, Agata and Sigrun Valderhaug, 'Legal Decisions, Affective Justice, and "Moving On"?' (2017) 7(2) *Oñati Socio-Legal Series* 337–364

Finder, Gabriel and Alexander Prusin, *Justice Behind the Iron Curtain: Nazis on Trial in Communist Poland* (University of Toronto Press 2018)

Fischer, Bernd J., *Albania 1943–1945: A View Through Western Documents* (Albanian Institute of International Studies 2014)

Fittipaldi, Edoardo and A. Javier Treviño (eds), *Leon Petrażycki: Law, Emotions, Society* (Routledge 2023)

Fitzpatrick, Sheila, *Everyday Stalinism: Ordinary Life in Extraordinary Times: Soviet Russia in the 1930s* (Oxford University Press 2000)

'For the Rule of Law', *Bulletin of the International Commission of Jurists* (1954), https://www.icj.org/wp-content/uploads/1955/03/ICJ-Bulletin-1-1954-eng.pdf

Foucault, Michel, 'Of Other Spaces: Utopias and Heterotopias' (tr. Jay Miskowiec) *Architecture/Mouvement/Continuité*, October 1984, https://web.mit.edu/allanmc/www/foucault1.pdf

Friedman, Jan, 'Interview with Nazi War Crimes Prosecutor: "I have never seen remorse"', *Spiegel Online International*, 10 May 2011, https://www.spiegel.de/international/germany/interview-with-nazi-war-crimes-prosecutor-i-have-never-seen-remorse-a-761639.html

Gami, Bavjola Shatro, 'A Stranger in Rome: Musine Kokalari and Her Memoir La mia vita universitaria in Twentieth Century Albanian Literature' (2022) 30(1) *Mediterranean Studies* 76–107

Ginsburg, Evgenia, *Journey into the Whirlwind* (Harcourt Brace 1975)

Ginzburg, Natalia and Alba de Céspedes, with an introduction by Ann Goldstein, 'On Women: An Exchange', *The New York Review of Books*, 22 December 2022, 55–57, https://www-pressreader-com.leedsbeckett.idm.oclc.org/search?query=ginzburg&newspapers=9khf&start=22%20Dec%202022&stop=22%20Dec%202022&hideSimilar=true&type=3

Godden-Rasul, Nikki, 'Portraits of Women of the Law: Re-envisioning Gender, Law and the Professions in Law Schools' (2019) 39(3) *Legal Studies* 415–431

Goodrich, Peter,'*Flores quae faciunt coronam* or the Flowers of Common Law', in O. Ben-Dor (ed.), *Law and Art: Ethics and Aesthetics* (Routledge 2011) 259–272

Goodrich, Peter, 'Vision and Decision' (2021) 40(1) *Rhetorik* 47–64

Goodwin, Charles and Marjorie Harness Goodwin, 'Contested Vision: the Discursive Constitution of Rodney King', (1997) in B.L. Gunnarsson, Per Linell, and Bengt Nordberg (eds), *The Construction of Professional Discourse* (Routledge 2014) 292–316

Gorys, Boris, 'The Border between Word and Image' (2011) 28(2) *Theory, Culture and Society* 94–108

Grzegorczyk, Tomasz, 'Mieczysław Siewierski (1900–1981)', in Agnieszka Liszewska and Anna Pikulska-Radomska (eds), *70 Lat Wydziału Prawa i Administracji Uniwersytetu Łódzkiego* [Seventy Years of the Faculty of Law and Administration at the University of Łódź] (University of Łódź Press 2015), 173–175

Grzebyk, Patrycja, 'The Role of the Polish Supreme National Tribunal in the Development of the Principles of International Criminal Law', in Morten Bergsmo, Wui Ling Cheah, and Ping Yi (eds), *Historical Origins of International Criminal Law:* Volume 2 (Torkel Opsahl Academic EPublisher 2014) 603–630

Gulińska-Jurgiel, Paulina, 'How to Punish National-Socialist Crimes in Poland', in Paulina Gulińska-Jurgiel, Yvonne Kleinmann, Miloš Řezník, and Dorothea Warneck (eds), *Ends of War: Interdisciplinary Perspectives on Past and New Polish Regions* (Wallstein 2019) 346–370

Gumbrecht, Hans Ulrich, *In 1926: Living at the Edge of Time* (Harvard University Press 1997)

Gürsel, Zeynep Devrim, *Image Brokers: Visualising World News in the Age of Digital Circulation* (University of California Press 2016)

Halla, Barbara, 'Barren Landscape: Who is Afraid of Albanian Women?', *Asymptote*, 20 February 2019, https://www.asymptotejournal.com/blog/2019/02/20/barren-landscape-who-is-afraid-of-albanian-women/?fbclid=IwAR1Pc8-2EWx1vrNrRemeM8djbpe_gz-McahFWdNcVoVxSIwfOH0LidnhpSY

Hanganu, Gabriel, '"Photo-Cross": The Political and Devotional Lives of a Romanian Orthodox Photograph', in Elizabeth Edwards and Janice Hart (eds), *Photographs Objects Histories: On the Materiality of Images* (Routledge 2006) 148–165

Harrison, Lonny, 'Doctor Zhivago as a Response to the Weaponization of Soviet Literature and Mass Culture', *AUTHLANGUAGE*, 23 August 2017, https://thelanguageofauthoritarianregimes.wordpress.com/2017/08/23/2268/

Heard, Kathryn A. 'Unframing the Death Penalty', in Austin Sarat and Jurgen Martschukat (eds), *Is the Death Penalty Dying? European and American Perspectives* (Cambridge University Press 2011) 126–149

Hein, Christoph, *Der Tangospieler: Erzählung* (*The Tango Player: Writings from an Unbound Europe*) (Suhrkamp Verlag 2002)

Hirsch, Francine, *Soviet Judgment at Nuremberg: A New History of the International Military Tribunal after World War II* (Oxford University Press 2020)

Hirsch, Francine, 'Russia is Counting on the Media to Spread Propaganda about Show Trials', *The Washington Post*, 23 June 2022, https://www.washingtonpost.com/outlook/2022/06/23/russia-is-counting-media-spread-propaganda-about-show-trials/

Hodos, George H., *Show Trials: Stalinist Purges in Eastern Europe, 1948–1954* (Praeger 1987)

'The Innocent Victims of Germany's Postwar Soviet Special Camps', *DW*, https://www.dw.com/en/germany-postwar-soviet-special-camps/a-54759064

Jameson, Fredric, *Postmodernism, or, the Cultural Life of Late Capitalism* (Verso 1992)
'Jean François Lyotard', *The Stanford Encyclopedia of Philosophy* (21 September 2018), https://plato.stanford.edu/entries/lyotard/#LimiRepr
Jeffess, Dorothy Ames, 'Resolving Rival Claims on East German Property upon German Unification' (1991) 101(1) *The Yale Law Journal* 527–549
Jentes, William R., 'Petrazycki: Law and Morality' (1955) 54 *Michigan Law Review* 160–163
Kalemij, Ilir, 'Lustration in Albania: The Past and the Future' (2021), on file with author, https://www.academia.edu/45189580/Lustration_in_Albania_The_past_and_the_future?email_work_card=title
Kaloçi, Dashnor, 'The Official Letter of Enver's Sister', *Memorie.al*, https://memorie.al/en/the-official-letter-of-envers-sister-please-with-the-broken-heart-of-a-woman-fr-the-forgiveness-of-her-husband-bahri-have-mercy-on-her-in-exchange-for-the-capital-punishment/
Kearney, Richard, 'Bachelard and the Epiphanic Instant' (2008) 52 *Philosophy Today* 38–45
Kirchheimer, Otto, 'The Administration of Justice and the Concept of Legality in East Germany' (1958–1959) 68 *Yale Law Journal* 705–749
Kirchheimer, Otto, *Political Justice* (Princeton University Press 1961)
Klich-Kurczewska, Barbara, 'Luxury from the USSR and the GDR? Cameras and Photographic Equipment as Official and Unofficial Objects of Trade in the People's Republic of Poland', in Marek Maszczak (ed.), *Polski sprzęt fotograficzny z lat 1954–1995 w zbiorach Muzeum Historii Fotografii w Krakowie* [Polish Photographic Equipment from 1954–1995 in the Collection of the Museum of the History of Photography in Kraków] (Kraków 2006), 12–47
Klinke, Harald, 'Introduction: The Image and the Mind', in Harald Klinke (ed.), *Art Theory as Visual Epistemology* (Cambridge Scholars Publishing 2014) 1–10
Kochanowski, Jerzy, 'Zabrakło desek' [They Ran Out of Desks], 15 November 1997, 46 *Polityka* 80
Komska, Yuliya, 'On the Wire Above the Ruins', *Cabinet*, 4 March 2021, https://www.cabinetmagazine.org/kiosk/komska_yuliya_4_march_2021.php
Korkunoff, N., *Lectures on the General Theory of Law* (tr. W. S. Hastings, The Macmillan Company 1888)
Korkunoff, N., *Russian Constitutional Law* (St Petersburg 1893–1901)
Kornbluth, Andrew, *The August Trials: The Holocaust and Postwar Justice in Poland* (Harvard University Press 2021)
Kotkin, Stephen, *Stalin: Waiting for Hitler, 1929–1941* (Penguin 2018)
Kowalski, Grzegorz M., 'The Amendment of August 1926 to the first Polish Constitution of the Second Republic*' (2014) 7(2) *Krakowskie Studia z Historii Państwa i Prawa* [Cracow Studies in the History of State and Law] 317–322 (in English)
Kritz, Neil J. (ed.), *Transitional Justice: How Emerging Democracies Reckon with Former Regimes: Country Studies,* Volume 2 (United States Institute of Peace 2004)
Kurczewski, Jacek, *The Resurrection of Rights in Poland* (Clarendon 1993)
Lane, Rose Wilder, *The Peaks of Shala* (Chapman and Dodd 1924)
Lee, Hermione, 'What Is Biography?' *British Academy*, 7 July 2020, https://www.thebritishacademy.ac.uk/blog/what-is-biography/?gclid=CjwKCAjwoMSWBhAdEiwAVJ2ndh_L-Pi2fFStizzqSw6a3X_gKpa1k9iyWLQFCV9ywnqLU5G7PSVoBxoCJMsQAvD_BwE
'The Legacy of Kristaq Sotiri, Master of Photography' (2020) *Invest in Albania*, 28 February 2020, https://invest-in-albania.org/the-legacy-of-kristaq-sotiri-master-of-photography/

Leide, Henry, *Auschwitz und Staatssicherheit: Strafverfolgung, Propaganda und Geheimhaltung in der DDR* [Auschwitz and State Security: Law Enforcement, Propaganda, and Secrecy in the GDR] (Der Bundesbeauftragte für die Unterlagen des Staatssicherheitsdienstes der ehemaligen Deutschen Demokratischen Republik. Abteilung Bildung und Forschung [Federal Commissioner for the Records of the State Security Service of the former German Democratic Republic, Department of Education and Research] 2021)

Levine, Mark L., George C. McNamee, and Daniel L. Greenberg (eds) *The Trial of the Chicago 7* (Simon and Schuster 2020)

Lewin, Katiede Kuhna, 'Discover the Untold Stories of the Pre-Raphaelite Sisters: The Politics of Discovery' (2019) *LARB*, 17 August 2020, https://lareviewofbooks.org/article/the-politics-of-rediscovery/

Lichuma, Caroline Omari, 'Thinking outside the (Methodological) Box: Teaching New Dogs Old Tricks', 11 December 2020, *BAR Socio-Lab Blog*, https://barblog.hypotheses.org/?s=Lichuma

Lityński, Adam, 'Administracja, Polityka i Sąd Tajny w Polsce Ludowej' [Administration, Politics, and Secret Courts in People's Poland] (2010) 10 *Roczniki Administracji i Prawa* [Annals of Administration and Law] 21–37

Lityński, Adam, 'Obraz sądownicztwa karnego pierwszej dekady Polski Ludowej: Uwagi na marginesie ksiażek Andrzeja Rzeplińskiego i Marii Turleskiej' [The Judiciary and Criminal Law and Justice During the First Decade of the Polish People's Republic: Remarks from the Margins of the Books by Andrzej Rzepliński and by Maria Turleska] (1991) 43(1–2) *Czasopismo Prawno-Historyczne* [Legal Historical Journal] 153–170

Loebl, Eugene, *Sentenced and Tried: Stalinist Purges in Czechoslovakia* (tr. Maurice Michael, Elek Books 1969)

Löhning, Martin, 'Family Law in the SOZ/GDR I: Stalinism' (2020) 49(2) *Právnehistorické Studie* [Legal Historical Studies] 48–57

Lubecka, Joanna, 'German Crimes Tried in Poland', in Magnus Brechtken, Władysław Bułhak, and Jürgen Zarusky (eds), *Political and Transitional Justice in Germany, Poland and the Soviet Union in the 1930s and 1950s* (Wallstein Verlag 2019), 210–238

Lukina, Anna, 'The Soviet Court as a Propaganda Instrument II: The Semenchuk Case, 1936', *AUTHLANGUAGE*, 21 September 2017, https://thelanguageofauthoritarianregimes.wordpress.com/2017/09/21/the-soviet-court-as-a-propaganda-instrument-the-semenchuk-case-1936/

Malcolm, Noel, *Rebels, Believers, Survivors: Studies in the History of the Albanians* (Oxford University Press 2020)

Manderson, Desmond (ed.), *Law and the Visual: Representations, Technologies and Critique* (University of Toronto 2018)

Marat, Stanisław and Jacek Snopkiewicz, *Zbrodnia, sprawa generala Fieldorfa – 'Nila'* [A Crime, The Case of General Fieldorf – 'Nil'] (Warsaw 1989)

Markovits, Inga, 'Children of a Lesser God: GDR Lawyers in Post-Socialist Germany' (1996) 94(7) *Michigan Law Review* 2270–2308

Maripuu, Meelis, 'Cold War Show Trials in Estonia: Justice and Propaganda in the Balance', Tõnu Tannberg (ed.), *Behind the Iron Curtain: Soviet Estonia in the Era of the Cold War* (Peter Lang 2015) 139–196

Marxen, Klaus, 'Die Mediatisierung des Rechts als Gegenstand der juristischen Zeitgeschichte' [The Mediatisation of Law as an Object of Contemporary Legal History], in Klaus Marxen and Annett Weineke (eds), *Inszenierungen des Rechts: Schauprozesse, Medienprozesse und Prozessfilme in der DDR* [Staging of the Law: Show Trials, Media Trials, and Trial Films in the GDR] (Berliner Wissenschafts-Verlag 2006) 19–36, 19

Mcgiel, John, '"Frenzy and Ferocity": The Stalinist Judicial System in Poland, 1944–1947, and the Search for Redress' (1994) 1101 *The Carl Beck Papers in Russian and Central European Studies*

Mëhilli, Elidor, *From Stalin to Mao: Albania and the Socialist World* (Cornell University Press 2017)

Melsheimer, Ernst, 'Die Stalinische Verfassung' (1949) 3(12) *Neue Justiz* 299–302

Minow, Martha, Michael Ryan, and Austin Sarat (eds), *Narrative, Violence and the Law: the Essays of Robert Cover* (University of Michigan Press 1995)

Montefiore, Simon Sebag, *Stalin: The Court of the Red Tsar* (Weidenfeld and Nicolson 2003)

Moran, Leslie J., *Law, Visual Culture and Judges* (Routledge 2021)

Moran, Les, Gary Watt, Linda Mulcahy and David Isaac, 'Four Reflections on "The Art of Justice: The Judge's Perspective"' [book review] (2013) 7(1) *Law and Humanities* 113–128

Mulcahy, Linda, 'Eyes of the Law: A Visual Turn in Socio-Legal Studies?' (2017) 44(S1) *Journal of Law and Society* S111–S128

Mulcahy, Linda and David Sugarman, *Legal Life-Writing: Marginalised Subjects and Sources* (Wiley-Blackwell 2015)

Müller, Ingo, *Hitler's Justice: The Courts of the Third Reich* (tr. Deborah Lucas Schneider, Harvard University Press 1991)

Musaraj, Smoki 'Temporalities of Concrete in the Communist and Postcommunist Cities', in Nataša Gregorič and Smoki Musaraj (eds), *Remitting, Restoring and Building Contemporary Albania* (Palgrave 2021) 105–129

Myerhoff, Barbara, 'A Death in Due Time', in John J. MacAloon (ed.), *Rite, Drama, Festival, Spectacle: Rehearsals toward a Theory of Cultural Performance* (Institute for the Study of Human Issues 1984) 149–178

Novgorodsteff, P. I., *The Historical School in Jurisprudence* (1896) https://etherwave.wordpress.com/2012/08/19/paul-vinogradoff-historical-jurisprudence-and-the-critique-of-sociology/

Novgorodsteff, P. I., *Kant and Hegel* (1901) https://etherwave.wordpress.com/2012/08/19/paul-vinogradoff-historical-jurisprudence-and-the-critique-of-sociology/

Oushakine, Serguei, 'Performative Objects: How Things Do Things without Words', in Julie A. Buckler, Julie A. Cassiday, and Boris Wolfson (eds), *Russian Performances: Word, Object, Action* (University of Wisconsin Press 2018) 54–63

Oushakine, Serguei, 'Presence without Identification: Vicarious Photography and Post-colonial Figuration in Belarus' (2018) 164 October49–100

Pandelejmoni, Enriketa, 'Italian Fascist Modernisation and Colonial Landscape in Albania 1925–1943' (2021) *Perspectivas-Journal of Political Science* 43–56

Parker, Hannah, 'Face to Face Encounters: Letter Writers and Portrait Photographers in the Russian State Archive', *History* (3 November 2021), https://historyjournal.org.uk/2021/11/03/face-to-face-encounters-letter-writers-and-portrait-photographs-in-the-russian-state-archive

Pearson, Owen, *Albania in Occupation and War: From Fascism to Communism 1940–1945, Vols* 2 *and* 3 (The Centre for Albanian Studies in association with I. B. Tauris 2005)

Pepa, Pjeter, *The Criminal File of Albania's Communist Dictator* (tr. Vangjel Morcka, Shtepia Botuese Uegen 2003)

Petrażycki, Leon, *Fruchtverteilung beim Wechsel des Nutzungsberichtigten* (Berlin 1892)

Petrażycki, Leon, *Die Lehre vom Einkommen* (2 vols, 1893–1895) https://archive.org/details/dielehrevomeink00petrgoog/page/n15/mode/2up

Petrażycki, Leon, 'O dopełniających prądach kulturalnych i prawach rozwoju handlu' [On Complementary Cultural Trends and Laws of Commercial Development] (Nakładem Towarzystwa im. Leona Petrażyckiego 1936)

Petrażycki, Leon, 'Prawo a Sąd' [Law and Court] (Nakładem Towarzystwa im. Leona Petrażyckiego 1936)

Piekarska, Katarzyna Maria, 'Naruszanie zasady jawności w "sadach tajnych"' [Violation of the Principles of Open Proceedings in the 'Secret Courts'] (1995) 27 *Studia Iuridica* 25–41

Pipa, Arshi, *Albanian Stalinism: Ideo-political Aspects* (Columbia University Press 1990)

Polunina, Valentyna, 'Soviet War Crimes Policy in the Far East: The Bacteriological Warfare Trial at Khabarovsk, 1949', in Morten Bergsmo, Wui Ling Cheah, and Ping Yi (eds), *Historical Origins of International Criminal Law:* Volume 2 (Torkel Opsahl Academic EPublisher 2014) 539–562

Propp, Vladimir, 'Fairy Tale Transformations', reprinted in Brian Richardson, James Phalen, and Peter Rabonowitz (eds), *Narrative Dynamics: Essays on Time, Plot, Closure, and Frames* (Ohio State University Press 2002) 73–93

Propp, Vladimir, *The Russian Folktale* (tr. Sibelan Forrester, Wayne State University Press 2012)

'Prosecution of Nazi Crimes in the GDR up to the Fischer Trial in 1965', *Wollheim Memorial*, http://www.wollheim-memorial.de/en/nsstrafverfolgung_in_der_ddr_bis_zum_fischerprozess_1965

Rapper, Gilles de, 'Photography and Remembrance. Questioning the Visual Legacy of Communist Albania', in Jonila Godole and Idrit Idrizi (eds), *Between Apathy and Nostalgia: Private and Public Recollections of Communism in Contemporary Albania* (IDMC 2019) 103–119

Rapper, Gilles de, 'Photographs and Régime d'historicité: Past, Present, and Future in Two Photographic Albums on Communist Albania', in Nataša Gregorič and Smoki Musaraj (eds), *Remitting, Restoring and Building Contemporary Albania* (Palgrave 2021), 51–73

Rapper, Gilles de and Anouk Durand, 'Family Photographs in Socialist Albania: State Photography and the Private Sphere', in Eckehard Pistrick, Nicola Scaldaferri, and Gretel Schwörer (eds), *Audiovisual Media and Identity Issues in Southeastern Europe* (Cambridge Scholars Publishing 2011) 210–229

Resnik, Judith and David E. Curtis, *Representing Justice: Invention, Controversy, and Rights in City-States and Democratic Courtrooms* (Yale University Press 2011)

Richardson-Little, Ned, *The Human Rights Dictatorship: Socialism, Global Solidarity and Revolution in East Germany* (Cambridge University Press 2020)

Roberston, Cara, *The Trial of Lizzie Borden* (Simon and Schuster 2019)

Rogoff, Irit, 'Studying Visual Culture', in Nicholas Mirzoeff (ed.), *The Visual Culture Reader* (Routledge 2002) 24–36

Romanowska, Elżbieta, 'Procesy karne przeciwsko Mieczysławowi Siewierskiemu (1950–1956)' [Criminal Proceedings Carried Out against Mieczysław Siewierski (1950–1956)],

Witryna Historyczna blog, 3 February 2021, https://www.witrynahistoryczna.pl/artykuly/prokurator-z-pasja-procesy-karne-przeciwko-mieczyslawowi-siewierskiemu-1950-1956/
Romanowska, Elżbieta, 'Procesy karne przeciwko dr. Mieczysławowi Siewierskiemu w Polsce w latach 1950–1956' [Criminal Proceedings Carried Out in Poland against Dr Mieczysław Siewierski from 1950 to 1956] (2016) 9 *Z dziejów prawa* [History of Law] 99–130
Rosenberg, Carol, 'Inside America's War Court: Clothing and Culture at Guantánamo Bay', *New York Times*, 28 December 2019
Rosenberg, William, 'Kadets and the Politic of Ambivalence', in Charles E. Timberlake (ed.), *Essays in Russian Liberalism* (Columbia University of Missouri Press 1972), 139–163
Ross, Corey, *The East German Dictatorship: Problems and Perspectives in the Interpretation of the GDR* (Arnold 2002)
'Russia's Mariupol Show Trials', Editorial Board, *Wall Street Journal*, 30 August 2022
Rzepliński, Andrzej, *Sądownictwo w Polsce Ludowej: między dyspozycyjnoscia a niezawisłością* [The Judiciary in People's Poland: between Disposability and Independence] (Oficyna Wydawnicza 'Pokolenie' 1989)
Sands, Philippe, *East-West Street: On the Origins of Genocide and Crimes against Humanity* (Weidenfeld and Nicolson 2016)
Sarat, Austin, 'Rhetoric and Remembrance: Trials, Transcription, and the Politics of Critical Reading' (1999) 23(4) *Legal Studies Forum* 355–378
Sarat, Austin, Lawrence Douglas, and Martha Merrill Umphrey (eds), *Law and Performance* (University of Massachusetts Press 2018)
Schenk, Dieter, *Albert Forster: Gdański namiestnik Hitlera: Zbrodnie hitlerowskie we Gdańsku i Prusach Zachodnich* [Hitlerite Crimes in Gdańsk and Western Prussia] (Polnord 2002)
Schlögel, Karl, *Moscow, 1937* (Polity 2012)
Schneer, David, *Through Soviet Jewish Eyes: Photography, War, and the Holocaust* (Rutgers University Press 2012)
Sebba, Anne, *Ethel Rozenberg: An American Tragedy* (St Martin's Publishing Group 2021)
Sekula, Allan, 'Reading an Archive: Photography between Labour and Capital', in P. Holland, J. Spence, and S. Watney (eds), *Photography/Politics: Two* (Comedia Publishing 1986) 153–159
Sekula, Allan, 'The Body and the Archive', in R. Bolton (ed.), *The Contest of Meaning: Critical Histories of Photography* (MIT Press 1996) 343–388
Sharples, Caroline, 'In Pursuit of Justice: Debating the Statute of Limitations for Nazi War Crimes in Britain and West Germany during the 1960s' (2014) 20(3) *Holocaust Studies* 81–108
Shaw, Julia J. A. *Law and the Passions: Why Emotions Matter for Justice* (GlassHouse Books 2019)
Sheehi, Stephen, *The Arab Imago: A Social History of Portrait Photography, 1860–1910* (Princeton University Press 2016)
Silver, David,'East Germany Kept Nazi Past in Mind', Letter to the Editor at *The New York Times*, 22 January 1995
Simpson, Gerry, *Law, War and Crime: War Crimes Trials and the Reinvention of International Law* (Polity 2007)
Simpson, Gerry, 'History of Histories', in Kevin Jon Heller and Gerry Simpson (eds), *The Hidden Histories of War Crimes Trials* (Oxford University Press 2013) 1–9
Smith, Lindsay, 'The Wont of Photography, or the Pleasure of Mimesis', in Luisa Calè and Patrizia Bello (eds), *Illustrations, Optics and Objects in Nineteenth-Century Literary and Visual Cultures* (Palgrave 2010) 65–86
Snyder, Timothy, *Bloodlands: Europe between Hitler and Stalin* (Bodley Head 2010)

Soloviev, Vladimir, *The Crisis of Western Philosophy: Against the Positivists* (1874, reprinted by SteinerBooks 1996)

Sontag, Susan, *On Photography* (Penguin Books 1979)

Sontag, Susan, 'Remembering Barthes', *New York Review of Books*, 15 May 1980, https://www.nybooks.com/articles/1980/05/15/remembering-barthes/

Spierlich, Peter W., *The East German Social Courts: Law and Popular Justice in a Marxist-Leninist Society* (Praeger 2007)

Stacey, Robin Chapman, *Dark Speech: The Performance of Law in Early Ireland* (University of Pennsylvania Press 2007)

Starosolsky, George V., 'Basic Principles of Soviet Criminal Law' (1950) 28(4) *North Carolina Law Review* 359–374

Steinberg, Mark D., *Proletarian Imagination: Self, Modernity, and the Sacred in Russia, 1910–1925* (Cornell University Press 2002)

Steiner, Peter, 'Justice in Prague, Political and Poetic: Some Reflections on the Slansky Trial (with Constant Reference to Franz Kafka and Milan Kundera)' (2000) 21(4) *Poetics Today* 653–679

Steinke, Ronen, *The Politics of International Criminal Justice: German Perspectives from Nuremberg to The Hague* (Hart 2012)

Stevens, Edmund, *Russia Is No Riddle* (Greenberg 1945)

Stolleis, Michael, *The Law under the Swastika: Studies on Legal History in Nazi Germany* (University of Chicago Press 1998)

'Studio Marubi: Photographs of Albania 1858–1952' exhibition at the Museum of Cultures (Helsinki, Finland) 5 May 2010–23 January 2011, https://web.archive.org/web/20131002072425/http://www.nba.fi/en/museums/museum_of_cultures/exhibitions/studio_marubi

Strzembosz, Adam and Maria Stanowska, *Sędziówie warszawscy w czasie próby, 1981–1988* [Warsaw Judges during Rehearsal, 1981–1988] (IPN 2005)

Szász, Béla, *Volunteers for the Gallows: Anatomy of a Show-Trial* (tr. Kathleen Szász, Chatto and Windus 1971)

Tagg, John, *The Burden of Representation: Essays on Photographies and Histories* (Macmillan 1988)

Taylor, Telford, *The Anatomy of the Nuremberg Trials*(Little, Brown, and Company 1992)

Thurston, Robert W., 'The Soviet Family during the Great Terror' (1991) 43(3) *Soviet Studies* 553–574

Timasheff, Nicholas S., 'Introduction', in Leon Petrazycki, *Law and Morality* (tr. Hugh W. Babb, Harvard University Press 1955), xxxv–xxxviii

Tinkler, Penny, *Using Photographs in Social and Historical Research* (Sage 2013)

Todorov, Tzevtan, *A French Tragedy: Scenes of Civil War* (tr. Mary Byrd Kelly, Dartmouth College Press 1996)

Todorov, Tzevtan, *Hope and Memory: Lessons from the Twentieth Century* (tr. David Bellos, Atlantic 2004)

Torańska, Teresa, *Them: Stalin's Polish Puppets* (Harper Collins 1987). The Polish version is *Oni* [Them] (Mysl 1986)

'Trial of Gauleiter Artur Greiser', *Law Reports of Trials of War Criminals, selected and prepared by the United Nations War Crimes Commission*, Volume VII (London, 1948)

Turlejska, Maria, *Te pokolenia żałobami czarne…Skazani na śmierć i ich sędziowie 1944–1954* [These Generations in Black Mourning Dress … Condemned to Death and Their Judges] (2nd edn, Aneks 1989)

Ventrella, Francesco, 'Visual Turn', in James Wright (ed.), *International Encyclopedia of the Social and Behavioral Sciences* (2nd edn, vol. 25, Elsevier 2015) 207–213

Vickers, Marianne, *The Albanians: A Modern History* (I.B. Tauris 2008)

Viola, Lynne, 'The Question of the Perpetrator in Soviet History' (2013) 72(1) *Slavic Review* 1–23, https://www.jstor.org/stable/10.5612/slavicreview.72.1.0001

Vollmann, William T., *Europe Central* (Viking Press 2005)

Vorbaum, Moritz, 'An "indispensable component of the elimination of fascism": War Crimes Trials and International Criminal Law in the German Democratic Republic', in Morten Bergsmo, Wui Ling Cheah, and Ping Yi (eds), *Historical Origins of International Criminal Law:* Volume 2 (Torkel Opsahl Academic EPublisher 2014) 397–425, 405–408

Vyshinsky, Andrei (ed.), *The Law of the Soviet State* (tr. Hugh W. Babb, Macmillan 1948)

Waage, Henning, 'Der Staatsanwalt hatte das Wort. Zur Repräsentation des Gerichts im Fernsehen der DDR', in Klaus Marxen and Anneke Weinke (eds), *Inszenierungen des Rechts: Schauprozesse, Medienprozesse und Prozessfilme in der DDR* (Berliner Wissenschafts-Verlag 2006) 175–203

Wagner, Alina, *Musine Kokalari and Social Democracy in Albania* (Friedrich Ebert Stiftung 2016), https://library.fes.de/pdf-files/bueros/albanien/13145.pdf

Wallach, Erica Glaser, *Light at Midnight* (Doubleday 1967)

Weinke, Annette, 'Von den frühen Schauprozessen des "verschärften Klassenkampfes" zur fernsehkompatiblen Rechtsberatung der Honecker-Ära' [From Early Show Trials of the Intensified Class Struggle to the Television-Compatible Legal Advice Trials of the Honecker Era], in Klaus Marxen and Anneke Weinke (eds), *Inszenierungen des Rechts: Schauprozesse, Medienprozesse und Prozessfilme in der DDR* [Staging of the Law: Show Trials, Media Trials, and Trial Films in the GDR] (Berliner Wissenschafts-Verlag 2006) 37–80

Wieland, Günther, 'Judicial Punishment of Occupation Crimes', in Werner Röhr (ed.), *Europe under the Swastika. Analyses, Sources, Registers* (Heidelberg 1996), https://second.wiki/wiki/waldheimer_prozesse

'Women from the Marubi Archive' exhibition at the Marubi Museum 8 May 2016–19 January 2017, https://www.marubi.gov.al/exhibitions/temporary/women-from-the-marubi-archive

Wood, Elizabeth, *Performing Justice: Agitation Trials in Early Soviet Russia* (Cornell University Press 2005)

Young, Alison, 'From Object to Encounter: Aesthetic Politics and Visual Criminology' (2014) 18(2) *Theoretical Criminology* 159–175

Young, Alison, *Judging the Image: Art, Value, Law* (Routledge 2005)

Young, Alison, *The Scene of Violence: Cinema, Crime, Affect* (Routledge Cavendish 2009)

Zimmerman, Judith, 'The Kadets and the Duma 1905–1907', in Charles E. Timberlake (ed.), *Essays in Russian Liberalism* (Columbia University of Missouri Press 1972) 119–138

Film/TV

Diary for My Children (Márta Mészáros, 1984)

Diary for My Lovers (Márta Mészáros, 1987)

Diary for My Mother and Father (Márta Mészáros, 1990)

Dreharbeiten im Auftrag des ZDF in der Gedenkstätte Münchner Platz Dresden [Film Commissioned by ZDF in the Munich Square Memorial in Dresden], 3 September 2020, https://www.stsg.de/cms/dresden/aktuelles/dreharbeiten-im-auftrag-des-zdf-der-gedenkstaette-muenchner-platz-dresden

Enver's Bulb – A Short History of Albania's Electrification (Björn Reinhardt and Eckehard Pistrick, 2018)

Forster Trial (British Pathé, 1948), https://www.britishpathe.com/video/forster-trial

Hilde Benjamin – die 'Rote Hilde' [Red Hilde] (MDR, 2013)

The Martyrs (Saimir Kumbaro, 2012)

Olympia, Part 1: Festival of Nations; Part 2: Festival of Beauty (Leni Riefenstahl, 1938)

A Trial in Prague (Zuzana Justman, 2001)

The Trial (Sergei Loznitsa, 2018)

Triumph of the Will (Leni Riefenstahl, 1935)

An Unsung Hero: Musine Kokalari (2017) (Patrick Titley, 2017)

Index

Page numbers in *italics* refer to figures.

For Product Safety Concerns and Information please contact our EU representative GPSR@taylorandfrancis.com Taylor & Francis Verlag GmbH, Kaufingerstraße 24, 80331 München, Germany